GW01085529

Does It Matter?
The Unsustainable World of the Materialists

Graham Dunstan Martin

Does It Matter?

The Unsustainable World of the Materialists

Floris Books

First published in 2005 by Floris Books
© 2005 Graham Dunstan Martin

Graham Dunstan Martin has asserted his right under the
Copyright, Designs and Patents Act 1988
to be identified as the Author of this Work.

All rights reserved. No part of this publication may
be reproduced without the prior permission
of Floris Books, 15 Harrison Gardens, Edinburgh.
www.florisbooks.co.uk

British Library CIP Data available

ISBN 0-86315-533-2

Printed in Great Britain
By Cromwell Press, Trowbridge

Contents

To Anne for being
and to all those whose minds have wings

Introduction

> Henri Poincaré used to say to post-graduate students who covered blackboards with mathematical formulae: 'Put your chalk down, stand with your back to the blackboard, and tell me what it means in ordinary language.' Woe betide the student who could not satisfy this test.
>
> J.E. Charon[1]

I was probably not quite eleven when a frightening thought occurred to me. I know my age at the time because I can remember where I was — walking across the tarmac playground of my Grammar School in the autumn of 1943. I speculated that there is but one consciousness, and that it enters every single person in the world in turn.

I still think about this sometimes. The implications are terrifying, as I knew in that moment. Indeed, if it is true, I am you and you are me and we are all everyone else, and all the joy of the world would be ours but also all the suffering — which is immensely more than the joy. So none of us would want it. It should however be compared with the view (scientific speculations are just as strange as this thought of mine) that the whole Universe could be wrapped up in an equation — it could all be described as a single particle travelling everywhere at once and for ever.

My eleven-year-old speculation reflects a true question. (Children have the wisdom to ask true questions. We should listen to them more often.)

Some time later, I remember attending a philosophical discussion in an undergraduate club of the Oxford of 1950/1. It was about whether the Resurrection had occurred or not. My 1951 self firmly believed that it had not. Nor did I like supernatural theories at the time. But I would have enjoyed any theory, natural or supernatural, if it had had that special quality of the fantastic-credible, by which at once any true scientific theory can be recognized.

However, these clever students, imbibing the modish 'Oxford Philosophy' of the time, had no theories to propose. Nor were they looking for facts (unlike lawyers in a courtroom or policemen on a case).

They sought merely to demolish any belief, true or false, which might lie behind words. So that the words in which the Resurrection was described, replaced the Resurrection and 'became its reality.'

An unfortunate consequence follows. By the act of words replacing events, of words becoming everything, by that very act those same words are instantly emptied of all meaning. I am not surprised that Derrida became a fashion in this country in the 1980s, considering how, long before it, the Word had replaced the World. Derrideanism is the child and inheritor of Oxford Philosophy.

I think back to that memory. When I rose and objected that my fellow-undergraduates were discussing words, and not any facts to which those words might point — my friends attempted to pull me down. 'Hush! You know nothing about it! You're making a fool of yourself!'

My friends were being sensible and kind. But what a pity it is that truth is subject to fashion, and free speech can be prevented in the name of philosophy. What a pity it is that talk is worshipped at the expense of experience.[2]

Scientists on the other hand believe in facts, not words. Lewis Wolpert wrote a book called *The Unnatural Nature of Science,* in which he declared that:

> Doing science requires a conscious awareness of the pitfalls of 'natural' thinking.[3]

Commonsense views are seldom correct. Faced with a mystery, you should try to turn it upside down. As if this were a law of life, let us recall that the images of our outside world arrive through the lens of our eyes, as they arrive through the lens of a camera, upside down. Our brains convert them to the right way up. Thus, built into our physiology, there is, as it were, the parable of knowledge itself.

For it is often a revelation to see things upside down. Very few things in the world are as they seem. Our ancestors, looking at the world around them, claimed that there were four elements — air, earth, fire and water; that the Sun revolved around the Earth; that the Earth was flat or like an upturned bowl; that heavy objects reach the ground before light ones; that motion always requires a force driving it. All these things appeared for thousands of years self-evident, and it is only because of the obstinate creative scepticism of a few brilliant scientists that we have learnt that not one of these assumptions was correct.

This reflects Stanislaw Lem's opinion in 'Odysseus of Ithaca,' that there are three sorts of genius:

> First come your run-of-the-mill and middling geniuses, that is, of the third order, whose minds are unable to go much beyond the horizon of their times. These ... are often recognized and even come into money and fame. The geniuses of the second order are already too difficult for their contemporaries and therefore fare worse. In ... the Middle Ages [they were] burned at the stake; later ... they were allowed to die a natural death by starvation, and sometimes even were maintained at the community's expense in madhouses. ... In addition there exist ... geniuses of the highest category. ... They are creators of truths so unprecedented, purveyors of proposals so revolutionary, that not a soul is capable of making head or tail of them.[4]

These highest types of genius are consequently never heard of either in their own time or any subsequent one. Let us recall Wolfgang Pauli's famous remark at a nuclear physicists' conference:

> This theory is not crazy enough to be true.

Wolpert is right to preach the heretical. Unfortunately he believes the orthodox, namely that matter is all. These days, it is materialism which is the obvious, commonsense way of thinking. What used to be unconventional is now conventional, those who used to be burnt at the stake are now the Holy Church of Immortal Matter. It is high time we turned Wolpert and his fellow-reductionists upside down too.

For reductionism is a failed ploy.

Back in 5000 BC the builders of Callanish and Maes Howe believed we were immortal souls. Back in AD 1620 our Jacobean ancestors believed likewise. This faith was based on the instincts of the ordinary man, on the revelations of religion, on the arguments of theologians and philosophers. In all countries, in all societies until recently, the spiritual universe had been unquestioned.

Then, slowly, in the face of immense religious resistance, science began to transform our view of the world. People always quote Alexander Pope at this point, and so shall I:

> Nature and Nature's laws lay hid in night:
> God said, *Let Newton be!* and all was light.

Pope (rightly, I think) sees the true Creation as the coming of age of human intelligence. What had been darkness became light, what had been mystery became, still a wonder, but *a wonder comprehended.* The excitement of science cannot be overstated, nor can its light-giving, evil-dispelling, illuminating power. As over the years it grew and expanded, it came to explain things never previously understood or even suspected — the relation of the Sun to the Earth, of the Solar System to the Universe, the evolution of all living things, the physical details of sex and reproduction, the interdependence of the two sexes in this, the table of the elements, the kinetic theory of heat, the degrading of energy through entropy, the existence of magnetism, electricity, germs and microbes, the nature of matter and of light, radioactivity, nuclear forces, genes, enzymes, proteins, DNA. It achieved increasingly great feats — the prevention of the deaths of mothers in childbirth, the reasons for diseases and their methods of cure, the techniques of successful agriculture, miraculous methods of travel and of instant worldwide communication. The Earth has been transformed. Compared with what it was 200 years ago, ours is now a science-fiction world.

Moreover all this was done initially in the teeth of opposition by the spiritual authorities. Science, the saviour of the human race, has risen *despite* the churches.

The moral seems as clear as the method. The spiritual had sunk the human race in darkness for uncountable thousands of years. It offered a spurious knowledge, a superstitious belief in nonsense such as the soul, angels, devils, ghosts, gods and God. It offered stasis, immobility, permanent ignorant credulity. It preached obedience and incuriosity. Through persecutions, torture and burnings, it sought to suppress new questions and new understanding. It martyred Giordano Bruno, and sought to martyr Galileo. It sided with the rich against the poor, with the ignorant and complacent against the lively and inquisitive. Voltaire called it 'The Infamous.' If only the Roman and Byzantine

Churches had not suppressed the free thought of the Ancient World in the fourth and fifth centuries, would the history of humanity not have been happier?

Increasingly over the last 150 years it has begun to look as if science could solve all problems. The method was crystal clear: *Reject the Spiritual.* All you need to solve your problems is the scientific method. *Matter is all.*

Now I comprehend this viewpoint, and am second to none in my admiration of science. The achievements of science have been astonishing. Reductionism has been of the utmost value. The revolution which has transformed religion from a universally held truth into merely one opinion among many, has been an excellent thing. For no beliefs must ever be immune to challenge, and neither Church, Mosque nor Temple must be an exception.

And here is exactly where we turn things upside down again. Over the last 150 years, materialists, reductionists and atheistic philosophers have put in devoted work. They have shown that if you want consistent results, you should address yourself to the stolid consistency of dumb matter. They have understandably sought to show that there is nothing but matter, so that it is from matter that even consciousness derives.

All the other strongholds of religion have fallen before this kind of assault, so why not this one? Everyone remembers Gilbert Ryle ironizing about 'the Ghost in the Machine' and Alan Turing pretending that, if a machine could be made to imitate a human being, then it was one. And indeed the assault on the spiritual has, if anything, gained in intensity over the last two decades. Dennett, Dawkins, Crick, Hofstadter, Pinker are the warrior heroes of contemporary materialism, and I welcome their savage attacks. The more searchingly the soul is questioned, the more light is shed.

I would suggest the parallel of Quantum Mechanics, which has seemed so paradoxical that people have tested it (over perhaps 80 years) more intensely than any other theory in the history of science, and (in all its astonishing counterintuitive brazenness) it has stood up.

Tests of the soul cannot be so rigorous. But there is something similar, in that the intellectual fashion of the last century has been materialist. Dualism, idealism and soul-ism have been mocked and derided. The flood of criticism has been continuous, the hostility unrelenting. The attempts to 'construct' mind out of mindlessness, and consciousness out of unconsciousness, continue as I write. Nonetheless, during this entire period, not a crack has been made in the reality of consciousness. No mechanistic theory has the remotest chance of explaining consciousness, still less explaining it away, as I shall demonstrate in the following pages.

Now, as the philosophy of science attests, the more lucid and unforgiving the criticism which a theory survives, the better the theory. No-one can put out of court the unimaginable, that is what brilliant new idea might one day turn up. But for the moment, the reality of consciousness looks secure. It has survived, unscathed, so many searching and ingenious assaults that I conclude as follows. In this rationalist, materialist age, we are not *less* justified in being soul-ists than our prescientific forebears — but *more* justified. Today, at the dawn of the twenty-first century, *it is more sensible for me to believe in the reality of the soul than it was for my grandfather.* He believed in it as a matter of faith. I believe in it because, despite the arguments, it stands up.

Frequently, in the literature about consciousness, you come across statements that contradict all sense. Philosophers say things like:

> Thomas Nagel set out the essential problem of consciousness. He did so in a downbeat, stark and rather pessimistic way which still shadows the whole question.[5]

This is because Nagel pointed out that, quite likely, no reductionist account of consciousness is possible.

I should like to ask, 'In what way is this a "pessimistic" statement?' On the contrary, it is our great hope, and leads to optimism in the highest degree. It leaves open the possibility that there is a purpose in the Universe, that our concern for those we love is not a mere illusion produced by mindless chemicals, in short that we human beings are real.

'Unfortunately' — they will say of this book — 'unfortunately, he thinks there is hope.'

We do not know who or what we are. Are we mere mechanical contraptions evolved out of pure Darwinian chance? Purpose and meaning rule our lives, but are these mere delusions? Are we smashed at death into a myriad fragments, or do we have souls? We do not know whether, at life's ceasing, death is indeed the end of all awareness, or whether it is a door — a hard and heavy door, to be sure — which opens on another place. We do not know, in short, whether we are finite machines, toys of the indifferent gods, or immortal souls.

We are in no better case than that common soldier — a peasant and a wise man — who before the Battle of Blenheim was overheard praying: 'O God, if there be a God, save my soul, if I have a soul.'

I shall not appeal to revelation, but to argument, evidence and probability. I shall ask how much we may *know* or *guess,* and what the *probabilities* are of the reality of the soul and of a Universal Creator. As Tom Paine, with his customary no-nonsense clarity, wrote over two hundred years ago:

> No one will deny or dispute the power of the Almighty to [communicate a revelation] if he pleases. But admitting, for the sake of a case, that something has been revealed to a certain person, ... it is revelation to that person only. When he tells it to a second person, a second to a third, a third to a fourth, and so on, it ceases to be a revelation to all those persons. It is revelation to the first person only, and *hearsay* to every other; and consequently they are not obliged to believe it.[6]

In short, revelation cannot stand up in a court of law, and should be dismissed before we start. If we seek — ambitiously — to have some inkling of what the Universe's grand design may be, we are *obligated* to look for something more solid. Speculation is better than revelation. For the latter leads to the immobility of dogma, whereas the former leads to inquiry, discussion and ingenious conjecture.

I am not a professional philosopher, though I have been thinking about these things all my life. In my professional career I have taught poetry, literature and philosophy, usually in their French incarnations. But, as Mary Midgley observes:

> [Philosophical] problems are not private property. They belong to anyone who can help to solve them.[7]

As G.K. Chesterton wrote:

> If ordinary men may not discuss existence, why should they be asked to conduct it?

In this book we shall ask: How could Matter possibly turn into Mind? By what magic can the unconscious turn conscious? In any case, what exactly *is* 'Matter'? Is consciousness really computer-like? Is it really 'in the brain' at all? Are reductionists right to deny the existence of decision-making, free will, foresight, purpose and meaning?

Could dualism (the theory that mind and matter are both fundamental) be after all a perfectly tenable position? Could idealism (the ancient view that mind is the ultimate ground of the Universe) be correct?

What is the place of consciousness in the Universe? Was Creation purposive, or a mere accident? In taking up their austerely atheistic position, materialists appeal to science as their authority. But what does science *really* say?

With questions as momentous as these, we cannot expect to arrive at certainty; we can however hope to assess the probabilities. I intend in this book to give a tentative answer to three questions: Does this strange universe in which we find ourselves have a Designer? Are we living souls? Does materialism make sense?

Before starting upon this task, we need to offer some definitions. These are tricky things, and this is particularly true of basic experiences, for the latter, being the source of all our definitions, are themselves hard to define. I must utter a similar warning to that of Karl Popper, who says that of all definitions one might particularly expect scientific ones to be precise, but that in practice they are always rather fuzzy-edged and fluid.

> 'Unambiguous' concepts, or concepts with 'sharp boundary lines,' do not exist Thus ... every physicist knows exactly what the first and the second law [of thermodynamics] mean, but ... no two physicists agree about them.[8]

Moreover they would not be useful to us if they were entirely precise, for then they would be too rigid to be useful.

Nonetheless one must seek to be as lucid as possible, and so I shall set about defining some of the key terms:

— *Consciousness* is the simple fact of being aware as opposed to being unconscious. Consciousness is that which perceives (as opposed to everything else, including not only material events but thoughts, ideas and emotions — all of which fall under the heading of *that which is perceived*). I shall use 'consciousness' and 'awareness' as synonyms.

— *Pure consciousness* is pure awareness without being aware *of* any outside fact. Normally one is aware *of* something, and it is unusual for consciousness to have no content other than itself. Some have questioned the existence of such a state, and we shall discuss this in a later chapter.

— *Self-awareness* is a distinct modality of consciousness, that is being conscious of being conscious. In practice, when conscious of any experience, one is usually aware that it is oneself being aware, yet one's focus of awareness is on the content of consciousness, not on one's self-awareness. However, one may perfectly well reverse this and attend to the fact of being self-aware. When discussing this, Sartre says consciousness 'has circular existence,' for 'every conscious existence exists as consciousness of existing.'[9] Consciousness is the only thing in Nature which can be self-aware.

— *Experience.* In ordinary parlance it is often found linguistically convenient to expand the sense of 'consciousness,' that is to use it as meaning consciousness *plus* the contents of consciousness. Strictly speaking however this is 'experience,' i.e. conscious awareness of events, things, facts, thoughts, emotions, memories, etc., as these are lived through.

— *Mind* is the whole 'world' of conscious experience, that is that faculty or region of which consciousness is the central fact. I shall sometimes use 'mind' as a synonym of consciousness, particularly when contrasting it with matter, or when speculating that the world is fundamentally 'mind-stuff' rather then 'solid matter.'

I do not use 'mind' as a synonym for 'brain': the former is the mental aspect of thinking, experiencing, etc.; the latter is the physical organ.

For clarity let me show all this in diagram form:

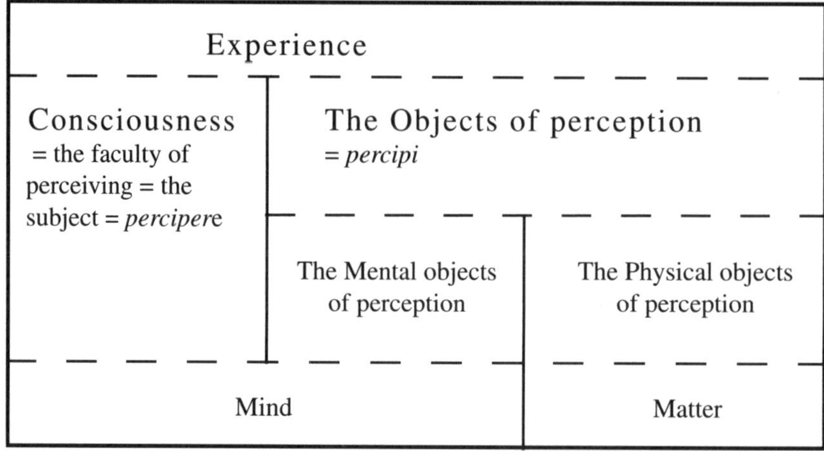

Thus consciousness is, fundamentally, separate from the objects of consciousness, whether these are mental or physical. 'Mind' however includes consciousness and the mental objects of perception; 'Matter' is a term used only for the physical objects of perception.

1. Can Computers Be Conscious?

> It is impossible to awaken someone who is pretending to be asleep.
>
> Navajo Proverb[1]

> The exploration of the external world by the methods of physical science leads not to a concrete reality but to a shadow world of symbols.
>
> Sir Arthur Eddington

The invention of cheap, handy computers and their rapid propagation around the globe has not merely been useful. It has produced experimental ferment in the Artificial Intelligence community, metaphysical effervescence among philosophers of the mind. It is hard to say how often one comes across the claim, 'Soon we'll be able to build conscious computers,' or 'The human mind is nothing but a computer,' or 'Soon we shall know what consciousness is.' None of these things can be affirmed as yet, but some scientists and philosophers are panting with excitement like dogs on a hot day. In this chapter I shall therefore be discussing whether these claims are reasonable, or even rational.

We shall not, however, talk about computers in the early pages of this chapter, for I cannot go into these issues 'cold.' Before we can have the least idea whether a computer can 'know' in the way a human being knows, or whether the 'information' a machine 'contains' in any way resembles the information we live and breathe, we must look at the experience of 'knowing' and the meaning of 'information.' We shall find that conscious beings possess a mode of knowing and of information which is inconceivable in computers. The whole assertion that machines might be able to think rests upon a crude reduction of human experience to abstraction — even perhaps upon the loss (back in the seventeenth century) of a vital piece of vocabulary from the English language.

We therefore cannot ask yet 'whether computers might become conscious.' First we have to consider two quite distinct and different kinds of knowing.

Tacit versus explicit

As far as I am aware, every European language except English has at least two words for 'to know': German has *wissen / kennen,* Norwegian has *vite / kjenne,* French has *savoir / connaître,* Spanish has *saber / conocer.* The first element of these pairs means 'to know (a fact),' the second 'to know (by acquaintance).' Europe's non-Indo-European languages also have similar pairs. Basque has *jakin* and *ezagutu;* Hungarian has *tud* and *ismer.* In Finnish the clarity of the distinction is particularly pleasing, there being three verbs: *tietää, osata* and *tuntea.* The former means 'to know (a fact),' the second 'to know (how to do something),' and the third 'to know by acquaintance.' A clear lexical distinction between abstract knowledge and knowledge by acquaintance used to exist in English (the verbs were respectively *to wot* and *to know),* but the verb *wot* got mislaid at some time during the sixteenth century. It is not exactly the same distinction as the one I am about to discuss, but its loss from the English language can hardly assist the clarity of British and American philosophy. Oxford Philosophy long held that truth could be arrived at by exploring the language we speak. But its practitioners spoke only English. And what if that language lacks certain essential distinctions?

The distinction in question is that drawn by Michael Polanyi between *explicit knowing* and *tacit knowing.* He first discussed this important difference in a little book called *The Tacit Dimension.* There are, he said, at least two kinds of knowledge: knowledge that can be put into words, and knowledge that cannot. Explicit knowing can be expressed in words or in formulae, in mathematics, or in symbolic systems.

Tacit knowing, on the other hand, cannot be put into words. Take for example the following incident. John meets Jane at a party tonight, and talks to her for ten minutes. On the following day as he is walking down the city street past thousands of faces, he sees her coming towards him through the crowd and infallibly recognizes her. How does he do that? On the other hand, if John describes Jane's face to his friend Philip, and Philip is walking down the street past these thousands of faces — he has no hope of recognizing Jane; not for a moment will he notice her. Our recognition of faces — and of course of most other things — cannot be put into words. Yet without it, how could we operate in the world?[2]

Other examples of tacit knowing are : (a) learning to play the piano. Verbal advice may be useful, but only to a very limited extent. 'Practice makes perfect,' as we say. (b) Riding a bicycle. The process can be more or less perfectly described by a mathematical formula. However, you cannot learn to ride a bike by knowing the formula. It may represent to a large extent what the bike-rider does, but *not what he knows how to do and not how he knows what to do.*

Another of Polanyi's examples is that of a lecture-hall full of medical students being shown a set of X-ray photographs of healthy lungs and of lungs with tubercular 'shadows' on them. To begin with, the students can't see the shadows, and can't distinguish the healthy lungs from the diseased ones. Nor can they be told how to see them, but merely shown where they are. This knowledge (though, note, it is scientific) cannot be communicated explicitly, but only tacitly.

This perception is by no means new. We have already seen that something very like it is embedded in most European languages. The great Muslim philosopher Ibn Al-Arabi (1164–1240) made a distinction between three forms of knowledge — knowledge by information, by experience, and by being:

> He likened the first form to knowing a fruit by reading about it, the second form to knowing a fruit through direct experience of its qualities (its weight, texture, odour and taste), and the third form to consuming and assimilating the fruit into one's being.[3]

Among neuroscientists who study human memory a similar distinction to Polanyi's is made between procedural (similar to tacit) and declarative (similar to explicit) memory.[4]

All experience is basically tacit. Experience is like a landscape, whereas our explicit statements about it are like a map. What is a map? It is a set of *simplifications* — symbols and pointers which enable us to make our way over the terrain of life. Thus, when we talk about our experience or write about it, and 'reduce' it to words, we are indeed *reducing* it. For it is impossible for words (as it is for mathematics) to describe any natural object completely.

I hope I do not appear to be attacking language, and particularly poetry, whose especial virtue is that it often gives an impression of not being abstract at all. However, language *is* fundamentally abstract, that is to say it is general, selective and imprecise. It is

(a) *general* in that any single word covers a whole range of things. Thus, 'blue' stands for a whole gamut of different shades of blue. It is (b) *selective* in that any word selects one feature from a whole set of features. Thus, 'blue' selects a particular hue rather than other qualities (tones, densities, etc,) present in the light. It is (c) *imprecise,* for one can always ask, '*How* blue? How *precisely* blue? What *exact* shade or quality does the word mean in this case?' We may of course specify the sort of blue more definitely by using words such as 'pale,' 'dark,' 'indigo,' 'azure,' 'cerulean,' etc. But these words too are infinitely imprecise, for the shades to which they refer can also be divided into an infinite number of gradations. Any particular experience of blue will have a precise quality which no words will be able to pin down.

As for poetry, it provides devices and stratagems for avoiding (or rather seeming to avoid) these problems. But that is another, much longer story, and I must put it aside, for it is not what concerns us here.[5]

Take the example of my hand. What object in the world could be more familiar to me? Yet any attempt on my part to describe it is doomed to failure. How can I find the words to express its particular shape, appearance, texture, movements, etc.? However good my description, moreover, I could never get to the end of describing it. Logically, I can never reach a point where my description will be complete. For it is always possible to extend the description by adding some detail or other. A moment's thought will show us that the same is true of any phenomenal object.[6] An abstract circle may be described rapidly and simply. But an abstract circle is not a phenomenal object, but a perfect shape created in the mind. Insofar as this perfect shape corresponds to actual real objects, it is only approximately, for actual real objects possess no such perfection. If, on the contrary, one tries to completely describe a phenomenal object such as a tree — it cannot be done.

Linguistic description *fails* at this point. As Polanyi observes, 'perception has this inexhaustible profundity.' The tacit is ineffable because experience is ineffable. It is not possible to express it totally. Indeed, the very phrase 'linguistic description' is radically misleading. Words do not 'describe' objects. They *point* to them. They do not 'describe' colours. They name them. If the listener does not *already* know what the word points at, or what experience the colour names, he cannot understand this alleged 'description.'

There are also aspects of experience which it is more or less impossible to express at all, for instance (a) what it is like to be conscious; (b) what the experience of the colour red is like; (c) how freshly-ground coffee smells; (d) what pain is like; (e) what joy is like; and to tell the truth all the most important experiences in life. None of these can be defined except ostensively, that is by pointing or appealing to a person's own experience of them.

Nonetheless these experiences are perfectly ordinary and everyday. Without them we would be unable to perform the least action in the real world. Yet they are impossible to reduce to the explicit. They are beyond definition or description. Words such as 'red,' 'coffee,' 'pain' do not, in essence, point to abstract entities, but on the contrary to dense, intense, concrete, tacit experiences. Ordinary reality is ineffable. As we shall see, the things computers cannot do are perfectly banal — such as smelling an apple, feeling the skin of a baby, seeing a sunset, or appreciating and enjoying these things.

The distinction between the tacit and the explicit, and the observation that ordinary experience is ineffable, casts a glaring light on the quite common misapprehension among some philosophers that, without language, we would not be conscious. Thus, I have heard someone seeking to explain away *cogito ergo sum* by its being allegedly parasitic on language. He claimed that 'I' is a learnt category belonging to grammar, that the notion of being a subject is due to the learning of human language in infancy. His claim was therefore that there is nothing in reality corresponding to 'I.' It is purely linguistic — a delusion imposed upon us by the language we speak.

How then does the notion of 'I' arise at all? If it is merely language that causes the belief in 'I,' then one ought to be able to find a language among the thousands which flourish on Earth, where there is no notion of 'I,' 'you,' he,' 'we' or indeed any of the grammatical persons. But, just as the semantic distinction between 'pig' and 'dog' reflects reality, so grammar too reflects reality. There is no human language that lacks the notion of 'I,' 'you,' and of a variety of other persons. This notion is sometimes expressed by a pronoun, sometimes by a suffix, but the notion of 'I' is always present.

Our speaker therefore had it all backwards. To hang a coat up, there has to be a peg to hang it on. If we had no experience of I-ness to hang the word 'I' on, then we would not be able to understand the word 'I.' If there were not an experience of I-ness, the persons of the verb could not be understood — and could not therefore have survived in language. Indeed, if we had had no experience of 'I'-ness, then language could never have introduced it.

As for the issue of whether one could be conscious if one had no language — and therefore whether tiny infants are conscious, or animals are conscious, or whether Helen Keller (who had become in early childhood blind and deaf)[7] was conscious before she learnt sign-language — one can see that not only is consciousness prior to language, but that many of consciousness's most remarkable features are of the tacit (and therefore non- or pre-linguistic) kind. These, being *inexpressible* in language, cannot be *dependent* on it. Any argument which wishes to reduce consciousness to language thereby reduces consciousness itself to the explicit, that is to abstract dust and ashes; and in so doing disproves its own ambition.[8]

It can be seen from this brief account of tacit and explicit knowing that the distinction casts light on many puzzles. It is indispensable to our understanding of our own minds, and should be introduced into philosophy as a fundamental distinction. To achieve this revolution in our thinking may however be especially hard for English speakers. For although the distinction can be expressed in our language, as the difference between 'knowing a fact' and 'knowing by acquaintance,' the stubborn fact that both these expressions misleadingly use the verb 'to know' means that the insight is not *embedded* in English as a fundamental distinction, as it is in other European languages.[9]

Now, the explicit is always incomplete, because it is always an abstraction from any true experience. Consequently, it is always a reduction, a distortion, a falsification of reality. Explicit knowing is a structure of abstract approximations. It also is necessary, indeed invaluable in the business of everyday life — for, just as we need concrete experience, so also we need abstract knowledge, that is we need language, mathematics, maps — but it is still abstract, approximate and often misleading.

The argument can be put as follows:

(1) Does the abstraction allow the original object to be completely reconstructed from it? Can one for instance reconstruct a painting from a verbal description of it?

No, one never can.

Therefore the abstraction is not a total representation of the object.

(2) Since the explicit is never a completely accurate representation of the object, therefore an element of vagueness, uncertainty, imprecision and even ambiguity resides in all abstract assertions. All abstract assertions are, by the nature of the explicit, (a) general, (b) selective and (c) imprecise. One can see therefore that certainty has gone right out of the window.
(3) Reductionism therefore cannot be right, because by its nature it cannot know what it left out of account when it 'reduced' the rest.
(4) The 'real' in any case is always left out, because abstraction is always merely a simulacrum of the real.

Now, science is an explicit system consisting of explicit processes and principles, that is it is abstract. Hence, as the quantum physicist David Bohm believed, it cannot provide total freedom from error:

> All abstractions, according to Bohm, are at most nothing more than approximations, for we cannot hope to encompass conceptually the qualitative infinity of nature. Science, in this view, cannot lead to error-free knowledge.[10]

And if science cannot, then what can?

Arthur Eddington, in his classic *Nature of the Physical Universe,* cites the example of an elephant sliding down a grassy slope:

> If we search the examination papers in physics and natural philosophy for the more intelligible questions, we may come across one beginning something like this: 'An elephant slides down a grassy hillside ...' The experienced candidate knows that he need not pay much attention to this; it is only put in to give an impression of realism. He reads on: 'The mass of the elephant is two tons.' Now we are getting down to business; the elephant fades out of the problem and a mass of two tons takes its place. What exactly is this two tons, the real subject matter of the problem? ... Two tons *is* the reading of the pointer when the elephant was placed on a weighing-machine.
>
> Let us pass on. 'The slope of the hill is 60°.' Now the hillside fades out of the problem and an angle of 60° takes its

> place. What is 60°? [It] *is* the reading of a plumb-line against the divisions of a protractor. Similarly for the other data of the problem. ... By the time the serious application of exact science begins we are left with only pointer readings. If then only pointer readings or their equivalents are put into the machine of scientific calculation, how can we grind out anything but pointer readings? But that is just what we do grind out. ... The whole subject matter of exact science consists of pointer readings and similar indications. [11]

Science is humanity's most majestic creation. On the one hand it has taught us rigour, on the other it has magnified our sense of wonder. But it neither replaces nor replicates reality. It merely gives us an abstract account of reality, which enables us to manipulate it better. The world is not the same as statements about the world. The concrete is not the same as the abstract. You cannot sleep on the word 'bed,' you cannot make love to the word 'woman,' and you cannot eat the word 'fish.' The chemical formula for salt is not the same as tasting it. The equation which describes the structure of the Universe is as yet to be found. In his *Brief History of Time* Hawking seems to think that if we knew it, 'we would know the mind of God.' But supposing it ever is discovered, we would merely know *explicitly* one thing that God knows *both explicitly and tacitly;* and knowing one thing that He said is not the same as experiencing His mind.

The most such a formula could express would be the Universe's abstract structure. It would not and could not explain why the Universe, for sentient beings like ourselves, is the kind of experience it is. An equation is not the same as the Universe, and cannot 'replace' it. It is not usually realized that Hawking himself (on the last pages of his book) recognizes this. He (even he!) asks 'What is it that breathes fire into the equations and makes a universe for them to describe?' [12] In other words, how does the tacit emerge from the explicit? How does the concrete emerge from the abstract? Hawking has not even the beginning of an answer to this question.

We may compare Douglas Adams's *Hitchhiker's Guide to the Galaxy,* where (understandably puzzled by the absurdity of the Universe) they ask the greatest computer what the meaning of everything is. The computer replies, '42.' This is just what a computer *would* think. But when it is discovered what the original question had been, this turns out to be 'What is 7 × 8?' — which doesn't make its answer any more sensible. Besides, we must remember that the original question was 'What is the *meaning* of the Universe?' — a question which for some unknown reason seems to have been turned into 'What is 7 × 8?' Douglas Adams is making the point that, though a question and an answer about the *functioning* of the Universe might be expressed mathematically, a question and an answer about its *meaning* cannot be. 'What is 7 × 8?' is not a translation into mathematics of 'What is the meaning of the Universe?'and if it were so every schoolchild would know the answer. Indeed, it is immediately plain that no question about meaning and purpose can be translated into numbers.

It is therefore unsurprising — though it remains shocking — to find Hawking saying:

> If you take a positivist position, as I do, questions about reality do not have any meaning. All one can ask is whether imaginary time is useful in formulating mathematical models that describe what we observe. This it certainly is. Indeed, one could even take the extreme position and say that imaginary time was really the fundamental concept in which the mathematical model should be formulated. Ordinary time would be a derived concept that we invent as part of a mathematical model to describe our subjective impressions of the universe.[13]

Hawking is a great theoretical physicist. However this statement of his is an extraordinary muddle. Questions about reality 'have no meaning.' Does reality then not exist? Is reality for Hawking only the abstractions of higher mathematics? How can a mathematical *model* of reality become (by some sleight of hand) that reality itself? How can the abstract replace the concrete? Why is experience — real experience — to be pushed aside in favour, not even of a shadowy simulacrum, but of a mathematical codification? In Hawking's statements we can see the disastrous result of taking the explicit to be exclusively the real.

Armed now with these distinctions, let us look at our contemporaries' most popular model for the mind. The brain is, in the view of many thinkers, a kind of computer; and if the brain (as they believe) creates consciousness, surely consciousness is derived from computational machinery?

The computer model of consciousness, or, mind into box doesn't go

Now, *it's a fallacy that a computer could be conscious.*

I am sorry to be so downright, but to see why, we should look at what actually goes on in a computer. As Raymond Tallis writes:

> In essence a computer is an electronic device for performing high-speed arithmetical and logical operations, calculating quantities, truth tables and weights. These operations lie at the heart of the most sophisticated or powerful computer — irrespective of whether it is digital-serial or a parallel-processor.

He goes on to ask: 'Why is a mathematical model said to be 'like' consciousness? What is quasi-conscious about 2 + 2 = 4 ?'[14] In what way, for instance, could my tacit experience of 'red' resemble such a sum? As Sir Arthur Eddington asked on one occasion, 'Is my wife a rather elaborate differential equation?'

Now of course mathematical operations can occur in a conscious mind. But because this is one of the things a conscious mind may do, this does not mean that the other activities of consciousness can equally be reduced to number-crunching. It is easy to think of experiences which simply cannot be translated into mathematics. How do you compute:

— the joy you feel as you reach the summit of your favourite mountain?
— the love you feel for your child?
— the sensations of a hangover? (From the sublime to the ridiculous, but the point remains just as good, for all these things are equally non-computable.)
— the difference between the smell of coffee and the taste of coffee, or between the smell of coffee and that of tea?

We have already seen that these experiences can't be put into words, for they are tacit experiences. How then do you *translate* such tacit and ineffable experiences into a mathematical formula?

Some processes in a computer, that is certain *explicit* processes, may indeed reflect certain mental activities. But let us not be taken in by valid observations *which are then fallaciously extrapolated.* We must not take some small part of what the mind can do (that is some of its computing and mathematical abilities) and puff this up in an attempt to explain all of the rest. It's as if you were to attribute my pleasure at walking among mountains to the fact that I can count up to ten.

Roger Penrose is inclined to think that the entire physical world might be described in terms of maths. Nonetheless he believes that mind and consciousness cannot so be described, and could not be simulated computationally.[15] Even mathematical reasoning is not a matter of computation.[16] Penrose devotes more than half of his 457-page book *Shadows of the Mind* to trying to make this argument watertight.

Information theory versus information

But 'consciousness,' we will be told, 'is simply information.' Thus the cosmologist Frank Tipler tells us quite categorically, in his *Physics of Immortality,* that life and consciousness are 'nothing but information.'[17] If this were so, and if 'information' meant the same in information theory as it does in ordinary experience, then our descendants might (as Tipler in all seriousness suggests) end up as an electronic form of life — though one cannot be sure what the word 'descendants' might then signify.

Reductionists are fond of saying that non-reductionists suffer from 'folk-beliefs.' In all communities, including that of the Artificial Intelligence community, there are beliefs whose origins are social. It is an AI folk-belief that consciousness is information, and that information is what you feed into a computer.

This view is due to a confusion between two senses of 'information,' namely 'information' in the ordinary sense and 'information' in a scientific sense. The two are quite different. Warren Weaver (one of the founders of information theory) says:

> Information in this theory is used in a special sense that must not be confused with its ordinary usage. In particular, information must not be confused with meaning. In fact, two messages, one of which is heavily loaded with meaning, and the other which is pure nonsense, can be exactly equivalent from the present viewpoint as regards information.[18]

As E.J. Lowe says, 'information' in the theorist's sense contains no *understanding,* no *interpretation,* it is merely a scatter of data lying around waiting for a conscious interpreter to arrive:

> Consider the pattern of rings exposed by a horizontal cut through a tree's trunk: such a ring pattern is, in the sense of 'information' employed by Chalmers, an *informational state* of the tree — it carries 'information' about the tree's age, amongst other things. Clearly, though, it is *not* a state with *conceptual* content: it would be ludicrous to suggest that the ring pattern somehow embodies the concept of *number* and *time* ...[19]

The rings of a tree-trunk are not 'information' in a human sense till a conscious being realizes they can provide it.

The neuroscientist Steven Rose similarly points out:

> Brains do not work with *information* in the computer sense, but with *meaning.*

He goes on to use the example of a restaurant meal:

> I read the menu, chose and ate the meal, and can now tell you that it included broccoli soup and poached salmon. Information in the printed text of the menu was transformed into recollections of earlier tastes, then the spoken order to the waiter, and then the material reality of the food and its actual taste. And now when I tell you [all this] I further modify last night's experience by translating it into spoken words. At each point in this sequence there has been more than just a switch in the modality in which the information has been expressed: there has been an input of work on that information which has irreversibly transformed it ...[20]

'Information' (in the computer sense) is merely the label on the drawer, concealing behind it a whole mass of experiences, many of them tacit or ineffable.[21] 'Information' is what is left when you *don't* open the drawer and have the experiences, that is it is a mere label.

Moreover, as Rose points out elsewhere, when you listen to a well-known piece of music, *it is never the same twice.* Your mood will be different, it will seem subtly different to you. *Its meaning is transformed for you.* How different this is from the computer, which (given the same command) provides the same reaction every time.

In point of fact (as my reader will have surmised by now) there are three senses of the word 'information' lurking here. Information–1 is the unrealized potential of some phenomenon for having extracted from it an explicit piece of information; Information–2 is when that explicit piece of information is extracted by a conscious mind; Information–3 is the tacit type of information, of which the explicit Information–2 is merely an abstract label.

We must remember the extraordinary richness of human sensation, which is so dense, so much itself, so incapable of being expressed in other terms that the word 'information' seems quite absurdly *narrow* for it. Experience cannot be *reduced* to 'information,' to abstractions, to mechanisms, to anything indeed but itself.

The term 'simulation,' or, the confusion of imitation with thinking

Another term which causes confusion in AI circles is the term 'simulation.' As Tallis points out, the word 'simulate' is ambiguous, and is so in ordinary speech. For instance, 'simulation' may mean 'imitation, model or representation' in some contexts, as in a war game. However nobody thinks a war game is a real war. On the other hand, 'simulated' may mean 'easily mistaken for.' Tallis's example is that of a *trompe-l'œil* painting, say, of a violin hanging on the back of a door. One may well be unable to see that it is not a real violin until one gets very close indeed to the door. However, as everyone agrees, such a painting is a painting, and not a violin. Thirdly, 'simulate' may mean 'do the same job as.' Thus, a machine might be built which could produce the same results as a blacksmith. It would not, however, for that reason *be* a blacksmith.[22]

A principal source of these errors is one of the founding geniuses of AI, namely Alan Turing himself. For Turing argued in his famous 1950 paper[23] that the question whether a computer could think would be settled by an operational test: 'Can a computer imitate the performance of a human being so well that no-one could tell the difference between them?'[24]

This must be one of the most bandied-about fallacies ever to be proffered. It is immediately evident that an appearance of thinking is not the same as thinking; that one may appear to think without thinking; and that one may think without appearing to do so. It is a fallacy to suppose that if an imitation is good enough to deceive then it is no longer a deception. On the contrary, it is only if an imitation is good enough to deceive that it *becomes* a deception.[25]

There is, however, an ironic consequence to Turing's view. If it were indeed possible to simulate all the external appearances of being conscious, to such a degree that no difference could ever be detected between a conscious person and an unconscious machine, then what would follow? What would follow is this: it would then become inexplicable what the purpose or function of consciousness is, that is *why consciousness is present in the world at all.*[26]

Parallel distributive processing / neural networks

What however of those other kinds of computers whose functioning is referred to as 'parallel distributive processing' or as 'neural networks'? This latter term is metaphoric — or even wishful thinking — for the mechanisms in the brain and those in these computers have actually very little in common. The behaviour of a PDP or 'neural network' is determined:

> by varying the strength of connectivity among a (usually large) number of simple switch-like elements. At a given time, each of these elements is in one of two output states: quiescent (=0) or firing (=1). [... These kinds of machine] compute in parallel by sending waves of activation through networks of such elements.[27]

It can be seen at once that PDP is as helpless as the digital computer to incorporate tacit knowing in its circuitry. Fundamentally both kinds of computer consist of on-off switches.

Although Steven Pinker ambitiously entitles his book *How the Mind Works,* he himself often lets slip the gravest doubts about this whole project. He starts for instance on page 5 with a diagram of how the world would look 'through a robot's eyes.' Naturally this diagram shows us *a set of numbers.* It does not show us an experience of kissing someone. Least of all does it show us *how* the robot would 'see' the world through its 'eyes.'

On the other hand, he trots out this familiar tale:

> The computational theory of mind ... says that beliefs and desires are information, incarnated as configurations of symbols. The symbols are the physical states of bits of matter, like chips in a computer or neurons in the brain.

But, as we have already seen, it is precisely beliefs, desires, and other things of this sort, which do *not* fall under the computer definition of 'information–1.' To be sure symbols may be *incarnated* as 'bits of matter,' as pictures or as words; but they are not symbols by virtue of their physical incarnation — but by the fact of a conscious human mind's attribution to them of a human meaning. It is our conscious minds which *choose* to interpret them as 'symbols.'

Pinker admits, much later, that 'We get to decide what the symbols mean.' Indeed yes, though he has telescoped two or three processes here. (a) They are not symbols until we decide that they will be. (b) They do not have meanings until we decide what those meanings will be. (c) Usually we look around for a suitable symbol before ascribing a meaning to it. Intrinsically, they are neither symbols, nor do they have meaning.

Another error is made when he claims that the PDP machine contains 'internal representations.'[28] These are *not* however 'internal representations' in the sense that a mind possesses such. They are merely machinery which operates further machinery. They are 'internal' only in the sense that they lie within the computer. Similarly, a mirror could be said to contain a number of 'representations' of the objects it reflects. The mirror is not, however, representing these things to itself, for it is just as unconscious of them as are the walls of the room upon which it hangs.

The terminology of 'inner representations' is wishful thinking and wilful misreport. There is certainly internal communication of Information–1 (in the information-processing sense). But nothing is 'represented' till it comes to the human consciousness of the operator. There simply is no inner consciousness in the computer to represent to itself its own internal procedures. The only 'representations' which the computer provides are not to itself but to its human users — those which the latter have in *their* heads.

Searle's Chinese room

One of the most famous thought experiments in modern philosophy revolves around these issues. I refer to John Searle's 'Chinese Room' argument, about which more ink has been spilled than about the Al-Qaeda network. In his recent *Mystery of Consciousness* Searle himself puts it as follows:

> Imagine that you carry out the steps in a program for answering questions in a language you do not understand. I do not understand Chinese, so I imagine that I am locked in a room with a lot of boxes of Chinese symbols (the database). I get small bunches of Chinese symbols passed to me (questions in Chinese), and I look up in a rule book (the program) what I am supposed to do. I perform certain operations on the symbols in accordance with the rules (that is, I carry out the steps in the program) and give back small bunches of symbols (answers to the questions) to those outside the room. I am the computer implementing a program for answering questions in Chinese, but all the same I do not understand a word of Chinese. And this is the point: *if I do not understand Chinese solely on the basis of implementing a computer program for Chinese, then neither does any other digital computer solely on that basis, because no digital computer has anything I do not have.*[29]

Searle's is an absolute knock-down argument. This is why opponents can't accept it. In fact, anyone who honestly rejects Searle's Chinese Room argument thereby shows that he has failed to understand it. One can see how worrying reductionists find it, from the fact that there have been over a hundred published attacks on it since its original publication. Searle's own account of the structure of his argument is this:

> (1) Programs are entirely syntactical.
> (2) Minds have a semantics.
> (3) Syntax is not the same as, nor by itself sufficient for, semantics.
> Therefore programs are not minds. Q.E.D.[30]

He goes on to say that he now believes this argument concedes too much to computers. The computer does not even contain computational symbols, but merely electrical pulses:

> What fact of physics and chemistry makes these electrical pulses into computational symbols? No fact whatever. The words 'symbol,' 'syntax,' and 'computation' do not name intrinsic features of nature like 'tectonic plate,' 'electron' or 'consciousness.' The electrical impulses are observer-independent; but the computational interpretation is relative to observers, users, programmers, etc.[31]

In other words, no information communicated to us by a computer can be called information until a human observer is there to interpret it.

Does Searle's argument equally knock down the pretensions of the PDP to be a mind? Clearly it does. As Pinker reminds us, it has been derisively suggested that the PDP operates, not like a Chinese Room, but like a Chinese Gym. It's exactly the same story except that in the Chinese Gym the messages are thrown around the room by people pretending they are neurons and sending signals to each other all over the place. These signals however are still entirely mechanical, and the athletes in the Gym still understand no Chinese.

Pinker tries to get out of this by arguing that Searle 'is merely exploring facts about the English word "understand."' This is simply not so. Searle is exploring facts about what 'understanding' *means* and *is*. And by the way the words for 'understand' in Arabic, Chinese, Hindi, Spanish and Tlingit are all understood in the same sort of way.

Pinker however has a more open mind than sometimes appears, and his final conclusion is striking:

> Our thoroughgoing perplexity about the enigmas of consciousness, self, will and knowledge may come from a mismatch between the very nature of these problems and the computational apparatus that natural selection has fitted us with.[32]

What an excellent remark! If there is such a mismatch, then consciousness, self, will and knowledge are beyond computation, which means that they must be non-arithmetical, non-explicit, and non-mechanical.

Building minds?

Rodney Cotterill's *Enchanted Looms* produces in the end a similar impression. Although he writes that 'consciousness will be seen in computers,' he wishes to suggest only that consciousness could be simulated in a computer, without its being conscious. This is like weather being simulated in a computer, without its being weather. As Searle puts it: 'The simulation of mental states is no more a mental state than the simulation of an explosion is itself an explosion.'[33] In other words Cotterill and Searle are in accord with Tallis about the various (and confusing) senses of the word 'simulation.'

Consciousness, Cotterill believes, is dependent on having a body. Computers will never possess consciousness, for they will never be:

> capable of giving an appropriate answer to the excellent question composed by Martin Fischler and Oscar Firschein: 'If a young man of 20 can gather 10 pounds of blackberries in one day, and a young woman of 18 gather 9, how many will they gather if they go out in the woods together?'[34]

Let us next examine the statements of another important researcher in this field, namely Igor Aleksander. The title of his recent book *How to Build a Mind* gives an impression of vast ambition. Perhaps his publishers imposed it, for in fact he admits that computers are never going to be anything like us, and is already writing on page 5:

> Consciousness ... is possessed by living organisms [and] surpasses by far anything we can engineer in our laboratories. This is likely to be true for a long time, if not forever. But ... that which makes my consciousness different from that which can be built is an important part of the discussion.

Thus, at a conference where all the important philosophers believed consciousness could be explained 'in some material way,' Aleksander preferred to ask the crucial question: 'What distinguishes a neural structure that generates consciousness from one that does not[?]' Indeed, then one might make some progress.

> People talk far too glibly about 'recognizing' things and then build machines that simply label patterns. There is a vast difference between recognizing patterns by labelling them correctly and knowing the objects that are perceived.

And of course this is precisely the difference between a machine and a human consciousness. Similarly he points out the huge gulf between what his brain does and what computers do, that is processing long lists of numbers. His ingenious creation the computer WISARD can 'recognize' faces but it is (he says) just a 'massively dumb image-labelling system.'[35]

It is intensely interesting that, upon investigation, one finds that the practical scientists actually engaged in computer research rarely make excessive claims. It is the theorists who do so.

Jerry Fodor, one of America's most penetrating philosophers, is also highly critical of these mind-building ambitions. He points out that the reason why people get so excited about the 'computers-are-exactly-like-brains theory' is that the sentences of human language seem to have a structure which is independent of their meanings. This structure is the syntax of each sentence. Thus the idea is that a computer could simulate the workings of the human mind.[36] But to suppose that the entire workings of the human mind can be based on the logical structure of sentences is to forget all the other things that the mind does — its perceptions, emotions, passions, its qualia, its mysterious relationship to time. To suppose that the mind is built exclusively on syntax is like saying that one of the toes on the duck's webbed foot is the whole of the duck.

Electronic conclusions

Digital computers plainly fall under the objection of tacit / explicit. So do PDP computers.[37] Reality is not mathematical, any more than it is linguistic. It is not made of words, or numbers, or symbolic systems. It is made of what the symbolic systems *stand for,* namely itself. Mathematical formulae describe certain features of it, as do words, but neither the former nor the latter provide anything even approaching a total description.

The prologue of that splendid book *The Emperor's New Mind* relates the following story. And indeed this story explains Penrose's title. There is a great gathering in the Grand Auditorium to mark the ceremonial switching on of the new Deep Thought computer. The President is looking forward to this moment, for now he has a wonderfully intelligent machine to make decisions for him. (One wishes that politicians were really like that, but this President is a fiction who prefers golf to power.) The audience wait with bated breath. The Chief Designer nears the climax of his speech:

> This computer has over 10^{17} logical units. That's more than the number of neurons in the combined brains of everyone in the entire country! Its intelligence will be unimaginable. But fortunately we do not need to imagine it. In a moment we shall all have the privilege of witnessing this intelligence at first hand!

The switch is thrown, the dials light up and wink. Here comes the long awaited moment. The assembled dignitaries are asked: 'Now, is there anyone in the audience who would like to initiate our new ruler? Anyone who would like to ask it its First Question?' Oh what a privilege! And how intimidating privileges are! What question would be clever enough for the Omnipotent Consciousness? What question would not show its human asker up as a human fool? There is a clearing of throats followed by an embarrassed silence. The tension builds and still no smart aleck has posed the First Question to That Which Knows All the Answers.

So there pipes up an innocent child, sitting there with his mother among the throng. 'What does it *feel* like to be a computer?' he asks. There is a moment's expectant silence. A long moment's mortifying silence. The Great Brain replies that it doesn't understand the question.[38]

As it takes a little child to point out in Hans Andersen's famous tale, the Emperor is naked.

From the argument of this chapter we should conclude that it is impossible, even in principle, for a computer to become conscious. For the contents of a computer are explicit, not tacit. Even supposing that you could feed our explicit knowledge into a computer, you couldn't feed our tacit knowledge in. For it has to become explicit before being fed in, and it would then cease to be itself.

As Babbage, inventor of the first computer, foresaw, — If the rules of calculation can be incorporated into a machine, then there is no need for the intervention of conscious thinking. In short, *the whole point about computers is that they are not conscious.*

This is also why Cryonics is in principle impracticable. I refer to that peculiar modern American dream of feeding our consciousnesses into computers so that we may become immortal. In preparation for such future inventions, it would appear that some ex-citizens of the USA are at present lying frozen in what they hope are their merely temporary coffins. For not only is there a belief among some that medical science will one day develop so far that dead bodies may be resuscitated. But another form of this belief is that the consciousnesses of the dead might be transferred into computers, in which they (transformed into electronic 'information') might live again in a simulated electronic heaven created by the brilliant technicians of the future.

In many cases, since preserving the whole body is expensive, it is only the head which is preserved. Thus we are told that many citizens of the USA are currently being beheaded just before death. For if they were beheaded just after, that would be too late. Needless to say, this practice has caused some legal problems.[39]

Ethics in Artificial Intelligence

Finally, let me shift the basis of this whole argument in a direction which, though blindingly obvious, has to my knowledge never been discussed in the Artificial Intelligence (AI) community.

In Stanislaw Lem's masterly collection of 'reviews of imaginary books' entitled *A Perfect Vacuum*, let's seek out the chapter 'Non Serviam.' It relates how, at some future date, scientists invent the new science of 'Personetics.' They succeed in creating, through electronic means, true consciousness. (Lem's irony here is so accomplished that for a while his explanation remains half convincing.) They set up whole communities of conscious beings within computers. They give their 'personoids' a complex and rewarding environment in which to live, to undergo rich sensations and experiences, and to die. The personoids' environment, though 'virtual,' is as interesting as our own world. Moreover they are really conscious, and *therefore* moral issues arise. Can one imagine what the results of any such experiment would be?

Lem writes, with withering irony:

> Before long, the experimenters came to the conclusion that contacts between personoid and man, via the inputs and outputs of the computer, were of little scientific value and, moreover, produced moral dilemmas, which contributed to the labelling of Personetics as the cruellest science.[40]

Soon the personoids, in their computer environment, are discussing morality and theology, and are giving lessons to their inventor the unfortunate Professor Dobb on the duties of a God to his creatures, on the problem of evil, the question of suffering, the ins and outs of morality. He never replies to them: he dare not. On account of the exigencies of his scientific programme, suffering is necessarily imposed on them; and on account of the expenses of his university, he will soon have to switch off the whole experiment, thus killing all his innocent victims. For (as experiments do) it has outrun its budget.

Is this why, like Dobb, *our* God does not make contact with us? Is he too ashamed?)[41] Poor Dobb admits his own 'final villainy in a situation of total domination over innocents.'[42] To create conscious computers has turned out a moral disaster.

Now here comes a peculiar twist to the whole argument. For it is precisely on moral grounds that the philosopher Dawkins proclaims the rightness of materialism. Since the world, he says, is full of suffering, we must therefore reject belief in God, since any such Creator must be evil.[43]

All the evidence seems to show that the creation of consciousness inside a computer is impossible. However, if by any chance that were not so, a warning needs to be issued. I would challenge Dawkins as follows: *If, for moral reasons, you think God to be evil and therefore unthinkable, then forbid human experimentation with consciousness for those same reasons.*

What could explain the silence of the AI community, and also of that part of the philosophical establishment (one thinks of Dennett, of Hofstadter, of Blackmore) who believe so firmly in the capacity of matter to create mind? The answer seems evident. Despite the apparent certainty with which they hold their views, deep down they do *not* really believe in our ability to fabricate consciousness; they do *not* believe that this project can ever be brought to fruition. Otherwise they would, for clear and evident moral reasons, be seeking *not* to create conscious machines.

2. Robots and Zombies

> If your theory results in the view that consciousness does not exist, you have simply produced a *reductio ad absurdum* of the theory.
>
> John R. Searle

> Why should one wait for science to produce a coherent explanation of mind when it has not yet produced a satisfactory explanation of matter ...?'
>
> Richard E. Cytowic[1]

In view of the arguments above, we may put the theory that mind may be explained into oblivion as merely a form of 'information' — right out of court. Computers are not minds.

But they are not brains either. What is really at issue is how much may be known or guessed about the relationship between brain and mind. At first sight it seems that the mind simply *must* be dependent on the brain. This arises from the simple fact that, when people lose bits of their brains, they often (though not quite always) lose bits of their minds.

Robert Charman expounds this case with especial clarity:

> The central nervous system (CNS) is a physiological system like any other bodily system, such as the digestive and respiratory systems. But, unlike any other system, the brain end of the CNS is credited with the property of being a *conscious mind* as well. ... Every finding from the neuro-science laboratories can be reasonably interpreted as supporting this one substance hypothesis. All mental activity [is associated with] brain activity. Mentation requires real units of electro-chemical work to be done. [Body and brain] are so united that a physiologically distressed brain results in a psychologically distressed mind and vice-versa.[2]

To assert this is however not to assert very much. That there is a connexion no-one can doubt. The problem is the nature of that connexion.

It is clear that damage to the brain damages the mind. As, however, McTaggart pointed out many years ago, this fact does not prove that the mind is brain-dependent. For 'the fact that an abnormal state of the brain may affect our thoughts does not prove that the normal states of the brain are necessary for thought.'[3]

This connects with the difficulties of trying to ascribe functions to various parts of the brain. Steven Rose quotes Richard Gregory's analogy:

> If one removes a transistor from a radio and, as a consequence, the radio emits a howl instead of a symphony, one cannot therefore infer that the function of the transistor is a howl-suppressor. ... When one studies the radio in the absence of the transistor, one is doing just that — studying the system minus a component, not the missing component itself.

Hence defining what the missing bit does is neither obvious nor easy.[4] We should also attend to what John Smythies has to say:

> The evidence from neurology and neuro-psychiatry that lesions of the brain can interfere with and indeed abolish for all intents and purposes, mind in all its manifestations, has long been held to provide conclusive evidence that mind and brain are identical. This however is a logical mistake. [For] you cannot show a movie without the film. But the film by itself is insufficient. You must have a projector and a screen too.[5]

In other words, for mind to act in this world, brain is certainly necessary. But is it sufficient? If the brain is the individual mind's computer, then it is understandable that, if the computer breaks down, we can no longer function normally. But this does not prove that the mind is not still there. In the present state of our knowledge we cannot show the brain to be sufficient for the activities of the mind. We cannot therefore show mind to be made of / created by matter.

Science & matter?

What is matter? Considering that it is held by scientific orthodoxy to be the one and only basic material of the Universe, one would think that scientists might have a lucid answer to this question. For how can one assert that one knows that the Universe is made of X, when one does not know what X is?

We have already seen Sir Arthur Eddington discussing the nature of scientific knowledge. It consists of measurements, pointer-readings, etc. It is of course intensely useful, even invaluable to us. But that is not the point at issue. The point at issue is what is the nature of such pointer-readings? Discussing whether a scientist could in principle give a complete description of a human being, Eddington writes:

> I can make an exhaustive physical examination of Mr X and discover the whole array of [scientific] symbols to be assigned to his locality. Will this array of symbols give me the whole of Mr X? There is not the least reason to think so. The voice that comes over the telephone wire is not the whole of what is at the end of the wire. The scientific linkage is like the telephone wire; it can transmit just what it is constructed to transmit and no more.

For even if the physical universe is all there is, our scientific data, that is pointer-readings, do not tell us of what it is made. For the nature of that physical universe lies hidden always behind the pointer-reading. Thus the claim that matter is all that there is amounts merely to the following assertion: 'What is measurable as a pointer-reading we shall call primary. What is not measurable we shall dismiss as an illusion.'[6]

But there are many things in the world other than pointer-readings.

Moritz Schlick points out that what is normally called 'subjective' is the given and the known; what is normally called 'objective' is 'not given and not known.' We know it and experience it only indirectly, *through* our subjective experience. The words 'Physical' and 'Matter' are:

> not a special kind of reality, but a special way of describing reality. ... 'Physical' should not be misunderstood as being an

> attribute which belongs to one part of reality and not to another: it is rather a word for a kind of abstract construction ...[7]

This is entirely in accord with Eddington. 'Matter,' in science, simply means 'what science is (so far) capable of measuring.'

The materialists' claim is quite the opposite. They assert that matter:

— 'is real in itself, apart from any mind's perception or conception of it.'[8]
— is devoid of anything 'mindful,' that is it experiences and is conscious of nothing, and
— that there is nothing but matter.

Let us contemplate this treble proposition, and let us do so by means of the fundamental definition of consciousness and of matter, as given by Bishop George Berkeley in the eighteenth century. No statement could shed more light than his, nor be more profound in its implications.

Berkeley starts by asking what 'to be' means. He replies that it has only two experiential meanings: (i) *percipere* (to perceive) and (ii) *percipi* (to be perceived). That is to say, there are (a) things whose *whole nature is* to perceive but which cannot be perceived; and (b) things whose *whole nature is* to be perceived but which cannot perceive. The world can be neatly divided into these two things, which have nothing in common except their total opposition. The one is everything the other is not and nothing the other is, and vice-versa. The extraordinary mystery at the core of reality is laid bare in Berkeley's description. There is an absolute division and contradiction between these two basic elements of reality — (1) consciousness which perceives but never can be perceived,[9] and (2) matter which is perceived but never can perceive.

Could this total opposition be a way of reconciling them, for they are opposed along the one dimension of 'conscious perception'? For these two fundamental things to be, each, everything the other is not, is for them to exist in a very precise and symmetrical relationship, namely that of complementarity.

The world's two greatest philosophical systems are the European and the Indian. In the West, the dual aspect of the world is termed (1) mind and matter; in India (2) consciousness and appearance. (In the Indian system, both 'matter' and 'the contents of mind' are included in 'appearance.')[10] The Indian system resembles Berkeley's, in that it makes no initial assumptions about the nature of this 'appearance' — calling it 'matter' does not make it any less mysterious — but starts from the basic observation of a duality between perceiver and perceived.

Now let us emphasize this key point: the contemporary reductionist view is that, fundamentally, there is only matter. Their definition of matter *exactly* corresponds to Berkeley's definition, namely that it is devoid of consciousness. By their definition, consciousness is 'derived from it.'

Let us ponder this in the light of the distinction between *percipere* [the active verb *to perceive]* and *percipi* [the passive verb *to be perceived]*. If, according to reductionists, consciousness must be a product of the mechanical processes of unconscious matter, that is *seeing* can be causally and logically derived from *being seen*, then according to them, *seeing* is not primary. *Being seen* is primary.

Intuitively, one feels there is something wrong here. *How can reality be derived from a passive verb?*

For the notion of 'being perceived' is inconceivable without the more primary notion of 'perceiving.' *Being seen* logically implies an active *seeing*. How can reality be derived from the *object* of an action, from which the acting *subject,* and therefore the action itself, has been removed? How can the *acted-upon* exist in the absence of any action whatever? How can inertness be seen as the essence of being, whereas activity is seen as a secondary creation, produced by inertness? How can inertness 'produce?' Does this make sense? Why, in our contemporary Western philosophy, is *suffering or undergoing some event* regarded as fundamental? Such philosophers have not realized the strangeness of their world — one in which 'doing' is regarded as impossible, whereas 'being done to' is all that there is.

Thus the philosophy of reductionism is the philosophy of the passive verb, the denial of the active verb, the denial of one half of the Grammar of Existence.

As Berkeley argues:

> But something whose whole essence is to be perceived is simply an idea in a mind because it by definition cannot exist except by being perceived by some mind.[11]

The conclusion is inescapable. It is that consciousness is logically prior to unconscious matter. Without consciousness, nothing can exist.

Let us also ask the following question. How can a thing be 'real in itself' if it isn't the least bit aware? What is 'real' supposed to *mean,* in the absence of any mind *to judge whether it is illusory or not?* How could something be 'real in itself' if there is nothing in itself *to* which to be real? Berkeley's analysis of 'what matter is' is here sharply pertinent. Things which cannot be perceived (for there is nothing to perceive them), but whose whole nature is to be perceived, simply cannot have independent existence.

Materialists also assert that matter is devoid of anything 'mindful' — experiences and is conscious of nothing. As Griffin points out, materialism 'is merely a decapitated version of [dualism], having returned to the former's "nature" while lopping off its "mind."' In addition they claim that matter is all there is.

All this is already implicit in Democritus:

> *The Intellect to the Senses:* Ostensibly there is colour, ostensibly sweetness, ostensibly bitterness. But in reality only atoms and void.
>
> *The Senses to the Intellect:* Poor intellect! You get your evidence from us, and you hope to overthrow us? Your victory is your defeat.[12]

Democritus is here making a point against himself. For it was he who first enunciated the Ancient Greek version of the atomic theory, he who first declared that 'there is nothing but atoms and void.'[13] Yet it is precisely on the basis of having sensations of various sorts that Democritus himself — or any of us — came to understand the world and have theories about it.

Having removed all consciousness, all experience and all perception from the universe, and having further reduced it to a set of unconscious miniparticles behaving according to mathematical formulae, the materialist then expects that it will magically fill again with density, with experience, with colour, taste, smell and sound, with emotion, passion and understanding. Despite his providing not the faintest hint as to how this could be done, he claims there is no problem.

As Jerry Fodor writes:

> Nobody has the slightest idea how anything material could be conscious. Nobody even knows what it would be like to have the slightest idea about how anything material could be conscious. So much for the philosophy of consciousness.[14]

Occasionally this is admitted by materialists themselves. Colin McGinn confesses that the problem may be permanently insoluble.[15]

De Quincey challenges materialists to explain (a) how 'consciousness or experience is ontologically identical with matter-energy' and/or (b) how consciousness could emerge from unconscious nothingness.[16]

Whence subjectivity and sensation?

Let us examine one such explanation, namely the much discussed theory recently put forward by Nicholas Humphrey. This philosopher rightly recognizes that any satisfactory materialist theory 'must address the problem of getting *subjectivity from wholly non-subjective raw materials.*'

Humphrey offers an account of evolution in which there is an increasingly complex development of mechanical processes — which (though they are unconscious) he carefully terms 'sensitivity, response, reactivity to good or bad stimuli.' He gradually builds towards a point where the animal (he claims) begins to be *conscious* of 'sensations' and begins to 'store representations.' Can one assume at this point that Humphrey has triumphantly proved his case?

No, I'm afraid not. In a detailed critique, de Quincey shows how, for the incautious, Humphrey has *created the impression* of a proof. For where does the animal's ability to *feel* these sensations and *experience* these 'representations' come from? From where does Humphrey derive that aware subjectivity that suddenly enters his account when he divides time into two kinds: a) the 'physical present' and (b) his nicely-named 'thick moment' of the 'subjective present'? *Either* this ability to have subjective experience was lying in wait from the beginning of time, hidden in the heart of matter — a proposal that Humphrey rejects — *or* Humphrey has suddenly inserted it at this point, hoping that we won't notice his sleight-of-hand. His account is well-written and rich in detail. Nonetheless we must conclude along with de Quincey that:

> he still ends up with coloured water, thinking he has produced the 'wine of consciousness'[17]

Exactly the same sleight-of-hand is present in *Consciousness*, a book by the Harvard neuropsychiatrist Hobson. For let us consult pages 95f. Here he explains that 'sensation could emerge simply as the sensation of sensation.' 'Simply'? Analysing his argument we see he is claiming that sensation–1 (meaning 'aware experience') could spontaneously arise from sensation–2 (meaning 'unconscious mechanical reaction'). We must ask, *How?* He gives no explanation of any such thing, and has confused two incompatible senses of the word 'sensation.' Indeed, his second sense of 'sensation' (= unconscious mechanical reaction) is not an admissible meaning of the word. For (by definition) a sensation cannot be insensible.

When he writes therefore that:

> It follows that, given sensation, awareness could emerge simply as the sensation of sensation,[18]

we must read this as meaning:

> It follows that, given no-sensation, awareness emerges as sensation of no-sensation.

Hobson is committing a conjuring trick. He starts by calling mechanical responses which (he admits) cannot be felt, 'sensations.' Then, because he has called them 'sensations' he claims they can be felt. Like many reductionist arguments, this one attempts an act of magic: it claims to conjure living sensation out of dead sensationless matter, and it does so by equivocation and the slippery use of words.

In the ancient Arabian tale, there was a genie who emerged — most alarmingly — from a bottle. He had been imprisoned there many centuries before by the magic of King Solomon. Materialists need to explain how the genie could pop out of the bottle, when he had *not* been put in the bottle in the first place. How can consciousness arise from what is, *by definition*, incapable of consciousness? The materialist position resembles superstitious beliefs about perpetual motion machines, where no energy is put in yet an infinite amount of it emerges.

Indeed, the resemblance is exact.

Zombies, or, what is consciousness for?

Daniel Dennett's strategy is different from Humphrey's. In the face of conscious activity he seeks to provide a totally mechanical explanation, that is to show that, to explain human activity, there is no need of consciousness. He claims that 'conscious experience is an illusion' or 'a user's illusion.' He is, as Jaron Lanier remarks, 'a philosopher who claims not to be conscious.'[19]

To have an illusion, however, you have to be conscious, for all illu sions are necessarily conscious experiences. Thus Dennett, a professional philosopher, is guilty of an obvious self-contradiction.[20]

Even if we were to take Dennett seriously, this leads to further problems. Firstly, since he claims that all conscious behaviour is really unconscious, then he is claiming that there is no way of distinguishing a zombie from a conscious person. In that case then zombies might be amongst us now. (Such hypothetical human beings are termed in the literature 'zombies' after the Haitian tradition that corpses can be raised from the dead. A zombie in the philosophical context is an insentient being whose lack of consciousness is the sole thing that distinguishes it from ourselves.)

But in that case, where are zombies to be found? Anyone who proclaims that there is no such thing as consciousness, qualia, or subjective experience, must be a prime candidate, and the most likely place to look for such zombies is the professorial seats of materialist philosophers such as Susan Blackmore and Daniel Dennett. Thus, as Jaron Lanier (inventor of the term 'virtual reality') facetiously remarks, 'Dennett is obviously a zombie [and] arguing with a zombie is generally futile, of course.'[21]

Secondly, if the whole of human behaviour could be explained away as mechanical, then what does consciousness add to this process? As I wrote in *Shadows in the Cave*:

> In such a universe whatever can consciousness be *for*? It is reduced to the status of a mere helpless observer. It is like a man strapped to a chair, ... a living, feeling being helplessly imprisoned in a machinery that may, indifferently, according to its own impersonal laws, provide him with the bliss of Krishna or break him on the wheel, confer on him the ecstatic visions of a saint or the despairing agony of poor Giordano Bruno dying in the Inquisition's flames.[22]

If consciousness is pointless, then why do we have it? Our possession of it is inexplicable. According to orthodox neo-Darwinian thinking, if it has no point *it is a mystery that it should ever have evolved.* In short, Dennett's argument does not even *explain* consciousness *away*, it simply fails to explain it.

Chalmers and 'the hard problem'

David Chalmers is one of the philosophers who has been instrumental, not only in restarting the discussion about consciousness, but in bringing it back into the centre of our concerns. It is he who single-handedly popularized the notion of the 'hard problem' in consciousness.

Chalmers mentions seven so-called 'easy problems of consciousness' and includes among them the following:

> The ability to discriminate, categorize, and react to environmental stimuli;
> The integration of information by a cognitive system;
> The focus of attention;
> The deliberate control of behaviour.[23]

However I hardly think that (to take one instance) the last of these is an easy problem. It is the issue of free will, and being so is likely to remain exceedingly mysterious for a long time yet. Indeed, E.J. Lowe challenges Chalmers on this question and says there are no 'easy problems of consciousness.'[24]

Nonetheless Chalmers' contribution is splendid, as he unerringly seeks out the very heart of the issue:

> The really hard problem of consciousness is the problem of experience. When we think or perceive, there is a whirl of information-processing, but there is also a subjective aspect. As Nagel has put it, there is something it is like to be a conscious organism.[25] This subjective aspect is experience. When we see, for example, we experience visual sensations: the felt value of redness, the experience of dark and light, the quality of depth in a visual field. Other experiences go along with perception in different modalities: the sound of a clarinet, the smell of mothballs. Then there are bodily sensations, from pains to orgasms: mental images that are conjured up

> internally; the felt quality of emotion, and the experience of a stream of conscious thought.

He goes on — and this is the nub of it: —

> It is undeniable that some organisms [for instance we] are the subjects of experience. But the question of how it is that these systems are subjects of experience is perplexing. ... It is widely agreed that experience arises from a physical basis, but we have no good explanation of why and how it so arises.

As Chalmers goes on to say, papers by philosophers and scientists usually begin with 'an invocation of the mystery of consciousness.' But by the second half of their article:

> the tone becomes more optimistic, and the author's own theory ... is outlined. Upon examination, this theory turns out to be a theory of one of the more straightforward phenomena — of reportability, of introspective access, or whatever. At the close, the author declares that consciousness has turned out to be tractable after all,

but they are trying to pull the wool over our eyes, and 'the hard problem remains untouched.' Indeed, we saw this above in the cases of Humphrey and Hobson.

Chalmers is exceptionally lucid about this problem. Science and reductive philosophy find it easy to explain abilities and functions, for all they have to do is specify a mechanism which can perform such a function. The hard problem on the other hand 'is not a problem about the performance of functions.' It goes *beyond* such problems:

> To see this, note that even when we have explained the performance of all the cognitive and behavioural functions in the vicinity of experience ... there may still remain a further unanswered question: Why is the performance of these functions accompanied by experience? ... Why doesn't all the information-processing go on 'in the dark' free of any inner feel? ... We know that conscious experience *does* arise when

> these functions are performed, but the very fact that it arises is the central mystery. ... Experience may arise from the physical but it is not entailed by the physical.

In other words:

> An analysis of the problem shows us that conscious experience is just not the kind of thing that a wholly reductive account could succeed in explaining.[26]

We need to stand back and admire this statement.

Thus, the conclusions of Chalmers' impressive book *The Conscious Mind* could be expressed as follows:

(1) Conscious experience exists.
(2) Conscious experience does not emerge entirely and exclusively from the physical properties of the fundamental particles.[27]
(3) If there are phenomena of this kind, then materialism is false.[28]

Conclusion

The reductionists cannot provide 'a theory of everything.' It looks as if, even in the present state of our knowledge, materialism is untenable.

3. The Symphony of Consciousness

To tell the truth is dangerous.
To listen to it is enraging.

Danish Proverb

Qualia

There are however further difficulties with the materialist view of the brain. Some of these revolve around the question of *qualia*.

What is meant by 'qualia'?

Just as, before discussing computers, we were obliged to consider the modalities of knowing, so here, before discussing the brain, we need to discuss the modalities of experience. *Quale* (singular), *qualia* (plural) is the Latin origin of the word 'quality.' In modern psychology and philosophy *qualia* are the actual *feel* of sensations — for instance the 'feel' and 'look' of colours, the 'feel' and 'flavour' of musical sounds in all their infinite variety, the felt texture of objects, the rich (but literally indescribable) tastes and odours of things. The examples are endless. Qualia are the raw sensory material of conscious experience, they are what we *feel* and *how* we feel it. Though evidently the essential centre of all our most vivid experiences, they are however incommunicable to others, for the reason that we have no means of transmitting these 'feels,' these 'experiences,' directly from one brain to another. Talking about them is quite inadequate. For instance, how do you describe the particular green of a Granny Smith apple, or the special joy of that moment of dancing? You can appeal only to other people's similar experiences — provided they have had such. If we have not had the experience of a particular *quale*, then we cannot imagine it.

Evidently, in the case of a colour-blind person, and when mentioning a particular shade of the colour 'red,' such an appeal will necessary fail. This is still more evidently so with someone blind from birth, as Bertrand Russell wrote many years ago:

> It is sometimes said that 'light *is* a form of wave-motion,' but this is misleading, for the light which we immediately see ... is not a form of wave-motion, but something quite different — something which we all know if we are not blind, though we cannot describe it so as to convey our knowledge to a man who is blind. A wave-motion, on the contrary, could quite well be described to a blind man ... But this, which a blind man can understand, is not what we mean by light: we mean by light just that which a blind man can never understand, and which we can never describe to him.[1]

Ramachandran and Hirstein have a neat way of explaining qualia. Imagine a superscientist who has complete knowledge of the workings of the brain, but who is colour-blind. He examines the brain of X, who has normal colour perception. He comes up with a complete description of the laws of wavelength processing, of the neural events from the receptors all the way to the brain. He has now 'completely understood the laws of colour vision, and [is] able to predict correctly which colour word X will utter when you present him with a certain light stimulus.' But this description is incomplete, because the actual experience of colour is missing from the diagram, and the colour-blind superscientist will never, despite the 'completeness' of his account, be able to know what that experience is like.

> Second, imagine ... a species of electric fish in the Amazon which ... has something we lack: the ability to sense electrical fields, using special organs in its skin.. You can study the neurophysiology of this fish and figure out how the electrical organs on the sides of its body transduce electrical current, how this is conveyed to the brain, what part of the brain analyses this information, how it uses the information to dodge predators, find prey, and so on. If the electric fish could talk, however, it would say, 'Fine, but you'll never know what it *feels* like to sense electricity.'[2]

Unfortunately, despite the excellence of their examples, the co-authors go on to suggest that the barrier is due to language, which *translates* the experience into words. This irrational suggestion completely misses their own point. A person who is colour-blind cannot 'translate' the word 'red' into his own experience of redness, because he has no such experience. Qualia are real. The arguments against them do not hold water.

A *quale* is a primal experience. In consequence it cannot be described. It is experienced as having a certain very distinct quality; it can be named,[3] and the appeal made to others: 'You know what I mean.' This is 'internal ostensive definition,' because one cannot show one's interlocutor by pointing, but has to ask him to refer to his own inner sensations. A *quale* (such as the colour red, the smell of hot coffee, the sound of a clarinet) is an experience that cannot be broken down into more elementary components.[4]

One consequence is that I cannot be sure I see colours, hear sounds, taste flavours, etc. in the same way as you do. A famous thought-experiment states that, if someone were to see all the seven colours of the spectrum, but in reverse order, seeing yellow therefore where I see blue, and violet where I see orange, then it would be impossible to know this fact, simply because it is impossible to step inside someone else's consciousness and see things 'through their eyes.'

But the situation is even more fascinating than that. As Max Velmans writes:

> But what is it that a bee sees? Is there a colour more 'ultra' than violet? If there is, we cannot visualize it. And what do the moth and the dolphin hear? If there is a pitch 500 times higher than middle C ... we cannot imagine it. ... What is it like to experience an electrical field [or] the sensed changes in the magnetic field experienced by the pond snail, homing pigeon, and wasp [?] The data from comparative psychology and zoology suggest that the 'physical reality' perceived by humans is only one of many possible perceived realities. The precise mix of sensory, perceptual, cognitive and social capacities in each species is unique. ... Consequently, the 'physical reality' that we perceive is actually a peculiarly human world.[5]

Again we find that consciousness sets a limit, a narrow but variegated boundary around our possible experiences.

How do the *qualia* relate to *tacit knowing?*

'Experience' is the whole of what we perceive, remember and undergo: this includes both the explicit and the tacit. What we know tacitly, comes to us through the qualia, which are a set of different modalities *within* conscious experience, that is the sensory modalities of colour, sound, taste, touch, etc., which present themselves to consciousness in all their qualitative (and ineffable) individuality. The qualia are *what* the tacit is *of*, and *how* it shows itself. Contemplating the qualia we see why the tacit is ineffable; for they *are* raw experience in all its variety. Moreover, it is not simply that they are ineffable; each is ineffable in its different way. The qualia of taste in no way resemble those of sight, the qualia of touch in no way resemble those of hearing. Moreover in no way do any of these experiences resemble the physical brain processes which give rise to them. As we shall see therefore, materialist explanations of the qualia face, not one severe problem, but at least ten.

The Sensory Qualia

Qualia are the very ground of our experience. The most obvious among them are: the *sensory qualia*. Conventionally there are supposed to be five senses: touch, sight, hearing, smell, taste. However, all the modern authorities admit that this is an incomplete list. Awareness of hot and cold has a quite different sensory quality from any of the traditional five, and should therefore be treated as a sense. Pain again has its own particular quality. A further (and indispensable) sense, first described by Sherrington in 1906, is proprioception:

> Proprioception is being inside, aware of, and 'knowing one's way about' one's own body; it is awareness of one's own equilibrium, of one's movement through the spatial reality around one, and also of the other forces moving through it. For instance, when you see someone walking towards you, you brace and balance yourself for avoidance, etc. You do so of course, as with every one of our senses, part unconsciously, part consciously. And it is only if, as we are walking rapidly forward towards the other person, a problem of decision emerges, that our proprioceptive awareness emerges too into full consciousness.[6]

Muscle-feeling is either a part of this sense, or may be separated to some degree from it.

Of the senses, vision is strong, smell weak (it is of course much stronger in most animals), and so forth. Pain may achieve the most horrifying intensity, and has causal force, leading to efforts to avoid it. Without the qualia of pain, its Suchness, we would not be moved to avoid injury, as can be seen in the case of those rare individuals who do not feel pain at all, and who tend therefore to ignore even those injuries of which they are aware.

Importantly, as Kripke points out, '*all it is* for something to be pain is for it to feel like pain.' That is to say, pain *is* the feeling of pain. It is not a brain state of any kind whether or not that brain state accompanies the pain. Nor is there a *necessary* connexion between any brain-state and the experience of pain.[7] Indeed, pain is well known to be a medical mystery: sometimes it occurs for no apparent physical reason, often it fails to occur when every physical reason would make one think it should. Pain is *exclusively* a quale; it is a psychological, not a physical event.

Nonetheless, without it many efforts for survival in the living world would not occur. *This* quale *is essential for evolution.*

Perhaps the most remarkable thing about the senses is the striking differences between their qualities. The qualia of vision, hearing, smell, proprioception and the rest have nothing whatever in common with each other. The 'feel' of each of the senses is totally foreign to that of any other. Nor is it possible to describe in words in what these differences consist. For the buck of effability stops here: Qualia are indescribable, since it is *in terms of* qualia that we describe, so that no further analysis of them is possible either to language or to thought. We know what seeing is like, but we cannot express or analyse this 'being like.'

That the qualia are of such different qualities, hugely enriches our experience. This variousness is a particular difficulty for the reductionist. For the neural processes in the brain which are supposed to cause qualia to arise 'in the mind' are fundamentally identical. Yet the qualia are astonishingly various.

Reductionists have usually been fairly cautious about qualia. Nonetheless Dennett says in *Consciousness Explained:*

> There are no such properties as qualia.[8] ... But I agree wholeheartedly that there seem to be. ... Qualitative properties that are intrinsically conscious are a myth, an artefact of misguided theorizing, not anything given pretheoretically.[9]

Thus Dennett claims that qualia are an illusion. Now, how can one 'seem' to be having an experience? When something 'seems,' its seeming *is* the experience one is having. Even a misleading experience is still an experience, and still has qualities of its own. Moreover, our experiences may sometimes fit into theories and sometimes not; but they are not themselves theories; they are precisely what is pretheoretical. Dennett does his case no good by denying self-evident truths.

When my wife and I visited Turkey some years ago, the heat was at first so strong that you could see nothing but sea and haze. Slowly on the third day, the Greek isle of Samos emerged out of the mist. 'What's the name of that island?' we asked the Turkish waiter in our hotel. He looked through the window and declared, 'I see nothing.' Greece is a country the Turks would wish into non-existence if they could. The Turks have their political, Dennett has his polemical, reasons.

However there is a fundamental difference. When Turks say Samos isn't there, they know that both they and you can see it, and they expect you to share this excellent irony with them. There is no irony in Dennett. When he denies that qualia exist, he is simply denying, not merely what we all know, but *what we all see, feel, taste and smell, and how we manage to stand up and walk.* 'No, it isn't there,' he declares, as meanwhile he stares straight out on the grandiose cliffs and mountains of the Aegean.

Max Velmans takes Dennett's argument and neatly analyses it:

> (1) [Dennett] translates first-person accounts of *what it is like to experience* colour 'qualia' (the experience of Granny-Smith-apple-green, etc.) into third-person accounts of how systems might *perform tasks* (how they might achieve colour discrimination, colour naming, stop on red, etc.)
> (2) He shows how the task might be performed by brains or machines without the use of representations that are themselves coloured.
> (3) He concludes that 'qualia' are not needed for functional explanations.
> (4) He concludes that 'qualia' do not exist.[10]

Thus Dennett asserts that because qualia are not necessary to his theory, then they cannot exist, that is that his theory takes precedence over any possible counter-evidence. This is a fundamentally unscientific procedure.

Similarly we find the philosopher David Lewis writing:

> The most formidable challenge to any sort of materialism and functionalism comes from the friend of phenomenal qualia. He says we leave out [pain, feeling, awareness, redness, bird-song, etc. He points out that there is] a special subject matter of phenomenal information.

Lewis continues:

> Now we must turn eliminative. We dare not grant that there is a sort of information we overlook.[11]

It is admirably frank of Lewis to give his game away. He proposes to solve his problem by calling phenomenal information 'possession of abilities.' One can see that his only interest is in winning the argument (through a careful choice of words), not in finding the truth (through respecting facts and experience).

Qualia do provide information, indeed they are the sole carriers of information from the outside world. Without sensory experience, we would have no window on the universe.

The Qualia of Imagination

Unsurprisingly the qualia of imagination tend to resemble the sensory qualia closely. For how could they be useful did they not? Imagine a tiger. One hopes this image will resemble a tiger, though one hopes also that it will not resemble a tiger sufficiently to be frightening. (Unlike *le Douanier* Rousseau who, having painted his tiger, found himself so alarmed by it that he had to sit in the sun by his windowsill to recover.)

Thus the psychologist Kosslyn found in his researches that imagined tomatoes may resemble real tomatoes to such an extent that sometimes the viewer may be uncertain which they are. This is to be expected. My imagination would be useless, even dangerous, if my image of a tiger did not resemble a real tiger. The laws of survival must ensure that human mental imagery evolves to resemble visual imagery.

Cotterill claims that 'In the face of such results, the imagination begins to appear rather less independent.'[12] One must disagree. When real objects are involved, then it is understandable (for evolutionary reasons) that images should resemble them. If cases of fantastic imagining had been investigated, however, Kosslyn might well have found that the imagination has a striking freedom.

We should not complain therefore but be grateful that many of our mental images so closely resemble reality. The main point is not that, but the fact that the imagination may be *independent* of outer stimulation. We are not passive victims of our sensory machinery. The latter can plainly be worked both from the outside (by events) and from the inside (by imagination). That is our imagination is almost as capable as 'our dear friend the world' of creating an experience in us.

The Qualia of Emotion

As Isaac Bashevis Singer has put it: 'When Descartes said *Cogito, ergo sum*, he should have been talking about the emotions.' After all, feeling proves the reality of consciousness more clearly even than thinking does. How can Romeo, experiencing his passion for Juliet, doubt that he exists?

Emotions, however, are hard to describe. The poets and novelists are the people to consult. Here it is all done by comparison, analogy, metaphor, and as always the appeal to our own experience. Here you will read of lulling breezes, calm moods, chasms of tedium — you will read of sexual fires, self-destructive explosions of anguish, volcanic angers. The meagre inadequacy in common speech of the vocabulary for our emotions shows their power, their reality, their distance from the banal, the readily nameable.

The Qualia of Thought

What is the 'feel' of understanding, the 'feel' of thinking, the 'feel' of having an idea? What is the *quale* that Dennett experiences when, feeling intellectual certainty, he denies he feels *in any way?* This issue has been little discussed, because compared with colours or tastes, it is harder to get a grip on. Thoughts are 'cool' and 'temperate' compared with feelings, which are 'icy,' 'colourful' or 'hot.' But different forms of thinking do have different 'feels.' This again highlights the difficulties that face the inventors of Artificial Intelligence machines. As P.M.S. Hacker writes:

> If [a machine] can think, it can also reflect, ponder, reconsider. It must make sense to say of it that it is pensive, contemplative or rapt in thought. It must be capable of acting thoughtlessly as well as thoughtfully, of thinking before it acts as well as acting before it thinks. If it can think, it can have opinions, be opinionated, credulous or incredulous, open-minded or bigoted, have good or poor judgment, be hesitant or decisive, shrewd, prudent, or rash and hasty in judgment.[13]

I fear that AI machines can, as yet, achieve none of these states of mind. For no-one has the ghost of an idea how to produce either consciousness or qualia.

We construct the world from ten sources: namely, the qualia of what we see, hear, touch, taste, smell, etc. How do these relate to the world described by physics? Not only is this an unresolved mystery, it is hard to see what kind of explanation would do.

Thus, as Dawkins asks, since nerve impulses are all similar, why do the senses of sight, hearing and smell turn out so different?

> The sensation of seeing is for us very different from the sensation of hearing, but this cannot be directly due to the physical differences between light and sound. Both light and sound are, after all, translated by the respective sense organs into the same kind of nerve impulse. It is impossible to tell, from the physical attributes of a nerve impulse, whether it is conveying information about light, about sound or about smell.[14]

Given the astonishing monotony of the behaviour of neurons, how is the wonderfully colourful and various experience of the senses produced? Theorists talk of 'encoding,' but they cannot explain how this might be done, nor point to where 'encoding' is being performed.[15]

A further difficulty is the famous 'binding problem' (as it is rather cryptically termed). According to modern brain research, the different features of an object are 'encoded' in quite different areas of the brain. These areas are separated by some distance from each other. 'Crick, for example, cites evidence for the existence of more than seventeen distinct areas in the visual system, which encode different visual features.' It is far from evident how at any given moment, our consciousness presents us with, not a mere seventeen, but the complete range of sensory experiences wrapped up in a single whole — this integrated three-dimensional phenomenal world — which is our everyday experience every moment of our lives.[16] No 'higher centres' in the brain have been identified which could account for such integrated experience.[17]

Cytowic asks how the different sense modalities arrive in consciousness as an integrated whole:

> In contemporary terms this is the binding problem. Thus, I see an apple as a unity, not as something red and round, or I perceive honey rather than something yellow and sweet. The binding problem has so far remained unsolved.[18]

The processing of colour and that of shape (for instance) go on in quite different parts of the brain. We still do not know how the brain melds these processes into a unified experience.

What, therefore, do we conclude? It has not been shown — or even suggested — how any physical mechanism or neurological process might cause the qualia to be experienced. Indeed the gulf between neurological events and the *quality* of what they result in seems unbridgeable. *That* qualia are caused by neurological events cannot be doubted. *How* qualia might be caused by neurological events is however impossible to understand, and no plausible explanation has ever been proposed. Moreover the nature of these qualia is so unlike the neurological events that it cannot be seen how any explanation could be given, or what sort of explanation it might be. Furthermore the differences in nature between the qualia of, say, vision, hearing, etc., are so large that, again, any explanation seems quite out of reach. *We require a theory which would explain at least twelve different sorts of disparity*, that is the disparities between the ten senses and between them and the qualia of feeling emotions and of thinking. No such explanation has ever been offered.

Thus, not only does the reductionist fail to explain (a) how there can be conscious experiences at all, and (b) how these conscious experiences do not resemble the neural events which transmit them, but also (c) how apparently identical neural processes produce conscious experiences of so numerous and diverse a sort. Of course the evolutionist will tell us, quite correctly, that the senses must have very different qualia, for if they did not we might mistake a sight for a sound, or a taste for a shape. And this would create problems for our survival. His observation is correct, but inadequate in that it explains neither *how* this diversity is produced, nor the *qualities* of the different qualia.

There are no acceptable theories as to how the trick is done. Moreover no location has ever been found for consciousness. It has not been located anywhere in the brain. It has even been suggested that it may have no locality at all.

Conclusion

Chalmers points out that there are two sorts of problem connected with consciousness — those which might in principle be solved by materialist explanations, and those which so far look insoluble. He concludes that conscious experience is of a *sort* that reductionist arguments are powerless to explain.[19] Physics does not provide a theory of everything. He says he finds this result disappointing.[20] I am not sure whether to believe in *his* disappointment, and certainly *we* should be encouraged. Consciousness cannot be either explained or explained away. It may be a fundamental reality; it is certainly not an epiphenomenon or secondary creation. This is not a cause for despair, but for hope and delight. Three possible steps can be taken from this point: (a) either there are two primary creations, consciousness and matter; (b) or there is one primary creation which produces out of itself both matter and consciousness; (c) or there is one primary creation, consciousness, which in turn is the source of 'appearance' or 'matter.'

Ken Wilber recently noted that Chalmers had been published by *Scientific American,* 'bastion of physicalist science,' where he stated that 'subjective consciousness continues to defy all objectivist explanations.' 'It never ceases to amaze,' says Wilber drily, 'how Anglo-Saxon philosophers greet the reinvention of the wheel with such fuss.'[21]

4. Do Brains Think?

> People are all in favour of new ideas, provided they are exactly like the old ones.
>
> Charles Kettering

> All the body is in the mind, but not all the mind is in the body.
>
> Swami Rama[1]

Some astonishing statements

Might the Universe contain something in addition to unconscious matter? Even the merest suggestion of such a view will be greeted with horror by materialists, reductionists and physicalists — and with the intolerance they show to all heresies. But what do materialists believe?

Much innocent entertainment can be obtained through collecting statements from the more extreme materialists. Thus a recent Dictionary of Psychology asserts:

> Consciousness is a fascinating but elusive phenomenon; it is impossible to specify what it is, what it does or why it evolved. Nothing worth reading has been written about it.[2]

Views of this sort were for two or three generations the reigning orthodoxy — imposed in the early twentieth century by the behaviourists. This school believed that it was contrary to scientific principles to admit the existence of inner states of mind. Thus one of their leaders, Burrhus F. Skinner, was still declaring in 1953:

> that mind and ideas are spurious entities invented for the sole purpose of providing spurious explanations.[3]

We are often told that behaviourism is dead. However, it is easy to find recent examples. Thus, Thalberg in 1983 refused to believe that

(a) there could be such a thing as mind and its contents observable by oneself alone, and that (b) one has privileged access to one's own state of mind.[4] In 1999 Susan Blackmore wrote:

> There is no truth in the idea of an inner self inside my body that controls my body and is conscious. ... Since this is false, so is my idea of my conscious self having free will.[5]

Thalberg is a professional philosopher and Blackmore is a reader in psychology.

Since, according to these authorities, consciousness does not exist, neither do any of its accompanying experiences, such as knowing, willing or intending. G. Vesey asserts that phrases like 'I know,' 'I hope,' 'I remember,' 'I mean' and 'I understand' do not refer to anything at all. Ramachandran claims that free will is 'a superstition.'[6] Olson suggests we stop speaking of ourselves as selves, 'because the word "self" has no agreed meaning.'[7]

Can Olson please suggest a word which *does* have a permanent stable agreed meaning? It's not just the meaning of the word 'Self' but the meaning of any word at all which has to be agreed every moment of the day, pragmatically, approximately, as the subject, context, and metaphoricity of our conversations keep changing.[8] Olson's objection applies to all language, and if taken seriously would prevent us from talking about anything at all.

A rather similar dismissal is made by Sharf, who attacks the word 'experience' as being a 'rhetoric' unfairly used to disqualify reductionism.[9] He claims that 'experience' can't be clearly defined, and that anything that can't be clearly defined doesn't exist. But, as the philosopher Karl Popper showed, nothing can be defined with total clarity. This is true even of scientific concepts, for:

> Every physicist knows exactly what the first and second law [of thermodynamics] mean, but ... no two physicists agree about them. ...
>
> It is impossible to speak in such a way that you cannot be misunderstood.[10]

If this is true in science, *a fortiori* it must be true of the concepts of everyday speech.

Blackmore insists that her book is not the result of conscious action on her part, but is 'a combined product of the genes and memes playing out their competition in [my] life.' (For 'memes,' read 'ideas seen as having independent existence.' We might compare them to viruses, but of a mental kind. Thus, according to meme-ists, we do not have ideas, we are 'infected' with them.) Genes and 'memes' are of course blind pieces of machinery concerned, not with truth, but with survival.[11] A book based on such a theory can imply no claim to truth, for by its author's own proud admission, *she does not know what she is saying*. Nonetheless, we cannot believe for a moment that she has written her book in a state of blind automatism, and she and other neo-behaviourists are a striking example of what they themselves declare to be impossible, namely the activity of consciousness.

Mind into brain doesn't go

Far from intimidating us, these extreme statements should encourage us to speculate.

Wilder Penfield was a great innovative neurosurgeon, founder of the Montreal Neurological Institute and Hospital, a pioneer in modern brain surgery and in mapping the functions of different regions of the brain. In 1975, having retired, he issued a book called *The Mystery of the Mind* in which he tells us:

> Throughout my own scientific career I, like other scientists, have struggled to prove that the brain accounts for the mind. But now, perhaps, the time has come when we may profitably consider the evidence as it stands. [He explains] how I came to take seriously, even to believe, that the consciousness of man, the mind, is something not to be reduced to the brain-mechanism.

To his own surprise, he confesses, he has ended as a dualist.

He describes how patients whose language ability had been partially 'turned off' attempt to deal with linguistic demands. One patient couldn't 'get' (as he put it) the word 'butterfly,' so he tried to 'get' the word 'moth.' He had no success, but explained to the doctor later what his experience had been. From this and many other experiences, Penfield concluded that there were at least two processes at work: one that 'knows' the word in the sense of being able to recognize it when found; the other that provides the word. The first was still active, while the second had been deactivated. During his physical manipulations of the brain he was unable to discover any site for the former process, and he was tempted therefore to think of it as mind, not as some other part of the brain.

Surgical treatment of the brain in Penfield's hospital was typically preceded by exploration of parts of the brain while the patient was conscious (for the brain does not feel pain). The doctor could therefore (by applying electrodes in various places) produce reactions in the patient, getting him to move his hand for example, or utter a sound. The patient however always knew that this was not an action willed by himself. He would say to the doctor, 'I didn't do that. You did.' Or: 'I didn't make that sound. You pulled it out of me.' The patient's will is thus clearly separate from the doctor's activating of his cortex, and the patient is plainly aware of this fact. Penfield writes:

> The patient's mind ... can only be something quite apart from neuronal reflex action. ... The fact that there is no confusion [between (1) the sensory information coming in and (2) the 'aloof and critical' thoughts judging the situation] suggests that, although the content of consciousness depends in large measure on neuronal activity, awareness itself does not.

Penfield's conclusions were these. He could discover no site in the brain for higher and non-mechanical actions such as believing or deciding. His experience and his findings all came together to make a consistent picture — namely that the brain is a computer. The controller of this computer is the mind, an entity not to be located in the brain. After all his experience, he concluded that 'mind-action' cannot be provoked by any part of the brain. He writes:

> But what the mind does is different. It is not to be accounted for by any neuronal mechanism that I can discover. ...
>
> There is no place in the cerebral cortex where electrical stimulation will cause a patient to believe or decide.[12]

Penfield's argument accords with first-hand accounts of migraine and of strokes. These constitute precious evidence of the relationship between mind and brain — a 'physiological experiment in the human being,' as one doctor puts it. Migraines may often result in a temporary loss of speech. The usual rhythmic zigzag patterns flicker in the air, enlarging progressively as the phenomenon advances, and eventually becoming so wide they disappear from view. If the experience goes to full term the subject cannot properly comprehend what others say to him, and cannot control what he is himself saying — though he knows what he would like to say. Thus a sufferer writes:

> I endeavoured to speak ... but found that I spoke uniformly other words than those intended.

Thinking he would use this wasted time to write a letter:

> I seated myself and wrote the first two words, but in a moment found that I was incapable of proceeding, for I could not recollect the words which belonged to the ideas which were present in my mind. ... I tried to write one letter slowly after the others ... but remarked that the characters I was writing were not those which I wished to write ...[13]

On the other hand, nothing except speech is lost to him. Objects are not apprehended differently; the sufferer knows what everything about him is, and what it is for; the world is perfectly comprehensible. Each object remains meaningful, and its purposes are clear. He or she merely lacks the word which refers to each object (though knowing there is such a word). There are thoughts in his mind, but his brain refuses to provide the right words and syntax for them. It must be like being a speechless animal — a fox for instance. He knows about rabbits, warrens, streams, hedgerows, dens, vixens and men in scarlet coats pursuing him with hounds. He has a mental map of his neighbourhood, and can find his way around with great skill. He has no words for such things — but his tacit knowing suffices perfectly. In other words, what sufferers experience during a migraine is the equivalent of losing the power of the explicit. Tacit experience, however, remains just as it was before.

The situation of stroke patients suffering aphasia is much graver. Language may be completely lost. Nonetheless, as Antonio Damasio, a professor of neurology, writes:

> As I studied case after case of patients with severe language disorders caused by neurological diseases, I realized that no matter how much impairment of language there was, the patient's thought processes remained intact in their essentials, and, more importantly, the patient's consciousness of his or her situation seemed no different from mine. ... In every instance I know, patients with major language impairments remain awake and attentive and can behave purposefully.[14]

This is born out by the testimony of patients. Thus one writes of his experience:

> I had suffered a stroke. I found myself thinking clearly enough but deprived of the ability to speak and to write. ... My speech became involved and deteriorated almost completely. I could not write my own name nor letters of the alphabet.[15]

Another writes:

> It is all very frustrating, as I know all I want to say or write but not being able to do it.[16]

As Dr Jay comments:

> It must be emphasized that a hemiplegic who has a defect of speech is not stupid or insane ... He has not lost the ability to think and reason but merely to talk or write.[17]

Sir John Hale who, after his stroke, was never able to speak comprehensibly again, communicated to his wife the following:

> John insists not only that he thinks as before, but that he thinks in language: that is why he is so surprised when people fail to understand his meaning. Dr Wise has no problem with this claim. John, he says, hasn't lost his language, he's lost his language *processing*.[18]

Core consciousness (which Damasio defines as the possession of one's own self-aware perspective, thoughts and freedom to act) is not affected by brain damage.[19] In short, sufferers are locked inside a machine whose controls no longer work — which is exactly the impression given by countless first-hand accounts. This is one major reason why, by hard work and practice, many sufferers may learn to speak again and to function much more normally. 'The aim of treatment is the re-education of the brain,' writes Charles Isted.[20]

Examining cases of aphasia allows one to resolve the old problem of whether thought is dependent on language. Aphasia cases show quite clearly that thought and language 'are neither identical nor parallel.'[21] Scott Moss (a professor of clinical psychology) relates of his own aphasia that:

> I even lost for the first two months the ability to use words internally, that is, in my thinking. ... I was rendered concrete in terms of my thinking ... Thus,. there seems to be a relationship between the loss of language and abstraction.[22]

This bears out what we have found about the tacit and the explicit. There is a difference between (a) thinking and (b) thinking which is dependent on words.[23]

We shall not know precisely what areas of mental experience 'belong to the mind rather than the brain' until a great deal more work has been done. Even under the most extreme supposition, however, it is evident that brain damage does not affect consciousness, identity, purpose and the will.

These findings harmonize with the investigations of Penfield. They suggest the possibility that certain important functions of core consciousness are distinct from the brain. The experiences of migraines and strokes certainly do not *prove* that this is so, for it is possible that the internal observer unaffected by these neurological electric storms is a separate brain function. Since, however, sufferers are not reduced to zombyism, and consciousness continues to affirm its independence, it seems that such functions are not subject to brain damage. It is therefore a tenable view that core consciousness is non-physical, or outside the brain. It was just such an internal observer as this that Penfield was unable to find in the brain.

And nobody has succeeded in discovering it since.

So far, then, we have seen that:

— no location has been found for consciousness, nor for any guiding 'witness' such as Penfield in his researches was seeking.
— No mechanism has been found to resolve the 'binding problem.'
— Moreover the manner in which the world is presented in experience is as yet inexplicable, on account of (a) the nature of qualia and (b) the variousness with which they present themselves (as sound, colour, taste, physical movement, etc). The problem of qualia not only has not yet been resolved, but may be incapable of resolution.

All this, though not conclusive, strongly suggests either (a) an extra-dimensional or (b) a dualistic / idealist solution. That is it suggests that consciousness (along with its experiential modalities, that is the qualia) *is outside the brain altogether,* either in some extra-dimensional space and/or in some separate mental space. We shall be exploring in due course what such a solution might look like.

Location of long term memory

There are however other major mysteries. Where are the forms of memory known as long term memory and tacit (or nondeclarative) memory located? In what part of the brain are they stored? Here I must point out that neurobiologists have distinguished several forms of memory. There is:

— short-term memory, much of which vanishes after a relatively short period; it does not survive brain-damage;
— long-term memory, which survives brain damage;
— explicit memory, which involves the recall of explicit information;
— tacit memory, which again survives brain damage.[24] Explicit memory and tacit memory appear to correspond in their natures to Polanyi's explicit and tacit knowing.

Again, Long Term Memory has as yet not been located. It seems clear that the hippocampus (and other components of the medial temporal lobe system) are needed for the laying-down[25] of long-term memories.

But where these memories are stored remains a mystery, for LTM, stored long ago, is not harmed by damage to the hippocampus.

Here we must return to Wilder Penfield. While preparing for operating on patients, and so as to enable the surgeon to localize the target area, it was necessary to explore their exposed brains, touching the latter with electrodes. Meanwhile the patients remained conscious, the brain having no pain receptors. He discovered that memories of extraordinary intensity could be evoked by touching parts of the patient's brain:

> On the first occasion, when one of these 'flashbacks' was reported to me by a conscious patient I was incredulous. On each subsequent occasion, I marvelled. For example, when a mother told me she was suddenly aware, as my electrode touched her cortex, of being in the kitchen listening to the voice of her little boy who was playing outside in the yard. She was aware of the neighbourhood noises, such as passing motor cars, that might mean danger to him.
>
> A young man stated he was sitting at a baseball game in a small town and watching a little boy crawl under the fence to join the audience. Another was in a concert hall listening to music. ... He could hear the different instruments. All these were unimportant events, but recalled with complete detail.[26]

Cytowic describes these restored memories as follows:

> ... Electrical stimulation could make patients relive the past as though it were the present. ... The recollection ... proceeds in a normal time frame. ... The evoked memory is more than an ordinary memory, appearing to be a full somatic participation in the original experience.

(That is it is a complete *tacit* restoration of experience, not a mere abstract simulacrum.)

These experiments suggested that our memories are (a) endless in number, (b) packed with as much tacit detail as the original experiences, and that (c) all memories, however banal or trivial, remain in the memory store. One might reasonably conclude that the mind preserves a complete record of the whole of our past experience.

Penfield's experiments are well known and have naturally been much criticized. For example, (a) the patients' brains were abnormal, since they were epilepsy patients; (b) they were not tested psychologically; (c) it was wrong to claim that the memory existed at the point of stimulation. To tell the truth (a) and (b) seem rather ill-targeted complaints. For, even if these patients' brains or psychologies were abnormal, the survival of memories in every detail remains hard to explain in physical terms. As for the point that the memories did not exist at the point of stimulation, this supports my case. The important objection is this: (d) how is one to determine whether these were true memories or mere 'confabulations' (that is products of the brain's imaginative powers)?

Nonetheless (as Cytowic reminds us) nobody has in recent years sought to repeat Penfield's experiments.[27] One hopes this is not due to reluctance to investigating facts which might refute materialism. Moreover, there is important other evidence to suggest that LTM is infinite or quasi-infinite. The great Russian psychologist Luria devoted a whole book to the remarkable case of S, who never forgot 'anything he had learned, even following a single exposure, and even after more than a decade.'[28] S was severely handicapped in the ordinary business of life by the permanent presence of so many memories, these being usually irrelevant to his immediate tasks. Thus most people have a mechanism which suppresses irrelevant memories, and indeed makes most of them hard to retrieve. This does not mean they are not still 'somewhere in the mind' however. Back in 1973 Lionel Standing set up a modern version of Kim's Game, in which subjects were shown a series of slides, then later examined on their ability to remember them. Standing was amazed by the success his subjects showed, and proceeded to increase the number of photographs up to an astonishing ten thousand. Even then the error rate was very low, and Standing concluded that 'there is no upper bound to memory capacity.'[29] Steven Rose comments that perhaps 'nothing is forgotten, provided we know how to ask if it is remembered.'[30]

What does all this imply? Does the mind indeed preserve everything that has ever happened to us, and moreover in the kind of tacit detail that the patients of Penfield and the remarkable S showed? Since the brain, being physical, is finite, how can it contain as much as this? The strong suggestion is therefore that *long term memory is not in the brain*. This is also strongly suggested by the fact that it survives brain damage. Once again we might draw the conclusion that the mind is either non-material or extra-dimensional.

We should note that this conclusion is not affected by the common modern view that (since it has proved impossible to locate memories in a particular store or 'receptacle') they are likely to be spread out across various parts of the brain.[31] For the question still remains, could the brain be capacious enough?[32]

Location of tacit memory

At this point I should remind you of Steven Rose's remarks, quoted in Chapter 1, about explicit and tacit memory — or to use the language more usual among neurologists, declarative and procedural memory. He points out that one never forgets how to ride a bicycle; 'yet it is possible entirely to forget, as a result of brain damage, that a two-wheeled object which one can sit on, pedal and move about with is actually called *bicycle*.' Steven Rose writes :

> The inescapable conclusion is that procedural and declarative memory are not merely localized, but localized to different regions of the brain, so that the one, declarative, can be lost, whilst the other, procedural, is spared. As it seems extremely difficult to lose procedural memory and relatively easy to lose declarative, it may also be that the actual biochemical, physiological or anatomical nature of the store is ... different in the two cases.[33]

Now, the location of tacit memory (TM) has not been found. It has been possible to identify parts of the brain which are utilized in the learning process, but not a location for the permanent storage of memories. Squire and Kandel wonder therefore whether memories are spread out over various parts of the brain.[34] Indeed, if one seeks a normal physiological explanation, this is the only alternative. It must be noted however that this makes the binding problem even more of a conundrum, and so also does these writers' identification of several different sorts of tacit memory, each of which calls upon different mechanisms.[35]

This again suggests that, as in the case of LTM and consciousness, an extra-dimensional and/or mentalistic explanation has not been excluded.

Moreover, the whereabouts of memories are not easy to trace. Bailey and Chen speak of 'structural plasticity' during memory formation.[36] Steven Rose (giving an account of one of his experiments with chicks) goes further in his 1991 article:

> Memory traces are not, it would appear, stably located within a single neuronal ensemble, but are dynamic and fluid, moving from site to site within the brain.[37]

Memory traces can't be pinned down. It's as if they move across and through the three-dimensional physicality of the brain. Such a picture would be in harmony with Smythies' extra-dimensional theory of consciousness, to be discussed in Chapter 12.

Memory for survival

Let me now tug the argument in an unexpected direction. One of the major difficulties about any religious or philosophical theory of life after death is the question of the survival of identity. It is normally argued that, if there is a soul, and if it is to survive death, then it needs a sense of identity, and that this must depend on a certain continuity of memory.

Now, as science has progressed, people have thought any such survival of the memory increasingly unlikely. For 'memory must depend on the brain,' and the brain dies with its owner. As we have just seen, however, this view is far from being proven. It is still perfectly possible to argue not only that consciousness and its qualia could be 'outside the brain' but also that certain areas of the memory, specifically long-term and tacit memory, could well be 'outside the brain' as well. Until neurobiologists can crack these problems, we are free to believe in the survival of memory.

Not perhaps in the survival after death of explicit memory, and therefore not in the survival of language. But this will not be too great a loss, provided the tacit, of which meaning is so important a part, and of which language is merely a semantic representation, will still be with us. Tacit memory and tacit knowing could perhaps be both/either extra-dimensional and/or mental and non-physical. This possibility cannot at present be refuted.

Many Westerners loathe the idea of survival. They claim they would not be able to live with themselves for ever. One can imagine the problem. George Bernard Shaw was one of these, though we cannot entirely take his point seriously, because so often his tongue was provocatively to be found in his cheek.

But survival does not necessarily have to entail the continuation of the *personality* (whether it be kind or ill-natured) of the survivor. The Buddha was impressed by the contingency of personality as such. He reasoned that purely personal qualities, subject to accidents of birth, locality and evanescent social customs, cannot be eternal. His theory of *anatta* (literally 'no-soul') proposes that all personal characteristics are eradicated after death.

Let us suppose then that LTM and TM are in the physical brain, and are indeed lost at death. This does not show that consciousness and its qualia-experiencing capacities are so eradicated. Pure consciousness (the impersonal) may be the survivor. What if the sense of simply 'oneself going on' is sufficient?

It is a fundamental mistake to suppose that my sense of identity and continuity are due to my characteristics as a *person*. It is true that many contingent features of my experience have built up throughout my life into a sense of 'my character and personality.' However, the word 'person' is revealing. Etymologically, it means 'mask' and relates specifically to the masks that actors wore on the Greek and Roman stage. It is not the essential part of oneself, but merely a rôle or self-invented 'part' that one plays, an outer surface, an externally visible set of behaviours. The deep self is not these outer and contingent aspects of my historical life, but most simply and profoundly my pure consciousness, lying behind and beyond the contingent.[38]

My sense of identity and continuity is due to the fact that I am a continuous viewer, experiencer and actor among successive events, and, as all experience shows, unfailingly connected to the onward progress of time. It has nothing to do with my contingent *existence* in the outside world, nor with my personality or character, but with my *experience* in my own inner world. The former is indeed relatively continuous and sequential, and so gives the false impression of being the source of my sense of identity. The mistake can be clearly seen if one turns to a tale from the *Thousand and One Nights* — one used by the Sufis — 'The Dreamer Awakened.'

Abu Hassan entertains at dinner a person whom he takes to be a merchant from Mosul, but who is really the irresponsible Caliph

Haroun al-Rashid in disguise. Abu Hassan expresses the wish that he could punish the malicious Mullahs of his local mosque. Haroun gives him a sleeping powder and transfers him to his own bed in the palace in Baghdad. Abu Hassan wakes up on the following morning, and after initial disbelief begins, as the day goes on, to be convinced he is Haroun al-Rashid. That evening he is given another powder, and wakes as Abu Hassan. Nonetheless he continues to claim he is the Caliph, for he can see that certain orders he issued the previous day are being carried out. He is taken away to the lunatic asylum. A month later he meets Haroun again, and again finds himself masquerading — temporarily — as Commander of the Faithful.

The moral of this story is not only the delusory nature of reality (though it is that too). It is the fact that we must not be deceived by the accidental appearances of continuity and discontinuity outside us in 'the real world.' We must not be taken in by their apparent *consistencies*, nor misled by their apparent *inconsistencies*. It is not from these appearances that our sense of identity and reality derives, but from the continuity of our inner experience. Real continuity is only to be found within the deep self. Consulting his experiences, Abu Hassan should not have supposed that his identity was *either* that of a citizen *or* of the Caliph, but rather that his true identity was his inner witness of himself, of his successive rôles and actions. Then he would have seen through it all, and realized that a game was being played upon him. Indeed, on the second occasion he begins to dance, the whole practical joke breaks down in laughter, and this demonstrates his new understanding of the situation.

Thus David Hume, who famously claimed that there is no 'I,' misunderstood the issue. As Hume says, whenever he searched about in his consciousness he could never find any 'I,' but merely sensations, images and thoughts. John Smythies ripostes that this shows us exactly what the 'I' is. For the 'I' Hume couldn't find was of course precisely what was doing the searching. That was why he couldn't find it. And Smythies adds that this will do as a definition of the 'I.'[39]

Subjectively, experience confirms that we in our essence are (a) an inner witness, (b) a guiding consciousness, (c) a will. There is no sign of the first two of these in the physical brain. With (c) we shall deal in the next chapter. In addition no location has been found for either LTM or TM.

Our conclusion is evident: namely that we do not yet know enough to conclude. We may confidently assert however that either (a) these items, some or all of them, will be found in the physical brain in future; or (b) we need some new theory, possibly physical in nature, such as a theory of extra dimensions; or (c) we need a mentalist theory.

In the light of our knowledge, dualism or non-physicalism remains a perfectly reasonable position. *Nothing has refuted it.*

Nonetheless, if we listen to a materialist such as Susan Blackmore, we might regard her as proving the reality of the non-material self. In her *Meme Machine* she asks three vital questions: 'What am I? Where am I? What do I do?' In response to the second, she replies:

> There is no centre of action where a self might reside. There is no one place into which all the inputs go, and from which all the instructions get sent out. ... The important point is that the description that neuroscientists are building up of the way the brain works leaves no room for a central self.[40]

She concludes that, because the physical world is all there is, there is therefore no self.

But we know there is a central self, because we are it. Thus if Blackmore's assertion is correct, then this proves, not that the central self is non-existent, but that it is not in the physical brain. She should abandon her materialism and conclude that either solution (b) or (c) must necessarily be correct.

The cerebral filter

Let us now take a radical step. Reductionists believe that consciousness is wholly a creation of the brain. But could the relationship be the other way around?

Could it be that the brain does not create consciousness, but on the contrary *limits* it? Is the brain a kind of valve or filter, which permits the entry to experience of only a restricted number of things? One can see the logic in this, for otherwise we would be radically overburdened, unable to choose or act under the welter of experiences descending upon us. And in one sense this is manifestly true. Our ears do not respond to the high frequencies which bats (for instance) can hear. Our senses do not convey the full range of possible sensory information to us — far from it. To take but one example, they do not convey to us the sorts of electrical experiences which an elephant-nosed fish has. Our visual sense does not respond to electromagnetic radiation except within a very narrow frequency range, namely that of visible light. We cannot see radio waves, nor even ultraviolet or infrared. Indeed the eye is sensitive to only about one percent of the electromagnetic spectrum.

The psychologist Ornstein, commenting on all this, refers to the ideas of Bergson:

> The suggestion is that the function of the brain, nervous system and sense organs is in the main eliminative ... [Their] function is to protect us from being overwhelmed and confused by this mass of largely useless and irrelevant knowledge, by shutting out most of what we should otherwise perceive or remember at any moment, and leaving only that very small and special selection which is likely to be practically useful.[41]

He then quotes Aldous Huxley:

> According to such a theory, each one of us is potentially Mind at Large. But in so far as we are animals, our business is at all costs to survive. To make biological survival possible, Mind at Large has to be funnelled through the reducing valve of the brain and nervous system. What comes out at the other end is a measly trickle of the kind of consciousness which will help us to stay alive on the surface of this particular planet. ... Certain persons, however, seem to be born with a kind of by-pass that circumvents the reducing valve. In others temporary by-passes may be acquired either spontaneously, or as the result of deliberate 'spiritual exercises' ...[42]

He then illustrates this view from an experiment done at the Massachusetts Institute of Technology, in which J.Y. Lettwin and his associates found that, out of thousands of possible kinds of message, a frog's retina can transmit only four kinds to its brain. 'The frog's brain presumably evolved to *discard* the remainder of the information available.'[43]

That the brain is a limitation on experience seems to have been the opinion of William Blake, who wrote in *The Marriage of Heaven and Hell:*

> How do you know but ev'ry Bird that cuts the airy way,
> Is an immense world of delight, clos'd by your senses five?[44]

lines which signify that the five senses are like peepholes permitting the entry of only small fragments of the wonder that is the Universe. Blake believes we would have awareness of the All were it not for the limitations of our physical senses.

Blake's lines are a mystical intuition, not a philosophical proposition. For the latter we need to turn to the French philosopher Henri Bergson and to his *Matière et Mémoire*, dating from 1896. As Stephen Robbins explains in an important article, Bergson seems to have foreseen holograms some fifty years before Dennis Gabor invented them. Bergson (who was intensely interested in the science of his own day) argued that the Universe is an immense field of mutual interactions, every detail of which is reflected throughout its whole space:

> Build up the universe with atoms: Each of them is subject to the action, variable in quantity and quality according to the distance, exerted on it by all material atoms. Bring in Faraday's centres of force: the lines of force emitted in every direction from every centre bring to bear upon each the influence of the whole material world.[45]

In short, comments Robbins:

> To Bergson, the universe was a vast holographic manifold — a 'photograph ... at all points in space.' In a hologram, it scarce needs repeating, the information for any given point of an object is spread throughout, while conversely, at any given point of the hologram is found the information for the entire object. ... Thus the state of any point-instant is in fact the reflection of the entire history of the holographic field. From this perspective the universal field has an elementary aspect of *memory*.[46]

Bergson proposed that remembering is really an aspect of perceiving — one of its modes.[47] The Universe is a single vast experiencing process, or 'perception-device,' of conscious and self-conscious activity. He audaciously turns the usual way of looking at things upside down, and so the problem, for him, is not the usual one: namely how perception could possibly occur. The problem, for him, is not how perception (and memory) arises, but how it becomes limited, in the case of individuals, to their own experience, and furthermore limited to their own experience in the here and now. The senses are a limitation on infinite perception, and therefore on infinite memory, confining us to a particular moving time and space, the present moment. The Brain is a mechanism concerned with our survival, and it rejects and shuts out anything which is at the moment irrelevant to that survival. *The Brain is a filter.*

> The past however has not ceased to exist in the permanent and total record of the mind. Bergson speaks of its 'integral survival.' When we seek to remember, we are enabled to make reference to the required (that is presently useful) pieces of the past.

The brain blocks off all recollections which are irrelevant to the present living moment, and allows only relevant memories to appear. Each person has his individual memory, and this is due to his possessing an individual brain mechanism, with its own history.[48]

Memory losses — amnesias, aphasias, etc. — are due to damage to the brain machinery. My permanent memory remains unaffected, but my 'I,' in its present state, finds itself disconnected from it through the malfunctioning of the cerebral valve, that is of the brain. It must be added that it was extraordinarily prescient of Bergson to anticipate our modern findings, namely that memory is quasi-infinite.

I suggested in my Introduction that we should turn everything upside down. This is exactly what Bergson did in 1896. If he is right, then the picture should be something as follows. The Universe is a One and All, is conscious and knows everything all at once. We however are individuals closed away from this total knowledge, 'polders' locked within our little lagoons, this enclosure / exclusion being caused by the divisions that the Universe has created in itself so as to produce a varied and quarrelling totality — this being much more interesting than temperate reason and flat calm. We are focused on action and survival in the present ever-moving moment and so, although our entire past history resides in our personal memory, we draw only upon those elements of it which may be helpful in the present. As Bergson himself observes, the structure of time is crucial to this picture.

This astonishing conjecture is at least equally plausible as that of the reductionist. Perhaps we may compare the latter to someone who thinks the wheels of the car control the pedals, which in turn control the movements of the driver. But this is quite simply the wrong way round.

We must next examine free will, that all-important companion of conscious awareness, to determine whether it can be argued away, or whether it too remains as a problem insoluble by materialism.

5. Free Will

Don't listen to your professors ...
especially if they are from Oxford.

Ramachandran & Blakeslee, p. 221

Perhaps the most important of the powers of consciousness is the making of choices. If we cannot defend free will, we cannot assert that consciousness 'makes a difference.' And if it does not make a difference, what is it for?

Defining determinism

Common sense generally agrees that, presented with a choice, we are capable of deciding between alternatives. Even with so familiar an action as crossing the road, we *decide* to do so at a preferred moment. My opponents here are the determinists, that is those who believe that all my actions are predetermined by an inevitable causal process, and that there is no room in nature for 'my will.'

The determinist's case against freedom might be expressed as follows: The human brain is part of nature, and nature is a system in which every event has a cause. Thus, at 7.30 John is powerless to alter his state of mind at 7.29. Suppose that, at 7.30, John decides to leave his wife. His decision depends on his state of mind at that moment. But this is caused by his state of mind at 7.29.59 seconds, plus anything that has impinged upon him in the meantime. These things are caused in their turn by things equally outside his control, that is his state of mind at 7.29.58 seconds, plus whatever caused the other things to impinge upon him. And so on backwards for ever into the infinities of past time. Indeed, without a shade of inconsistency we might run the same argument back before John's birth, back before the birth of his mother Joan, back before the births of the ancestors of their ancestors. For every event, according to this doctrine of the absolute empire of causality, comes about through causes, and these in turn through earlier causes, and all these causes are inevitable from the very beginning of time to its end. We are into the nightmare of Laplace's demon, in which the whole past and future of the universe is determined, absolutely, at the moment of its inception, including the precise place where every feather falls from every falling sparrow.

One can see the force of the determinist case. Nor is there any way out through saying (quite correctly), 'There are reasons for thinking that the brain operates (at least in some respects) at a quantum level. Now quantum events (taken in small numbers) are unpredictable.' This does not help the apologist of free will, for it merely transforms us from the puppets of causality into the playthings of chance.

Determinism self-refuted

Two twentieth century thinkers who have struggled with these problems are the French philosophers Jean-Paul Sartre and Henri Bergson. In Sartre, free will is called not *le libre arbitre* (a term he as an atheist may have disliked because of its religious overtones) but simply *la liberté* (freedom). To him free will is a fundamental datum. Consciousness is no doubt the most fundamental thing of all. But free will seems to come wrapped up in the same parcel with consciousness; to be conscious *entails* a knowledge of the freedom to choose and to act upon that choice. Now, suppose that someone has just performed an act which seems to us foolish, or morally dubious. We ask him 'Why did you do that?' and he replies, 'I had no alternative.' 'But look,' we say to him, 'you might have done B or C, not A.' He denies it: 'No, I could have acted in no other way.'

The man will then usually offer an explanation, for instance:

> The terrorist who kills and excuses himself by saying that he had no choice because the party ordered him to kill is in 'bad faith' because he pretends that his existence is necessarily linked with the party, while in fact this linkage is the consequence of his own choice.

Similarly with appeals to authority, for in every such case without exception the man's allegiance to such 'higher authority' is the result of a choice on his part and could be broken by another choice on his part.

This is part of the nature of human existence. 'Bad faith' *(mauvaise foi)*, says Sartre, 'is to pretend something is necessary that in fact is voluntary.'[1] Such a person is dissembling; he is withholding the truth from himself. We are 'condemned to be free,' as Sartre thought-provokingly puts it, because we are in our nature choosing beings. Consciousness cannot reject its power of choice, because even choosing not to choose is still a choice.[2] Only hypocrites deny they have free will.

Let us take a rather different case, someone who, asked why he betrayed his comrades under torture (a very Sartrean example), replies, 'I had no choice, I was forced to do it.' A character in one of Sartre's plays commits suicide because he fears to betray his comrades; plainly he recognizes this case as much more difficult. Nonetheless, some remarkable individuals have been known to remain silent even under the most horrible coercion. Thus, in Sartre's world (setting aside situations where drugs confuse the mind), there is nothing that can ultimately have compulsion over the human will. To claim otherwise is to be in 'bad faith,' for we all know as a matter of experience that we might have acted otherwise than we did. Sartre's world has a somewhat heroic flavour. One might say that, for him, free will is *proved* by the heroism of those who actually live up to it. And this is not unreasonable, for such cases may have a very unexpected look to them, which in itself tends to prove the case for free will.

Henri Bergson's argument against determinism arises from his analysis of the experience of time in his *Essai sur les données immédiates de la conscience* (Essay on the Immediate Data of Consciousness) published in 1889. Bergson contrasts time as we think of it with time as we experience it (*la durée*, which is usually translated as 'duration'). When we think of time, we imagine it in spatial terms, as a line. Now lines can be chopped up into lengths or divided into points which we call 'moments.' However this is a metaphor of, or an abstraction from, our experience of time, which is not space-like: it is a continuous boiling inextricable flow. Once time has entered the past, it solidifies: then, viewed in our memories, it appears to be analysable in spatial terms. But a map of the turbulent, molten present is impossible. It is simply not that kind of thing.

Similarly free will itself cannot be explicitly confined. It cannot be assimilated to a line drawn upon a map, as if time were at rest like space. Living in time is like a surfer riding a breaking wave: the actual experience of this cannot be analysed and chopped up into pieces as the surfer rides, though afterwards the camera might seem to confirm that delusion. Nonetheless, it is not the surfer's decisions, or the processes by which he came to those decisions, which are registered by the camera, but only their outcomes. Bergson's assertion is that the fluid, mobile nature of decisions is not laid out in time in the same way as the results of these decisions. Without demolishing causality, Bergson denies the absolute mechanical clarity of causation.[3]

The difficulty about Bergson's argument may be that it depends on our inner experience in which, indeed, the exact causal sequencing of events is often untraccable. This is of course perfectly good evidence, but unfortunately it is the opposite of the kind of evidence that will convince the determinist. The determinist, moreover, is a creature who is increasingly widespread. Colin Blakemore declares himself to be one:

> The human brain is a machine, which alone accounts for all our actions, our most private thoughts, our beliefs. It creates the state of consciousness and the state of self. It makes the mind. ... It seems to me to make no sense ... to try to distinguish between acts that result from conscious intention and those that are pure reflexes or that are caused by disease or damage to the brain.

This quotation is taken from Blakemore's *Mind Machine*. Its author however undermines himself by giving instances of people who, under the influence of a drug, explicitly stated that they *felt* controlled. One must conclude that, under the influence of the drug, they had noticed the difference from their normal state of *not* feeling controlled: that is they had noticed a diminution or an absence of their normal free will. Thus David Garabedian said: 'It just happened so fast. I didn't know who was doing this. I didn't feel in charge.' Julie asserted: 'This strange feeling would come over me, stranger and stronger than hell. A frightening feeling ... You had no control over how your body reacted.' Similar statements were made by Joseph B. Centifanti. One may equally well cite the statement of Al Ross, who declared he had 'chosen' to leave his criminal career behind.[4] Blakemore, very oddly, has failed to notice that his own selected examples of deterministic behaviour do not support his case.

Unfortunately it suits some people to claim they are zombies rather than responsible beings. The results can be alarming. It is increasingly the case (especially in the United States) that lawyers are using the new ideology of human zombyism to excuse their clients' crimes and 'get them off.' Alan Dershowitz in his *Abuse Excuse* discusses a disturbing number of such cases. For instance Jeremy Rifkin admitted to murdering seventeen women. His lawyer claimed he suffered from 'adopted child syndrome' because he had been 'rejected by his natural mother.' The symptoms of this alleged 'syndrome' include 'pathological lying, learning problems, running away, sexual promiscuity, an absence of normal guilt and anxiety, and extreme antisocial behaviour.' Dershowitz shows that 'adopted child syndrome' is at present being used as a defence in dozens of murder cases in the States. Eighteen-year-old Daimian Osby shot two men in cold blood. His defence lawyer claimed that because he lived in a dangerous neighbourhood which caused him to fear for his life, he was suffering from 'urban survival syndrome' and had become irrational and violent. Some of the jury were persuaded, so they split, and the case went to retrial. We must fear for a society whose members reject responsibility for their own acts, prefer to consider themselves the helpless puppets of their childhood or their chemistry, and who by the constant invention of imaginary 'syndromes' appeal to the prestige of science to support their irresponsibility.

It is well known that people who suffer from Parkinson's Disease, Tourette's Syndrome, Huntington's Chorea and even obsessive psychological compulsions to act in various ways — all these people are well aware of the difference between a voluntary act on their part and the unwilled and unwelcome actions of one of their bodily functions:

> A striking example is the 'alien hand syndrome.' Patients with a lesion in a fronto-medial portion of premotor area may find that the hand and arm on the affected side performs curious purposeful actions, such as undoing a buttoned shirt when the subject is trying to button it up; all this occurs without or even against the subject's intention and will.[5]

In other words people can tell the difference between willed and unwilled acts, and they are right about this difference. The determinist must not be allowed to shuffle the evidence under the carpet.

If choice and freedom of choice are not real, a whole sequence of questions and conclusions at once arises:

(1) Where then does the notion of 'choice' originate? Could it be a 'useful illusion'?

(2) But how can the notion of choice be useful if it is an illusion? Creatures who are deluded about the nature of reality must be, for that very reason, poorly fitted to survive.

(3) If choice is an illusion, then so is responsibility. Our actions are due merely to a mindless sequence of causes and chances. If we are to behave realistically, therefore, we must cease to consider our actions to be due to our own volition, and abandon the whole notion of responsibility.

(4) But if responsibility is abolished, so also is morality. It will no longer be valid to think in terms of doing good or doing evil. For:

(5) if we human beings have no responsibility, then it is not *we* who act, but the forces of chance and causation. The vital distinction we always make between what *we* do and what happens through the mysterious causal chains of nature, no longer exists. Thus:

(6) the whole notion of human action and activity would vanish. We are invited by determinists to adopt a passive fatalism.

In such a world, where the reigning philosophy is determinism, the following consequences should necessarily ensue.

(7) The author of the most horrific crimes would be regarded with indifference as if he were an accidental phenomenon of the laws of nature like a volcano or a flood.

(8) Equally the author of the most blissful happiness would receive no gratitude. For both of them would be no more responsible for their actions than would a stock or a stone.

(9) You wouldn't logically be able to say to anyone either 'Do that!' or 'Don't do that!' Still less would you be able to use the words 'shouldn't' or 'mustn't.' If free will is rejected, it is hard to see how anyone might bring up their children. Notions of good or evil would disappear. Notions of pain and suffering would of course continue, but the idea that anyone was responsible for these, or that anyone should try to amend them would vanish. Everyone would be free to do whatever s/he liked, under the excuse that there is no such thing as 'Doing whatever you like' but merely that:

> 'Everything just happens the way it must.' Perhaps this is what Susan Blackmore means when she writes that to be released from free will would make us really free.[6] Of course it would, but such 'freedom' is simply total moral irresponsibility.

To spell all this out shows how horrific such a situation would be. It is not only (1) unacceptable, but also (2) quite strictly unthinkable, that is to say *it is quite impossible for human beings to behave in the way I have just described.* This in itself proves that the determinist's picture of the human being is mistaken. We have, as it were, tested out the determinists' machine and found it doesn't work.

It may be that psychopaths are capable of behaving in this way, but they are fortunately a minority. There may be some other sick or pitiable people who might do likewise. If people started to *believe* it and *practise* it (as opposed to contemplating it in the philosopher's cold heaven) it would make impossible the love of parents for their children and render futile every human activity.

Determinism requires a credulous faith in the impossible.

We should also listen to Blauvelt's argument:

> Can belief in the overarching doctrine of determinism be seen correctly as anything but quaint or psychopathological? Belief in freedom, after all, is essential to our social institutions, with their emphasis on individual responsibility. Belief in determinism, to the extent it undermines that, is nothing but destructive of our social order ...[7]

And he goes on to warn us against the ideologies of communism, fascism and religious fundamentalism, all of which are determinist and deny humankind its freedom. It is clear from the entirely different behaviour of those who believe in such creeds and those who don't, that such beliefs make a difference — a fact which itself demonstrates the reality of Free Will.

In the light of the above it is not surprising that Cotterill relates that, 'when this awful truth dawned upon [him],' that is that he did not possess free will and was a mere passive spectator of his own actions, he was overcome with nausea.[8] Unfortunately he does not say what moral consequences he began to envisage after this negative epiphany. Perhaps he does not do so because such a description would itself undermine his alleged discovery. For can a helpless machine see why it would be better not to be helpless, and therefore feel appalled? I think not.

The determinist turns the clock back to that ancient view, fatalism — a view to which the Muslim world is to this day especially prone. By contrast we should attend to what Tim Mackintosh-Smith has to say. Bilingual in Arabic and English, this experienced traveller in the Middle East meditates on Islamic fatalism, and encapsulates a whole argument in this tiny parable:

> *Interviewer:* 'So, Mr and Mrs Bandersnatch, what made you choose the Algarve? Was it the direct flight? Or the childcare facilities? Or was it all this wonderful, guaranteed sunshine?'
>
> *Mr B:* 'Well, we certainly liked the look of the place in the brochure — didn't we, dear — but, to be honest, what really decided us was irresistible, inexorable Fate.'[9]

This is an effective *reductio ad absurdum* of fatalism and determinism, and demonstrates that causality, mediated by conscious beings, requires at the very least conscious assent, and therefore choice.

David Hume in the eighteenth century questioned the very notion of causality. Certainly we notice (he argued) that events succeed each other in an orderly way. However we can never observe just how one thing turns into another — only a succession of events: the causative process itself is invisible.[10] Kant, however, rethinks this. Without a notion of causality, he says, we cannot make sense of our experiences; we require it, or the world would be senseless; Kant even goes so far as to assert that a notion of causality is a precondition of our having any intelligible experience of the world.[11]

The roots of causality

Surely Kant is right. These considerations lead to the following question. Where does the concept of causality come from? It derives from observation, but perhaps most particularly from our personal experience. Do we not from earliest infancy *test out* our hunches about the nature of the world, by interacting with it? What is commoner than a child throwing its rattle over the side of its pram? The child repeats the act again and again as if to confirm its reliability: 'I do X, and Y follows. I am the cause of X which produces Y, and thus result follows cause.' Will and outcome. From this the whole notion of Cause and Effect arises. However tiresome this game may be to adults, we must treasure the delight and laughter in the child as he makes his rattle disappear — reliably — again and again.

I suggest therefore that *the idea of causality in the outside world is founded on a basic personal experience: namely that of exercizing our free will.* Causality is a notion that derives from our intimate acquaintance with free will. Causality therefore cannot be used as an argument against free will. Our application of it to the world is an extrapolation from our own experience. It is true that we cannot quite *see* how causation works. But we can *feel and know* it working as we raise our arms and cast the rattle or (when we are older) dance upon a surfboard off the Californian coast. It is self-contradictory to deny free will on the basis of a causal theory which is derived from the experience of that very same free will.[12]

Those who deny the causal efficacy of the will, should not, rationally speaking, accept the reality of causal processes in nature.

In their desire for objective truth, materialism and determinism have driven consciousness and freedom out of the picture. They have thereby brought about a strikingly ironic reversal. They have removed the conscious driver from the seat of his machine. But by thus asserting the subjection of the mind to its computer the brain, they have denied the very thing they sought — namely the possibility of attaining objective truth. For the statements of a determinist cannot possess truth, because the processes which produce it, that is perception, judgment, purpose, independent thought, discrimination, critical judgment, the weighing of evidence, disinterested objectivity, and moral responsibility — all these have been reduced to, replaced by, a haphazard chain of blind causes. The statements of a determinist are therefore, according to his own admission, not statements, but the mindless products of accident. They have no more claim to be statements than do the gushings of water down a mountainside according to the hazard of the showers of rain which fall.

The determinist is a self-refuting thinker. Or rather since, according to himself, he is a machine, he is a self-refuting machine.

Current state of the argument

The contemporary discussion over freedom and determinism is well represented by the authors collected in *The Volitional Brain.*[13] The centre of discussion is the repeating of Kornhuber's experiment by Libet and his associates, in which a subject is asked to flex the wrist at a time entirely determined by his or her will. Electrodes are placed on the subject's head to detect electrical activity in the brain. Brain activity in the form of a 'Readiness Potential' (RP) begins about 400 milliseconds before the performance of the act. However Libet found that the subject's conscious awareness of his or her intentions preceded the performance of the act by only about 200 milliseconds. Astonishingly therefore he had discovered that the brain's readiness to act occurs unconsciously about 200 milliseconds before the wish arises into consciousness.

So far the evidence seems to refute freedom of the will, since it looks as if the impulse to act is initially unconscious. However, as Libet explains, subjects were able, within the narrow perimeters of the time available (namely 100–200 milliseconds), to veto a planned act. No electrical activity has been detected *before* such a veto. Libet's conclusion is that this may be how free will operates — or at least how many free acts operate: an action is contemplated, but the will remains free to go along with it or to cancel it.

He also notes that there is no evidence of RP with acts that are not free and voluntary, such as Tourette's syndrome.[14] It must be added that voluntary acts are usually performed under conditions and contexts far removed from these rather artificial ones, and that these do not always resemble 'the simple one studied by us,' as Libet freely admits. There is thus no finality about his findings. Moreover whether or not these experiments tend to prove or disprove free will, they have evidently no bearing on decisions that are arrived at over a longer period than a second and a half.[15]

It is a universal experience that some impulses towards action seem to arise unconsciously, and then emerge into consciousness, though they are very often not acted upon. Libet's experiment would tend to show that we cannot help involuntary impulses arising, for they do so before conscious control can be exercised.[16]

There have been a variety of reactions to these findings, some claiming that they disprove free will, others, such as Goswami and John

Searle, claiming that Libet has triumphantly demonstrated its truth.[17] There can be no doubt that Libet does leave room for freedom. However, Roger Penrose's comment on these experiments is radical. He asks us to consider ordinary conversation. According to Libet's experimental calculations, he points out, it would take about a second and a half for any conscious response to occur. For conscious sensation seems to need about half a second, conscious willing about a second. Although some conversation may be automatic and unconscious, how could it take a whole second and a half to make a conscious response? The suggestion is quite counter-intuitive, and is in practice disproved by every conversation we have ever had.[18]

On the other hand, Libet's experiment is limited, as he himself agrees. The subjects knew *in advance* they were going to raise a hand, or not. It is hardly surprising therefore that they got ready to raise their hands .. and then on occasion did not. It is hardly surprising that there was a preparatory procedure in the brain — which could then be aborted.

Libet himself regards his experiment as tending to prove the reality of the will. He has proposed a further experiment to test whether conscious will could act on the brain without neuronal connexions, in a field-like way. However, the providers of research funds are repelled by experiments that might have a non-orthodox outcome. This later experiment has therefore yet to be performed.[19]

Further evidence for the will is put forward by the psychiatrist Jeffrey M. Schwartz. He describes the partial or complete curing of Obsessive Compulsive Disorder (instances of which are excessive handwashing, or ritualistic counting and checking). OCD patients can be trained to recognize these obsessive thoughts and urges, to realize they are caused 'not by me, but by the OCD.' They are encouraged to 'work around' the OCD by performing other behaviours. Eventually they may learn to 'separate' themselves from their compulsion and thus gain control over it. Physical changes in brain chemistry result. This seems a clear case of the power of mind over matter, and Schwartz assumes that we have a powerful 'Mental Force' at our disposal if we can learn to make use of it.[20]

Some conclude that we have the laws of physics wrong. Thus David L. Wilson writes:

> It is exciting to consider the possibility that a solution to the problem of consciousness might give us better insight into the nature of matter as well as free will.[21]

Elitzur says:

> The realization that consciousness is causally efficacious is devastating not only for all the theories that seek to preserve the completeness of the physical world but, ultimately, for physics itself. Which of the laws of physics will turn out to be wrong? Will it be the energy conservation law? The second law of thermodynamics? Is there a quantum-mechanical principle involved in this violation? Or perhaps quantum mechanics itself is violated? [22]

One thing is clear. Classical physics as understood by a mechanist would not permit such a phenomenon as free will. But many scientists think that quantum mechanics would *permit* it, or even *require* it. As Schwartz points out:

> The basic principles of physics, as they are now understood, are not the deterministic laws of classical physics. They are laws that determine only probabilities for events to occur. Other processes are needed to complete the ontological structure, if some definite sequence of physical events is to be actualized.[23]

That is to say, in quantum physics *the intervention of a conscious mind may be necessary for the misty probabilities of reality to emerge into actuality.* This most tried and tested of all scientific theories may be interpreted as supporting the ontological importance of consciousness and of free will.

But the findings of quantum physics require a chapter to themselves, and we must postpone this tempting discussion until Chapter 8.

Finally, we may ask a couple of pertinent questions. Can the unconscious mind make choices? Or are these (as philosophy would suggest) the privilege of consciousness? [24] A recent experiment described by Amit Goswami seems to show that the unconscious mind cannot make choices.

As Goswami points out, cases of 'blindsight' prove that we have unconscious vision. Thinking and feeling therefore do apparently continue in the unconscious. Not so however with choice. Tony Marcel set up an experiment in which the subjects were invited to sit in front of a screen. On this screen sets of three words would be shown one after another. They were asked to push a button each time they consciously recognized the meaning of the last word of the three. These triads were of the following kind:

> *hand – palm – wrist* (congruent: that is all three words belong in the same domain of thought / experience. Therefore there should be more rapid recognition of the final word.)
> clock – palm – wrist ('unbiased' that is the last two are associated in sense, but the first is not.)
> *tree – palm – wrist* (incongruent: that is the ambiguity of the middle word provides a bridge between the first and third words. Therefore there should be less rapid recognition than in the congruent cases.)
> *clock – ball – wrist* ('unassociated' — that is all three words are from different domains of thought / experience)

Sometimes, however:

> the middle word was masked by a pattern [25] so that the subject saw it unconsciously but not consciously. [In these cases,] there was no longer any appreciable difference in reaction time between the congruent and incongruent cases. This should be surprising, because presumably both meanings of the ambiguous word were available to the person, regardless of the biasing context, yet neither meaning was chosen over the other.

The experimenters explained these findings as follows. The unconscious holds off from resolving the ambiguity of the middle word. It does not choose. When the conscious mind is in control, however, it chooses between the two alternatives. Goswami continues:

> Apparently, ... choice is a concomitant of conscious experience but not of unconscious perception. ... *We choose, therefore we are.*[26]

This is a remarkable result. It bears out our instinctual belief that choice (and the will) are intimately connected with consciousness, and that in the absence of the latter the former cannot occur. Indeed it has often been suggested — by evolutionists among others — that the purpose of consciousness is to enable living things to make choices.

My second and final question relates to the theory of evolution. According to this, life is red in tooth and claw, survival goes to the fittest, the elimination of the unfit is pitiless, and all this explains the ascent of intelligence in the natural world, the ascent of man (as it used to be put), and now — according to fashionable theories — everything, from our sexual preferences to the taste of cornflakes.

Why then does the Universe present a picture of high drama if the actors in it are merely puppets? As the neuroscientist Smythies points out, one of the interpretations of special relativity is that the whole of the time dimension is already in being; the future is already determined. He is therefore moved to write:

> Why on earth the geometry of space-time should be arranged, if the [determinist] interpretation of special relativity is correct, so as to yield this entirely spurious appearance of an epic evolutionary struggle, is baffling.

Hence, he concludes, it is improbable that all is predetermined. Surely:

> World-lines might be more like ropes than tramlines, and so moveable by [mental] forces.[27]

For if free will does not exist, then consciousness must be a powerless prisoner of the torture chamber that is the Universe. And there is no point in that struggle either. For why *above all* pain?

Thus — and this is surely strange — the argument about free will *bears upon the nature of space-time itself.* On the one hand one particular interpretation of special relativity suggests that the entire Universe is predetermined from its most distant past to its most ultimate future. On the other hand, we can offer strong arguments against such determinism. For we *experience* free will; it is therefore an *empirical* finding. Therefore the geometry of space-time is likely to be arranged so that freedom is possible. Doubtless this is connected with the odd fact that time moves only forward, never towards the past. That time has an unknown future *makes no sense* unless free will is real.

Is purpose absent from the rest of the living world? Barry J. Hall of the University of Rochester has shown that bacteria may replace missing or faulty genes by mutating only those genes which they need. He experimented with *Escherichia coli* bacteria from which he had removed one of their genes. They mutated so as to produce a substitute enzyme. John Cairns at Harvard had similar results:

> Subsequently Hall could show conclusively that bacteria are able to mutate solely their defective genes. He tested specimens in which two of the five genes needed to synthesize *Trp* were defective, yet some bacteria survived the test by recovering the ability to synthesize this substance. It turned out that they mutated precisely and exclusively the two genes that were needed ...[28]

Orthodox neo-Darwinian theory states that mutations are entirely random. Thus, they (a) should not occur at a higher rate than normal even when needed; (b) should occur by sheer chance over the whole range of genes; (c) should be unaffected by the *needs* of the organism. Yet these bacteria mutated only those genes which they needed and mutated them 10^8 times more rapidly than expected. As Cairns says, nobody has the faintest idea how this trick is done.

Is it only highly evolved human beings who evince purpose? No. Such cases tempt one to assert the omnipresence of free will. Purpose, struggle and intention may be embedded in the most insignificant members of the Universe's living creatures. Thus it has been observed that:

> Protozoa are capable of complicated behaviour. For instance, H.S. Jennings has described the pursuit, capture and ingestion of one amoeba by another, the escape of the captured amoeba, its recapture and final escape. Mind and will, however rudimentary, appear to operate even at this low level of biological development.

The amoeba has no brain, it has nucleic acids. Is it these acids which are behaving 'cleverly'? As Firsoff comments later:

> Amoebae have no discernible organs of perception, but this does not mean of necessity that they have no perceptions.

> We may recall Jennings' amoeba ... which scampered off for dear life to escape being cannibalised by another 'dear amoeba.' 'She' thus demonstrated an *urge* to survive. ... This begs the question, how and why could a mere assembly of chemicals have had any urge to begin with? An urge implies a consciousness capable of experiencing it.[29]

Consciousness, will, purpose, etc, are claimed by reductionists to be explicable — but only *via* a machinery which has yet to be dreamed up. It would in any case be highly complex, and therefore inapt to this sort of problem. For the amoeba is tiny, it has no room for whatever bulky 'Machine of Conscious Identity, Will, Purpose & Survival' the reductionist might devise.

If purpose and the impulse for personal survival imply conscious awareness, and if they exist at the very 'lowest' levels of the Universe, then consciousness and free will are surely basic.

Conclusion

If consciousness (with its faithful companion Free Will) is real and if materialism does not hold water, what alternatives do we have? Throughout the twentieth century the word 'Dualism' was uttered with the same chill shudder of disgust as Christians (crossing themselves) when mentioning 'Satan.' As for Idealism, many seem to feel it has been consigned to history. Prejudice of this kind will not do — it is always the enemy of truth — and we shall confront these arguments in the next chapter.

6. Why Is One Better Than Two?

> There is a general social taboo on inner knowledge.
>
> Cytowic 2002, p. 19.

> If the body came into being because of consciousness, that is a wonder, but if consciousness came into being because of the body, this is a wonder of wonders.
>
> Jesus Christ in the *Gospel of Thomas*[1]

We have seen how materialism, reductionism and mechanism are powerless to explain conscious experience. In Europe the rejection of materialism has usually led to a dualistic standpoint — the view that there is on the one hand matter, on the other hand mind, on the one hand the body, on the other the soul or spirit. There is however a strong modern prejudice against dualism — a prejudice which both philosophers and scientists share.

There are at least three possible positions vis-à-vis these questions. Either:

(1) there are two fundamental entities, namely mind and matter — a doctrine termed 'dualism'; or

(2) one of these two is a subcreation of the other.
Thus either:

(a) mind is created by matter, a doctrine termed 'materialism,' or

(b) matter is created by mind, a doctrine termed 'idealism.'
Either of these doctrines is a 'monism' (a term meaning that there is only one fundamental entity).

(3) The above makes it plain there must be an alternative view, that is that both mind and matter are created by something deeper than both. This I shall term 'deep monism.'

No-one knows which of these doctrines is correct. If materialism is untenable, there has to be a solution from either dualism or idealism, or from deep monism. We may never know which is the truth, for possibly, though the questions seem clear to us, this is due to the limitations of our minds. And if the questions are indeed clear, it may be that insoluble mysteries have been wrapped around their answers. Good. This gives us occupation for the future.

The twentieth century has been contemptuous of dualism. There are indeed arguments against it, but this hostility is largely due to prejudice. After all, is 'One' meaningful without 'Two'? Is 'Two' thinkable without 'One'? As we shall see, dualism is a perfectly rational position. But let us start with some of its difficulties.

Problems of dualism

In the modern tradition, it is customary to treat Descartes (1596–1650) with *hauteur*. He is accused of making an elementary error in separating mind from matter. But it is absurd to lay this at the door of Descartes. All Christian and Platonic thinking views mind and matter, soul and body as contrasting aspects of reality.[2] So do Jews and Muslims. So do Hindus and Buddhists (though the way they conceive of this is different from ours).[3] The ancient Egyptians made a distinction between the body and various kinds of physical and spiritual souls. For thousands of years all the races of men have believed in a distinction of this sort, and although in all societies there have been atheists, such denials have been rare. It is the contemporary Westerner who is the odd-man-out, and when Gilbert Ryle (in his *Concept of Mind*) attacks Descartes as if he is solely and personally responsible for this alleged 'error,' he is being quite unfair.

Indeed, the real reason why Ryle attacks Descartes is that the latter has an absolutely knock-down argument for the reality of consciousness. 'I resolved to reject as false,' Descartes had written, 'everything in which I could imagine the least doubt, in order to see if there afterwards remained anything that was entirely indubitable.' Accepted beliefs and preconceived opinions are unreliable. Our senses may be deceiving us, and so we may doubt the reality of the physical world. We may be unsure whether we are, at any given moment, awake or asleep. He ends up certain of one thing only: in the final analysis, he cannot doubt that he is doubting. His thoughts, or at least some element of them, are therefore unmistakably real. Descartes proceeds to pronounce the famous phrase, 'Cogito, ergo sum.' ('I think, therefore I am.')

Yet Descartes' first step is too conceptual. The 'cogito' ('I think') is in part misleading. It leads to abstraction, to the apotheosis of pure thought. 'Conscio, ergo sum.' ('I am conscious, therefore I am') would have been preferable.

Nonetheless, his procedure is perfectly correct. He has sought certainty, and he has found the only certainty there can logically be. This first step is absolutely secure. The procedure has a curious analogy with the practices of Eastern meditation, in which the contemplative progressively withdraws his awareness from the world about him, to be left with nothing but the light of pure consciousness. In the East however what fines and refines itself away till it arrives at a fundamental consciousness is lived experience; whereas in Descartes it is reason.

The Islamic philosopher Al-Ghazzali had made the same observation hundreds of years earlier — and Descartes may perhaps have known his work. Ryle's intention in concentrating his fire on Descartes is a tactic so as to weaken the argument for consciousness.

Philosophers are no more immune to error than are ordinary people; and it has often been declared that the following is one of Descartes' mistakes. In distinguishing between mind and matter he declared that matter was spatially spread out, and that the soul was 'unextended.'

This observation is intensely interesting. It touches upon (a) the mysteries of our understanding of space, indeed upon (b) the reality, even, of space. However it may well be too simple. It is true that many of the contents of the mind (thoughts, ideas, emotions, perceptions) do not appear to be 'spatial.' Thus, my ideas of 'tiger,' 'jollity' and 'blueness' do not appear to be located in space vis-à-vis each other. On the other hand, my notion of 'tiger' is spatial, for my mental image of a tiger is laid out in imaginary space. Besides, our visual perceptions of the world are laid out spatially within consciousness; so are our tactile and proprioceptive perceptions; and one must assume that 'space' would mean nothing to us at all if 'space' were not 'in' our consciousness. On the other hand again, one can point to no space in the physical world where my spatial awareness is located. The issue is of great importance, as we shall see in Chapter 9.

The seventeenth and eighteenth centuries, however, obediently swallowed Descartes' distinction between matter as spatial and mind as non-spatial. They found it hard to see how a disembodied and totally non-spatial entity could influence an embodied spatial one, and vice-versa. On Descartes's account, the physical and the spiritual were two closed systems. He seemed to have cut the link between mind and body, leaving no means whereby the one could influence the other. The seventeenth and eighteenth centuries found this so difficult that they had to draw upon God's infinite power to provide solutions. Unfortunately these solutions were preposterous. Thus the 'occasionalism' of Malebranche (1638–1715) has been criticized as a bizarre theory which states that one has no control over one's own body. Thus, every time we will to do something it has to be God who (in his infinite kindness) performs the action for us. Malebranche's view, however strange, was arrived at for philosophical reasons which had nothing to do with Descartes.

Leibniz (1646–1716) proposed a theory of equal strangeness. His doctrine of 'pre-established harmony' declares that God had wound up the physical and mental universes in total accord with each other, so that they simply behaved *as if* they interacted. Such a suggestion would not persuade a one-year-old child, and seems almost more eccentric than Malebranche's proposal, for it contains the additional difficulty that it does not operate contemporaneously as events occur, but has to be set up in all its immense detail, *in advance*, through God's omniscience, at the very beginning of time.

These whimsical speculations draw attention to a fundamental problem. How can mind and matter interact? The two are of totally different 'stuff.' How can a feather press a button? How (as Ryle sarcastically asked) can a ghost work a machine? How effective such ridicule has been! It is almost always thought to be unimaginable that an immaterial soul might cause a material body to act. But is the analogy between a mind driving a body and a feather driving a locomotive (and others of this kind) really apt? To compare a mind with a feather, a mind with a ghost, is a problem in itself. In what way is a mind 'like' a feather or 'like' a ghost? These analogies have no basis in reality.

In one of its modern forms, the difficulty is often expressed in terms of the conservation of energy. For, no matter how different mind and matter may seem, if they exchange energy and momentum we will see them as interlinked, and interlinked *measurably,* through *process.* However, no such exchanges have so far been found, so that one may conclude, with Goswami:

> The Cartesian dualism of mind and body violates the laws of conservation of energy that physics has established beyond doubt. How could mind possibly interact with the world without occasionally exchanging energy and momentum? But we

> always find the energy and momentum of objects in the physical world to be conserved, to remain exactly the same.[4]

This is an ancient objection. The same was raised by George John Romanes[5] back in 1885. It is not however clear to me that the necessary experiments have been performed. Has anyone ever attempted to measure the levels of energy in a human organism both before and after a mental act? Do we have the necessary instruments to do so? Would such instruments be able to distinguish between changes in energy due to a mental process and to a physical process?

Here we should note Sir John Eccles' proposed solution: that the required interference at the level of the brain is so slight that we can presume it easy to occur, and well-nigh impossible to measure. The argument is that we know activity in the nervous system can be triggered by something as slight as three or four photons falling on the eye. Indeed a matter of a photon or two can make all the difference between our seeing a star or not seeing it — whence the flickering of the stars in the night sky.[6] This being so, the action of mind on brain could occur at the quantum level, would be well-nigh undetectable, and would entail no more expense of energy than is entailed by the uncertainty principle itself. By this I do not mean that it would be at the mercy of the uncertainty principle (for this would remove our control over ourselves and replace it by sheer chance). No, I mean that an exchange of energy which was as big as the uncertainty principle would allow, would be undetectable.[7]

But is the gulf between mind and matter any more mysterious than the gulf between electricity and magnetism, as seen in the nineteenth century before James Clerk Maxwell proposed his theories? Up till then, these were supposed to be two totally different things. Transformations of energy occur quite readily within the world — one thing turning into something astonishingly different. For instance, mass in Einsteinian physics is simply the ultimate type of condensed, passive or concentrated energy. Thus a transformation of energy with no corresponding loss or increase in it would suffice perhaps to solve our problem. One may therefore wonder whether the Quantum Vacuum might offer a solution. It is known that material is constantly emerging from the Quantum Vacuum into the normal world. Conservation of energy is however sustained by these subatomic particles being equally constantly drawn back into the Vacuum, or by an exchange of particles taking place. A small amount of inflow can be theoretically permitted from the QV, in the form of an *exchange* of energies. This therefore creates *change* without loss or increase of energy, and would solve the problem, for it would harmonize what we experientially feel — operative change — with what physicists claim on principle — no alteration in energy levels. We should note that small effects which *marginally* infringe the principle of conservation are already permitted to the QV. I submit that there should no longer be a difficulty of principle relating to these matters.

The case for dualism

These objections to Cartesian dualism are therefore of doubtful validity.

What, in any case, is the objection *in principle* to dualism? What is wrong with thinking that two might be more fundamental than one? The opposition to dualism is due to prejudice, reaction against the eccentric arguments of the eighteenth century, and the desire at all costs to take a materialist stance. For there are strong arguments on the other side.

For the metaphysical claim that One is more basic than Two becomes dubious once one starts to question it. It is not one of those things which can be resolved by experience, the findings of science, or the principles of mathematics. It is a metaphysical issue, though it is not particularly abstruse, for all one needs to argue it is simple common sense:

(1) For let us consider. It is true that there cannot be a notion of 'two' if there is not a notion of 'one.' But how can there be an idea of 'one,' if there is not an idea of 'two'? Surely 'one' as a notion exists only in opposition to 'two.'

(2) If unity is a simple and all-embracing 'pure unity,' then even an *idea* of such a unity is impossible, for the idea itself of the unity is separate from the unity. 'Two' has to be thinkable before you can think 'One.'

(3) It might be argued that the basic distinction is between 'none' and 'one' — or between 'nothing' and 'something,' as if between 'Yes' and 'No.' But any distinction implies twoness. And the distinction between what is and what is not is a distinction between *two*. Thus the moment that initial moment of realization arises: 'I am,' it follows that there are two: what is, and what is not. The very notion of existence entails the notion of twoness.

(4) Besides, *existence is always in relation;* there is no such thing as singular existence. 'It is,' we say. But 'It is' indicates two things, namely the 'something' that exists, and that something's 'existing.' Moreover, without one's being oneself 'two,' one cannot even have relation / communication with oneself. To know your own existence, you need an immediate duality: yourself *and* seeing yourself. 'Zen says,' according to Wilber, 'that spirit is "not-two, not one."'[8] He means by this that spirit is not a unity, but rather a non-duality. Without knowing your own existence, you are not conscious of it, consequently the initial step is not a oneness, but a duality appearing out of nothing, that is a consciousness of existence appearing out of unconsciousness, a light appearing out of darkness.

Monism is therefore mistaken, since duality is the fundamental. For how could 1 be meaningful if it did not already imply 1 + 1 = 2? Thus two is more fundamental than one, and one can, as it were, step back to 'one' only after envisaging the notion of 'two.' We discover 'two' first, and 'one' second, for the latter is discovered only *at the moment* one discovers 'two.'

Ken Wilber points out that subject / object dualism is the basic problem, 'the impassable gulf.' It is the start of the universe, 'the hallmark of all manifestation,' that is Descartes' dualism is not an error on his part, it is what is really there from the outset. It is the mystery hidden at the heart of *samsara,* a mystery that refuses to yield its secrets to anything other than meditational practices, mystical experience.[9]

Suppose that the first split made in the Universe's primal unity was that between *percipere* and *percipi*. Then how could any further split cast light on that first split? How can the less fundamental cast light on the more fundamental? Thus, we may be correct in asserting that the first essential things are (a) *percipere* and (b) *percipi*, but correct or not, we necessarily leave ourselves without any possibility of further explanation or analysis. As Schopenhauer says:

> The fundament upon which all our knowledge and learning rests is the inexplicable. It is to this that every explanation, through few or many intermediate stages, leads; as the plummet touches the bottom of the sea now at a greater depth, now

> at a less, but is bound to reach it somewhere sooner or later. The study of this inexplicable devolves upon metaphysics.[10]

Strangest of all, though this irresolvable distinction runs so deep, it is also immediately visible on the very surface of the world. As children we know (after but a little experience) that our self cannot be perceived in itself. We know almost at once that the rock cannot perceive us.

The prejudice against Dualism is thus entirely hollow. We still have no idea how Mind and Matter may interoperate. But that there cannot in principle be more than one ultimate thing has been shown to be a groundless prejudice.

My argument in the earlier part of this book has shown that materialism cannot possibly explain the facts. Moreover, it is only *half* a theory. For, as Velmans and others have often pointed out, it is actually what is left when you accept the Cartesian view of there being Mind and Matter ... and then throw away Mind.[11] Having accepted a dualist account of the world as accurate, materialists then seek to remove one half of it as a delusion. This is ironic. For it is exactly that part of the world which experience shows is often a delusion, *namely the apparently physical part of it,* which they seek to worship as truth — whereas that part of the world which, even when deceived by a delusion, is still indubitably there and still therefore no delusion, *namely consciousness* — this is the bit they seek to remove.

Panpsychism

An alternative view is that mind is everywhere, but that it is *hidden* within matter, as it were. This is the doctrine of Panpsychism, to which (under a variety of forms) a large number of thinkers have subscribed. Thus Teilhard de Chardin (1881–1955) suggests in his *Phenomenon of Man*[12] that particles possess two modes of energy, 'tangential' and radial.' Both seek complexity, but the former interacts with and connects outwards towards other particles; the latter has an inward quality and tends towards inner complexity. The former is essentially the form of energy that the scientist's instruments can measure; the latter 'can be regarded as a sort of psychic or spiritual energy.'[13] The former is entropic, the latter negentropic.[14] Both forms of energy exist in all forms of matter, and thus even the smallest particles of matter possess a sort of spiritual kernel, however rudimentary.

As Barrow and Tipler explain in their excellent account of this theory, the Law of Entropy declares that available energy will, over the course of the aeons, inevitably decline, bringing disorder and ultimately the end of the Universe in Heat Death. Now, living things appear to be negentropic, that is to develop increasing complexity, increasing order. The course of evolution on our planet gives a similar impression of increasing organization. Teilhard postulated therefore the intrinsically organizing properties of his 'radial energy.'

Barrow and Tipler claim that since Teilhard 'we have discovered in effect the "mechanical equivalent" for will or thought' in the form of 'information.' Unfortunately they define 'information' in computational terms. We have already found this claim to be mistaken. Thus, contrary to what Barrow and Tipler say, Teilhard has not yet been refuted. Nonetheless, these authors agree that his theory, by virtue of its being *capable* of refutation, is indeed a scientific theory.[15]

Many orthodox scientists have held similar views:

> In 1964, in the 25 April issue of *Nature*, D.F. Lawden, then professor of mathematics at the University of Canterbury, New Zealand, advocated the view that the continuity of nature necessitated consciousness or mind to be a universal property of matter, so that even elementary particles would be endowed with it in some degree.[16]

Eddington argued for a similar stance in the 1930s. One interesting proponent is the astronomer Axel Firsoff, who suggested that the only way to explain the mind was to suppose that there are 'mindons' — a word invented on the analogy of 'electrons, baryons, muons,' etc. — which interact with other particles only in one way — namely the mental. As such, their action would be hard to detect by the customary measurements of science. There may of course, as he says, be more than one mental particle or mindon — for in the physical world there are many different particles with distinct functions. He points out also that we already know of particles which interact so rarely with matter that they would — were it not for scientific ingenuity — be undetectable:

> Neutrinos interact so seldom with 'ordinary' matter that they can pass through the solid body of the Earth substantially as if it were so much empty space. A neutrino organism could,

> therefore, pass easily through walls and locked doors, and though ordinarily undetectable, it would be wholly physical and carry a substantial amount of energy.

Let us not mock at the notion of ghosts. By analogy with the elusive neutrino, they are entirely conceivable in terms of modern physics. As Firsoff reminds us, let us also not suppose that interactions between mind and body would necessarily be easily detectable in terms of energy gain or loss. To detect neutrinos, it was, historically, first necessary to have a theory which predicted their existence.

Similarly, we have as yet no theory of mind. Firsoff points out that 'mental entities have no locus in the space-time manifold.' As we have seen, consciousness is *not located,* and it is therefore possible that it is organized, as it were, outside space and time. He goes on, 'This already suggests a special kind of mental space, governed by different laws ...'[17]

More recently Chalmers has asked if there are hidden intrinsic qualities of the physical, enwrapped within it as the multi-dimensionalists of physical theory claim that there might be ten dimensions locked up in the four that we see. He makes interesting remarks about panpsychism in his 1997 essay, where he refers to a proposal by Bertrand Russell, to the effect that we may know (to some extent) what external events are 'like' 'in themselves' because they may be, from the inside, exactly like how we, from the inside, experience things. This proposal starts with the following observation:

> For everything that physics tells us about a particle ... it might as well just be a bundle of causal dispositions; we know nothing of the entity that *carries* those dispositions.[18]

This is the same observation as Sir James Jeans made in the 1930s:

> A mathematical formula can never tell us what a thing is, but only how it behaves; it can only specify an object through its properties.[19]

But the insight goes back long before Russell, to Kant and Schopenhauer. Kant had correctly pointed out that our understanding of the world is limited — for ever limited — by the categories of thinking through which we can grasp the world. The world's inaccessible true reality, its *noumenon*, lies therefore *logically* for ever beyond our understanding. At the time it seemed that it was impossible to advance further than this, and that an ultimate boundary had been placed around understanding. Schopenhauer however took a step further forward — though it must be admitted that his step is speculative. He observed that our understanding of the Universe divides into two: our understanding of the outer world, and our intimate acquaintance with the inner world of our own selves. These being the only two modes of knowledge known to us, he proposed that perhaps the world's inner nature resembles our own, resembles that is what we experience from the inside as opposed to what we perceive of the world from the outside. Thus Schopenhauer's great wager is that the inner nature of the Universe is experiential, or mind-like. A contemporary advocate of a similar viewpoint is the theologian David Ray Griffin.[20]

This is an attractive view. How it may be supposed to *work* on the other hand — how the material is transformed into the mental in consciousness — remains a mystery.

At all events Western materialism is a one-legged cripple, for it is in fact simply dualism lacking one of its own halves, namely the mental half. But before we can adjudicate between these standpoints, we must look at the prospects for good old plain idealism — that is, for the theory that it is not matter which is primary but mind.

7. Idealism and the Creative Power of the Mind

> The brain is wider than the sky,
> For, put them side by side,
> This one the other will include
> With ease, and you beside.
>
> Emily Dickinson

We have seen that it is inconceivable how matter could create mind. On the other hand, the converse is not true. It is quite conceivable that mind might create matter. We do it (or appear to do it) every night in our dreams. Moreover, there is (a) evidence drawn from medicine and from (b) reports of hallucinations, and there are (c) philosophical arguments. I shall not, by the way, be expecting the readers of this chapter to *believe* in Psi phenomena, but shall be using such reports to explore the relationship of reality to perception.

Creation of Matter by Mind

As we have seen, if matter is all, how mind could have been created from it is unimaginable. But could mind be all? Does our experience of the creative capacity of consciousness support that idea?

The first observation to make is this. Mind can create two sorts of thing, neither of which exists in nature. Firstly, abstractions. It is a matter of everyday experience that we can newly visualize relationships, inventing terms such as 'marginal value,' processes such as 'evolution,' hypotheses such as 'chaos theory.'

Secondly, the mind can create facsimiles of living experience. These come in at least two kinds: dreams, and hallucinations. In certain cases these experiences seem to be quite as powerful as 'the real thing.'

Let us look at the evidence.

Charles Bonnet Syndrome

This is a strange, but well-documented, medical condition in which the patient has lost sight in one or both eyes, or in a portion of their visual field. The humorist Thurber became blind in one eye after a childhood accident with a toy arrow. Later in his thirties he became completely blind, but vivid visual hallucinations replaced the darkness in his eyes. He would see 'a Cuban flag flying over a bank, an old lady with a parasol walking through the side of a truck, a cat rolling across the street in a striped barrel, bridges rising lazily into the air like balloons ...'

In a sense the Charles Bonnet syndrome is less odd than it may appear for, as Ramachandran points out, there is a blind spot in everyone's vision. It is filled in by the mind, and to prove this there are a number of visual illusions which are fun to play with. Nonetheless the blind spot remains and it is reported that King Charles II used to amuse himself by gazing sidelong at a courtier of his choice and perceiving him as headless.

Thus, in cases where there is a blind patch (termed a scotoma) in someone's vision, this may be filled in. Ramachandran's patient 'Josh' could actually *watch* his being filled in, for in his case the process was gradual. Ramachandran comments, 'Given how common this syndrome is, I am tempted to wonder whether the occasional reports of 'true' sightings of ghosts, UFOs and angels by otherwise sane, intelligent people may merely be an example of CB hallucinations.'

'Larry,' another of Ramachandran's patients, said to him, 'As I look at you, there's a monkey sitting in your lap.' Above a certain line 'Larry' saw the normal world. Below it, he was blind, and saw vivid and absurd hallucinations. The same patient told Ramachandran: 'Sometimes when I'm looking for my shoes in the morning, the whole floor is suddenly covered in shoes.' He could tell that his hallucinations were hallucinations because they were, as he put it, 'more real than real.' 'Nancy' saw images like film cartoons, that is line drawings filled in with flat colour. To these patients, seeing is *not* believing. The visions are incompatible with other more consistent areas of their experience. Rather, they manage the world by applying likelihood to their experience, and by supposing that much of what they see is hallucinatory.

Ramachandran quotes a report in the well-known medical journal *The Lancet*. '... Many older men and women with poor vision hide the fact that they see things which aren't really there. ... Out of 500 visually handicapped persons, 60 admitted they hallucinated ... [Some] experienced visual fantasies at least twice a day.' These hallucinators often 'see' children, and even 'hear' their laughter. Thus an aural hallucination may accompany the visual one.[1]

At times a Charles Bonnet hallucination may stray out into the normal field of vision.[2]

It has often been observed that when the mind is (a) cut off from outside reality, in a ganzfeld[3] situation, or (b) prevented from dreaming over a number of nights, it resorts to a frantic filling of the gap by producing hallucinations. The mind, says North, is a reality-producing machine. When outside stimulation from 'the real world' is cut off, then it creates.[4] Cytowic writes:

> The sensory-deprived brain starts perceiving things that are not there. Lacking input, the brain starts projecting an external reality of its own. ... Even simple boredom can produce hallucinations.[5]

Cotterill too has interesting things to say about visual illusions. He refutes with absolutely convincing logic Dennett's refusal to believe in 'filling in':[6] He notes phantom effects as Ramachandran does, and comments, 'the brain spontaneously generates its own experiences if it is denied sensory input for too protracted a period; [as nature was held in the old days to abhor a vacuum] the conscious brain appears to abhor idleness.' Some of the auditory and sensory illusions which Cotterill reports are quite sensational, as for instance the case of a woman who had lost a large part of both her vision and her hearing. On one occasion a circus was conjured up for her, and 'she was able to give a lively account of the various acts and the accompanying music.'[7] It should be noted that in cases like this, two senses are involved, namely hearing and sight.

The orthodox way of describing this is that 'the brain produces these hallucinations.' Well indeed this may be so. But *for what or for whom* does the brain produce them? For consciousness. The absence of conscious experience is causal: it *produces* hallucinatory events. Strangely, the brain does not resort to letting consciousness in on some of the manifold unconscious operations it is always engaged in. (For the unconscious activity of the brain is of vast proportions, yet very little of it emerges into consciousness.) Instead it produces 'entertainment' — an entertainment that is suited to the level at which consciousness operates.

SLEEP-DEPRIVATION

Stranger still, it may be held, is the mind's need for the fantastic. If people are deprived of sleep for several days, extraordinary distortions in their psychological stability begin to occur. Sleep-deprivation causes 'experiences that involve, or consist of, body-schema and weight alterations, time and space distortion, macropsias and micropsias [that is seeing things unnaturally large or small], tactile hallucinations, visual hallucinations such as seeing smoke rising from the floor or people standing in the room, and auditory hallucinations.'[8] These distortions in experience apply not only to human beings but also to animals, who quite soon die if deprived of sleep.

This is a very odd situation. It's as if we need madness so as not to become mad, require hallucinations so as not to hallucinate. A special system is set up, namely sleep, *so as to* allow hallucinations to be experienced. If this safety valve of sleep fails, then we are overcome by them, and become unable to live in the real world. It's as if our natural state is hallucination, and if we do not repeatedly revert to it, then we wouldn't be able to live in the normal world at all.

Hallucination is evidently a constant overpowering force which, unless it is steered away, overwhelms the person's consciousness. Or it is a drip, drip, drip of liquid into the vessel of oneself, in which, if it is not upturned every night, you will drown. Somehow, our coming into this apparently material world, hasn't turned this extraordinary process off. Indeed it is a condition of our being here. It's an unknown force of nature which surges constantly out of the depths behind consciousness. Consequently we live in a world which is constantly threatened by a deluge — like Noah's great flood. Such things as schizophrenia suggest much the same conclusion. We are surfers on a sea of vast incoming breakers beyond our ability to imagine.

This suggests the *all-powerfulness of mind* as creator of experience, and perhaps therefore of reality, and of what is called matter. This is what we have to be protected against, because otherwise our world's narrow possibilities would collapse, and we would find ourselves in a shifting unpredictable universe. Ours is a world of limited possibilities. Because all possibilities are given by mind, this is a world of limited mind. One is tempted once again to take Blake's and Bergson's view of the matter and say that our fundamentally illimitable minds have artificial valves or filters placed upon them, which limit us to the world of normality. But keeping the larger reality out is difficult.

Apparitions

At this point I must introduce the word 'eidetic.' An 'eidetic image' is a remembered visual image of the past, but which is identical with that past experience, being as complete, detailed and indeed capable of being moved about in the head as any real observed object.[9] Some eidetikers (that is people who are able to recall such detailed images) are able to hallucinate objects at will. Thus, Stromeyer & Psotka's eidetiker could:

> hallucinate at will a beard on a beardless man, leaves on a barren tree, or a page of poetry in a known foreign language which she can copy from bottom line to top line as fast as her hand can write. These visions often obscure a real object. Thus the chin on a beardless man may disappear beneath the hallucinated beard.[10]

Remarkably, this subject (a woman of 23, a teacher at Harvard, and a skilled artist) could superimpose a pictorial figure recalled from yesterday over a figure seen 24 hours later, and perceive the pattern that made sense of both images. Nothing could more clearly demonstrate the vividness and realism of eidetic images.

One of the most famous cases is that of 'Ruth,' the psychiatrist Schatzman's patient, who could produce at will an apparition of her daughter. When she did so, the stimuli in her eye were blocked off before they reached her visual cortex.[11]

Schatzman's work was assisted at various points by John Harris, Richard L. Gregory and Peter Fenwick. Ruth had been the victim, as a child, of an attempted rape by her father Later in her life, for reasons which seem moderately clear, she began to hallucinate her father's presence. Her father (who was in the USA at the time) was seen sitting at her breakfast table. She saw him, her husband didn't. Then he disappeared. Her father was an involuntary apparition, whom Ruth found terrifying. But with the help of her psychiatrist Schatzman she trained herself to 'bend his apparition to her will.' Having got control of the hallucination, he then ceased to haunt her.

The astonishing thing is that, during this process, she became aware of her ability to create apparitions at will. She was able at one point to hallucinate her husband — and her father saw the hallucination. She was able to increase her own body-warmth by hallucinating an electric heater. She caused an apparition to make her arm cold.

Dr Peter Fenwick, neurophysiologist at the Institute of Psychology and at St Thomas's Hospital in London, tested Ruth with sophisticated modern machinery. Her brain was pronounced perfectly normal [12] As Ian Wilson writes:

> Scientifically the oscilloscope was confirming that Ruth was quite genuinely seeing in her mind that which all along she claimed to see even though the vision had absolutely no reality. This is a striking result, and it confirms that, whether hypnotized or not hypnotized, it is possible for the mind to see an illusion as real.[13]

Ruth's case is remarkable. She was able to change her own world, and also *change it for other people.*

A striking instance of the ability of the human mind at times to control its own hallucinations is given by the form of dreaming known as 'lucid dreaming.' Here the dreamer is (unusually) aware of the fact that s/he is dreaming; and, once aware of this, s/he may be able to control the dream to a considerable degree.[14] Similarly, Mavromatis offers a great deal of evidence to the effect that hypnagogic imagery can be controlled by the subject.[15]

In discussing the nature and power of hallucinations — and in particular the number of senses which may be involved in their perception — I shall now be obliged to draw into the discussion the matter of allegedly supernatural hallucinations, such as 'ghosts.' The reason is that these have been subjected to searching analysis. I must however warn materialist readers that they may find themselves in a Catch 22. For either (a) Psi (that is parapsychological experience) is false, in which case nonetheless the reports of hallucinations remain true, and are excellent evidence of the nature, modalities, etc, of hallucinations imposed on us by the mind, or (b) Psi is true, in which case the materialist will be in trouble from a different angle, since parapsychological events are plausibly thought to be inexplicable in materialist terms.

I must here repeat Tyrrell's observation, that a hallucination is not a false belief, it is a percept.[16] Subjects may be perfectly well aware that it is not a 'real object' they are seeing but a hallucination; but that does not prevent them seeing it. The situation resembles that which obtains with optical illusions. Thus there is a famous optical illusion in which a hollow or concave face-mask seen from inside appears to be a convex face-mask seen from outside. As Richard Gregory comments, 'It is *impossible* not to see it as a normal face.' Our visual perceptions totally reject the possibility of its being concave, despite the fact that we have verified for ourselves, by sticking our hand inside the hollow mask, that it is so. The mind often feels acutely uncomfortable at this disagreement between appearance and knowledge.[17]

Hallucinations of the ghostly kind have been much reported throughout human history. They have also been much investigated ever since the establishment of the Society for Psychical Research in the nineteenth century. They have a number of puzzling features. For not only (a) they may provide convincing imitations of all the senses, but also (b) as Tyrrell pointed out, a complete hallucinatory environment may be produced.[18] For it is, once you start to think about it, very odd that, normally, hallucinations adapt themselves perfectly to their surroundings, for instance they have clothes, and may have horses, carriages and other appurtenances. Even more oddly they convincingly appear as they ought considering the light conditions, the perspective, etc.; and their surroundings may be subtly changed so that they appear to fit. Tyrrell underlines the strangeness of all this by saying, amusingly, that our psyches are like theatres containing a 'Producer' and a 'Stage-Carpenter,' who carefully build up all this false but convincing verisimilitude.[19]

Perhaps most puzzlingly of all, they are often perceived collectively. Braude writes that 'apparitions tend to be collectively perceived when there is more than one potential percipient present.'[20] Tyrrell claimed that in about one-third of the cases where there is more than one person, the apparition is experienced collectively. Hart's figures are even higher.[21]

Hallucinations are not always visible (or visible initially), they may speak, produce noises, changes in temperature, or even be solid to the touch.[22] Green and MacCreery's book *Apparitions* gives a statistical breakdown of the various senses affected in their group of subjects. It is as follows:

Sight	84%
Hearing	37%
Touch	15%
Temperature	18%
Smell	8%
None of these	4%

This adds up to more than 100 percent because many of the apparitions affected more than one of the senses, as is shown in the following table:

1 sense	61%
2 senses	25%
3 senses	9%
4 or more	5%

As the authors comment, it is unclear whether this really shows that visual apparitions are the most common, for one does not always get the *opportunity* to hear or touch the apparition. Besides, the word 'apparition' itself may bias the responses.[23]

One must point out therefore (and this is disturbing to our ingrained ways of thinking) that hallucinations may on occasion create a perfect illusion of material solidity. Although we saw above that (as Tyrrell says) it is most usual with hallucinations for there to be some flaw in them — something which gives away their status as hallucinations — nonetheless, the illusion of matter is at times entirely convincing. But if at times there is no way of telling the difference between reality and illusion, is it not the case that mind, to all intents and purposes, can create matter?

It might be claimed that it is the brain rather than the mind which creates such images. This however can be argued against. For in lucid dreams and hypnagogic phases the sleeper can consciously control whatever hallucinations are presented to him or her. Thus these experiences are not imposed by the brain but evoked by the mind in the course of acts of will.

We saw before that no convincing argument can be put forward to suggest that matter may create mind; we see now that there are experiences in which mind has the seeming power to create matter; that this appearance is so close to matter that we cannot tell the difference.

It has long been argued in many philosophies that matter is appearance. Indeed, this is implicit in much that has gone before in the present book. For Berkeley matter is simply that which has the sole characteristic of being perceived.

The quantum physicist Nick Herbert compares us human beings to King Midas who, having done a favour to the god Dionysos, ill-advisedly asked the latter, 'Pray grant that all I touch be turned into gold.' Unfortunately not only did flowers, stones, furnishings and palace walls turn to gold, but so did the food and drink that the King touched — and indeed his own beloved daughter. Midas would have died of thirst, hunger and grief if the ironic god had not taken pity on him.

Herbert writes that we, like King Midas, 'can't directly experience the true texture of reality because *everything we touch turns to matter.*'[24] How beautifully this is put! It agrees with Kant's view: we are made this way: it is the categories, those inborn restrictive senses and thought-systems of ours, which produce the quasi-illusion of matter. We are rich in matter, and our understanding of it makes us rich; but we shall starve in the end if we do not remember it is the things of the mind which count.

For how may we define matter, except as appearance? Matter is a conundrum without a point of access, a locked box without lock or key, a blank wall reaching to infinity, an enigma concealing its own enigma. It is a surface which — once one has cut away that surface, presents us with a further surface — and so on *ad infinitum.* Nothing lies within these surfaces but further surfaces. Nothing is to be found within them but outsides. *Matter has no inside.*

Whereas, in the case of consciousness, the tale is very different. There are outsides and there are insides. One can enter an area of one's mind, and exit from it. One can be inside and one can be outside. One performs this act a hundred times a day. Despite Berkeley's initial statement — and despite its being entirely true — in respect of the outside / inside contrast, mind has both, whereas matter has only one.

Thus consciousness is the only one of the two things (consciousness and matter) which is not deficient in respect of either. Consciousness has a dual view and standpoint, matter has a single limited blankness. Consciousness has potentially infinite understanding; and understanding is infinitely absent from matter.

As Sartre writes, 'L'*esse* du phénomène ne saurait être son *percipi.*' [The *being* of the phenomenal world could not be its *percipi.*][25] Whereas it is impossible that matter could create mind, *it is a fact of experience, that is an empirical fact, that mind may create appearance, that is matter.*

What, therefore, is the difficulty about idealism, that doctrine which proposes that mind is the ultimate origin of all things, including matter. and that some supreme consciousness created the Universe? There can be no difficulty. Practically speaking, such an act of creation is no more than we might expect from our own experiences.

In Idealism moreover there is no dualist problem of the interaction between Mind and Matter. Matter is 'imagined' or brought into being by consciousness, and therefore is observable by it. Matter is made of mind, *secreted* by it. Or to put it another way, Matter is one of the mirrors in which consciousness sees itself.

Thus, from an idealist perspective, the alleged mystery about the interaction of Mind and Matter is turned upside down. For, on the contrary, the fact that Mind can see Matter *shows the latter is the creation of the former.*

Deep Monism

An alternative theory of the ultimate nature of things is that of Deep Monism. Here, both mind and matter are held to be secondary creations of an essence more profound than either and productive of both. We must view this opinion too with the utmost respect.

First let us instance the philosopher William James, brother of the great novelist Henry:

> James's philosophy of 'radical empiricism' rejects the absolute duality of mind and matter in favour of a world of experience, in which consciousness *as an entity*, in and of itself, does not exist; nor is it a function of matter, for matter *as an entity*, in and of itself, does not exist either. According to this view, ... mind and matter are constructs, whereas pure experience, which is neutral between the two, is primordial. One implication of [this] hypothesis ... is that contents of consciousness can no longer be regarded as being 'in the mind' (let alone in the brain). Reality just *is* the flux of experience.

Experience is primary, and comes before mind and matter.[26]

A difficulty about this theory could be as follows. I do not regard my experiences as primary, but rather my experiencing them as primary, that is the presence of my consciousness comes in principle before what my consciousness perceives. Descartes's analysis is similar, and so is Sartre's when he writes:

> However the necessary and sufficient condition for a knowing consciousness to be knowledge of its object, is that it must be

> aware of itself as being that consciousness. This is a necessary condition: if my consciousness were not aware of being conscious of the table, it would then be conscious of this table without having awareness of being conscious of it ...[27]

This is logical, though it may sound tautological. Sartre is surely right about this. A knower must be a self-knower. The initial *given (datum)* is not experience, but self-awareness.

In short, I am not happy about mind and matter being 'constructs.' Though being two *aspects* to our experiences, they do not appear to be *constructed,* but rather offered to us as essential to the whole experience of experience (if I may put it that way).

Let us turn to another Western theory, namely that of Bertrand Russell — a theory which was practically ignored in Russell's own day. The philosopher writes:

> The stuff of which the world of our experience is composed, is, in my belief, neither mind nor matter, but something more primitive than both.

He agrees with William James:

> My thesis is that if we start with the supposition that there is only one primal stuff or material in the world, a stuff of which everything is composed, and if we call that stuff 'pure experience,' then knowing can easily be explained as a particular sort of relation towards one another into which portions of pure experience may enter.[28]

Russell was writing in the twenties. A contemporary proposal of a similar kind is that of Raymond Tallis. He argues that consciousness cannot be derived from matter, and that matter cannot be derived from consciousness. If therefore we start with these two there is no basis for the 'presence' of consciousness to matter or vice-versa. 'Presence, the interrelation between subject and object, cannot be derived from either matter or mind.' He argues that 'it must therefore be primary.' Thus, 'the original substance is neither mind nor matter,' but the interface between them, or 'presence' as he calls it. This, as he himself comments, is in fact Spinoza's suggestion — that the basic substance shows itself to us in two ways: (1) thought and (2) extension. This Tallis calls 'neutral monism.' He admits that he has not thought it out, and that it requires considerable elaboration.[29]

There are many other contemporary speculations of the Deep Monism kind. Thus the quantum physicist David Bohm has suggested in his *Wholeness and the Implicate Order* that matter and consciousness are an expression of the same fundamental reality, which is a higher-dimensional 'ground of all being.' He claims that 'mind and body [do not] causally affect each other, but rather that the movements of both are the outcome of related projections of a common higher-dimensional ground.'[30] Behind this ground (Bohm suggests) there may — again — lie concealed something even more fundamental.

Fritjof Capra, who started his career as an atomic physicist, takes a similar view, and it is apt that, summarizing the world view to which atomic physics has led him, he quotes an Eastern mystic, Lama Anagarika Govinda:

> The Buddhist does not believe in an independent or separately existing external world, into whose dynamic forces he could insert himself. The external world and his inner world are for him only two sides of the same fabric, in which the threads of all forces and of all events, of all forms of consciousness and of their objects, are woven into an inseparable net of endless, mutually conditioned relations.[31]

Eastern philosophy has propounded a number of different theories about the ultimate nature of the Universe. These include varieties of Materialism and Dualism. But this tradition is notable above all for its tendency towards Idealism, Non-Dualism and Deep Monism, and for its practice of meditation, that is the technique for investigating, through the mysterious levels of one's own inner consciousness, the ultimate nature of reality. This great tradition is an inexhaustible source. Here I shall cite merely a handful of views.

In the Shingon school of Japanese Tantric Buddhism, (founded by Kukai AD 774–835) absolute consciousness is the zero-point of Reality. Consciousness's self-determining nature is said to have spread itself out in all directions like waves, producing matter and everything else. In other systems however, matter and consciousness are thought of as being the two ends of a single continuum. In some theories, consciousness is not the starting point, but both matter and consciousness are the two initial things produced by the original One, at the zero-point of Reality, which is something beyond both of them. Thus, consciousness & matter both come from something beyond.[32]

Goswami's *Self-Aware Universe* (a book which seeks to compare and combine the insights of Eastern philosophy and of Western science) puts it as follows:

> The self of our self-reference is due to a tangled hierarchy, but our consciousness is the consciousness of the Being that is behind the subject-object split. There is no other source of consciousness in the Universe. ... It is the appearance of a world of manifestation that leads us to the experience of a self or subject that is separate from the objects of appearance.[33]

Allan Wallace gives a searching account of the philosophy of Padmasambhava (a teacher whose works he has translated). Here the mystic seeks through contemplation to transcend duality, reaching a state beyond both objectivity and subjectivity. Wallace writes:

> Tibetan contemplatives, like Augustine, declare that theories about the nature of consciousness and the manner in which introspection functions are ... artificial, conceptual constructions; for the experience of consciousness when the mind is settled in meditative stabilization is a state in which words and concepts are suspended. Any subsequent theory is nothing more than a conceptual overlay on an experience that is nonconceptual.[34]

I recently read a claim in *The Journal of Consciousness Studies* that the attainment of extraordinary states of consciousness through contemplation / meditation was not really a concern of traditional Indian philosophy.[35] This is completely untrue, as can be seen by giving the dates of some notable Eastern mystics, such as Asanga (fourth century), Vasubandhu, (fourth or fifth), Buddhaghosa (fifth), and Padmasambhava (eighth century).[36]

As another instance, therefore, of Deep Monism, let me refer to an account of Padmasambhava's theory and practice, as translated by Alan Wallace. This Buddhist thinker asserts the nonduality of appearances and awareness. Objective and subjective phenomena are of the same ultimate nature:

> ... If one attends primarily to objective phenomena, [they] appear more real; ... if one attends primarily to subjective phenomena, [these] appear more real. ... Contemplatives claim that ... there is a state of awareness that utterly transcends all conceptual constructs, including the dualities of subjective / objective, existence / nonexistence, self / other, and mind / matter; and this state is widely reported by contemplatives to be imbued with an unprecedented, enduring, great bliss.[37]

Thus, not only does the Eastern tradition of Deep Monism offer a satisfying hypothesis as to the metaphysical foundations of reality; but it also offers an invitation to seek, through meditation, experience of a higher and more primordial state of being.

Jean-Paul Sartre on consciousness

These findings (that the explanation of the Universe is either Idealism or Deep Monism) tend to be confirmed by the arguments of Sartre in *Being and Nothingness*. The key to his case is that consciousness must be fundamental, because (using introspection and reason) any other alternative is unthinkable.

It is fashionable to play down Sartre's contribution to philosophy, and to suggest that he is derivative from others. However, this is unfair. His importance resides in his being the only modern philosopher to have looked really closely at the nature of consciousness. He did this much more penetratingly than his masters Husserl and Heidegger, and he has important insights to convey.

Sartre writes as follows:

> (1) Consciousness is consciousness through and through. It could not therefore be limited except by itself ...

> (2) One must suppose that consciousness is prior to its own existence. Moreover one must not conceive of this self-creation as an act. ...
>
> (3) Consciousness exists of and by itself. And by this one must not understand that it 'derives from / draws itself out of nothingness.' There could be no 'nothingness of consciousness' before consciousness. 'Before' consciousness, one can conceive only of a fullness of being none of whose elements refers to an absent consciousness. For there to be nothingness of consciousness, it is necessary for there to be (1) a consciousness which has been and which is no longer, and (2) a witnessing consciousness which posits the nothingness of the first consciousness ... Consciousness is prior to nothingness and 'derives from' being.[38]

I need to comment on this in some detail. I have inserted letters in the text so as to make it clear to which part my comments refer.

(1) Pure consciousness is defined in Sartre exactly as it defined in Berkeley, namely as 'that which perceives and is incapable of being perceived.' And, just as in Berkeley, everything that is not consciousness is 'that which is perceived and is incapable of perceiving.' Consciousness is thus entirely of its own nature through and through. There is no element of *percipi* in it. It provides therefore no 'handle' whereby it can be manipulated by some outside force, least of all by an outside force which shares none of its nature. It thus cannot be limited by anything that is not itself — by for instance physical or non-conscious factors.

This way of arguing makes it once again hard to see how consciousness and matter (more precisely *pour-soi* and *en-soi)* can interact. However, the very definition of *pour-soi* is that it perceives *en-soi;* and the very definition of *en-soi* is that it is perceived by *pour-soi*. One might therefore argue that the split between *en-soi* and *pour-soi* is the original split in Being at the outset of the Universe.

(2) Since consciousness is *sui generis*, (of its own kind and of no other), it cannot derive either from something else or from nothing. It is conceived by Sartre as *causa sui* in the same way as God is *causa sui* in theology. This term does not mean 'self-caused' but 'not dependent on anything else for its existence': it has necessary existence in

and of itself. The picture here is of a self-sustaining, uncreated nature like that of God in orthodox Christian theology. Sartre writes also, 'Nothing is the cause of consciousness; it is the cause of its own manner of being.'[39]

(3) Nothingness is secondary to being, because it is possible for being to conceive non-being. But non-being (what is not) is incapable of conceiving anything, and therefore being cannot derive from it. For there to be nothing, there has to be consciousness aware of that nothing. Consciousness is logically prior to nothingness. Hence if there is anything 'before' consciousness — an 'anything' which Sartre names pure 'being' — then being must include consciousness within it.

Since both nothingness and non-consciousness cannot even be said to 'occur' unless there is a consciousness to be aware of their 'occurrence,' consciousness is more basic than either. Their occurrence in the absence of consciousness is unthinkable.

If the above argument is correct, we thus arrive at a startling conclusion: *for the Universe to exist, it has to contain consciousness*. We can then answer the old question, 'Why is there something rather than nothing?' Because there is not even nothing unless there is a knower. Consequently there has to be something, namely consciousness.

I shall not follow Sartre any further into the vast forest of his *Being and Nothingness*, for we have now dealt with the issues that concern us.

We must admit, of course, that these questions are of the utmost difficulty. At such airless heights who can be sure he is still thinking straight? The reason why Ryle, Ayer and Co. deserted this field of philosophy — and uttered anathemas against it — was because philosophical mountaineers explore areas where human language becomes as slippery as mountain ice. But why suppose it *should* be any different from this? At mountain summits the air gets thinner; but it cannot be denied that more landscape can be seen. Sartre's argument is surely correct.

Conclusion

If so, it fortifies our view that either Idealism or Deep Monism is the correct theory. It is surely not of great importance which we should prefer. What matters is that materialism is untenable, thus allowing us to perceive that consciousness is the essential building-block of the Universe.

The answer to the old question, 'Why is there something rather than nothing?' is 'Because there is not even nothing unless there is a knower.' The importance of consciousness will be borne out in our next chapter, when we shall turn to what Quantum Theory has to tell us about the laws of physics.

8. Consciousness and Quantum Theory

> The doctrine that the world is made up of objects whose existence is independent of human consciousness turns out to be in conflict with quantum mechanics and with facts established by experiment.
>
> Bernard d'Espagnat

Reductionists claim that science refutes the reality of mind and consciousness. We should look therefore at the theory which is at present (along with Relativity) the basis of scientific understanding of the Universe, namely Quantum Theory. A word of caution must be uttered here: the nature of scientific theories is (according to Popper) for ever incomplete, never finally verifiable. They are not definitive, and therefore succeed one another through time. Moreover they are doomed to be incomplete in another sense. They deal in the explicit, not the tacit, they tell us what the properties of things are, but not what things in themselves are, they grapple with the phenomenon but are powerless to deal with the noumenon.

We may however legitimately ask (a) whether modern science leaves room for a spiritual universe? (b) whether it leaves more room for a spiritual universe than nineteenth century science? (c) whether it hints at any possibility of such a universe?

For many years I used to teach a course on modern philosophy. This included an introduction to Quantum Theory, and I used always to warn my students before we started:

> Normally, when you're trying to understand a theory, you know that if you come up against a contradiction then you must have misunderstood something, and you'll have to go back and sort it out in your mind. In quantum theory, however, you know you must have misunderstood it if you *don't* come across a contradiction.

Some of the very foundation stones of Quantum Physics involve logical contradiction and paradox. Yet, as Mermin writes:

> ... the theory has enjoyed phenomenal success. It has accounted in a quantitative way for atomic phenomena with a numerical precision never before achieved in any field of science. When it was subsequently applied within the atom to the atomic nucleus — an object some hundred thousand times smaller — no further modification in the theory was needed. More recently, when applied within the particles making up the nucleus to describe their own internal structure -— an investigation on a scale as much smaller than atoms as atoms are smaller than us — the quantum theory still shows no signs of requiring extension or revision.[1]

Quantum Theory is the most tested theory in the history of science — largely because it is so bizarre that it offers a number of obvious challenges. Yet its predictions have, so far, never failed, and it is thus a more respectable theory than any other. Let us insist on this point: the most bizarre theory in the history of science is also the most successful.

I shall now try to present the main relevant elements of Quantum Physics as briefly and clearly as possible. The reader may readily find further information, for there are many excellent accounts. Particular favourites of mine are Paul Davies's *Other Worlds*. and Gary Zukav's *The Dancing Wu Li Masters*. Or the reader might like to turn to my own exposé in a previous book *Shadows in the Cave*.[2]

Quantum theory

Among its many fascinating features, Quantum Theory presents the following account of the bizarre behaviour of matter.

(a) *empty space:* Matter, as we know, is made of molecules, which are made of atoms, which are in turn made of a variety of smaller entities. This table at which I am sitting appears to me solid. Solidity however is a kind of 'phantom.' It is simply the way my senses convey my surroundings to my senses of touch and proprioception. It is due to the interaction of my own body particles and those of the table. From the physicist's point of view the table is almost entirely empty space. What is to be found in this space are myriads of minute particles which are in constant frantic motion. The entire known scientific world is made up of these 'objects.' To call them 'particles' however is quite inexact.

(b) *wave-particle duality:* At the subatomic level, the behaviour of these particles is quite counterintuitive. Their nature appears fundamentally ambiguous and paradoxical. In certain circumstances they behave like particles, in others like waves. They have for this reason often been termed 'wavicles.' Pagels writes:

> The quantum weirdness lies in the realization that as long as you are not actually detecting an electron, its behaviour is that of a wave of probability. The moment you look at an electron, it is a particle. But as soon as you are not looking, it behaves like a wave again.[3]

(c) *uncertainty*: Only a partial knowledge of the state of one of these wavicles is possible at any given time. If, for instance, one becomes 100 percent certain of the whereabouts of a wavicle, then one thereby becomes 100 percent uncertain of its momentum, and vice-versa. Partial knowledge of the one will permit partial knowledge of the other, and so on. Knowledge of the one *proportionally precludes* knowledge of the other.

(d) *probability:* Until they are observed, wavicles have neither a definite momentum nor a definite position in space. Their position (for example) is expressed as a wave of probability, or set of positions of varying probability.

(e) *superposition:* Most given quantum situations will necessarily involve large numbers of wavicles, each of which is subject to the same sorts of uncertainty. These interlocking uncertainties provide an overriding mix of potential interactions which is termed a 'superposition.' This can be calculated mathematically as the combination of their wave functions. Such a superposition is invariably paradoxical, that is it is a combination of Yes and No, both held in abeyance in a state of contradictory suspense until the final outcome (namely an observation) is made.

The situation is similar to that of a well-written play: dramatic tension builds up, an almost infinite set of possibilities, until suddenly the unpredictable *dénouement* arrives.

(f) *collapse of the wave function:* As long as the system is left to its own devices, its state function evolves deterministically over time, in accordance with Schrödinger's Equation. That is to say that the multiple possibilities of the situation continue their rational and causal progress — though this rational and causal progress contains all the contradictions of possible opposite outcomes. When a measurement is made, however, the state function is said to 'collapse,' providing a determinate outcome. This outcome is fundamentally unpredictable, or rather predictable only within the limits of the interwoven probabilities.

When an experiment is conducted and an observation made, this 'superposition' collapses out of its previous state of uncertainty into a definite situation. It emerges from potentiality into actuality. At this point the suspended contradictions resolve themselves into a single, non-paradoxical situation, and either Yes or No must emerge.

(g) *observation:* Since the outcome of the superposition cannot be predicted before the final observation is made, but only a set of more or less probable outcomes, the observation appears to be crucial to the emergence of reality. It is the observation which causes the (contradictory) potentials of the situation to turn into an event. The observation has no power over whether Yes or No emerges; it merely determines that there *is* an emergence. (However, see below.)

Different observations may however be made, or one could say that different questions may be asked of the system. Thus one may to some limited extent control what the responses of the system are, by choosing one's questions.

In Russell Stannard's enchanting rewriting of Gamow's *Mr Tompkins* books, we are introduced to an imaginary world where full-size objects behave as subatomic objects do in our own world. The effects are striking:

> As they entered the forest, Mr Tompkins noted that the leaves in the trees were rustling, and yet there did not appear to be a wind. He asked the professor why this was so.

> 'Oh, that's because we're looking at them,' was the reply.
>
> 'Looking at them! What's that got to do with it?' exclaimed Mr Tompkins. 'Are they shy?'
>
> 'I would hardly put it like that,' smiled the professor. 'The point is that in making any observation you can't help disturbing whatever it is you are looking at. ...'
>
> 'What if nobody is looking? ... Would everything behave properly then? ...'
>
> 'Who can say?' mused the professor. 'When nobody is looking, who can know how they behave?[4]

This leads us neatly on to the next point.

(h) *the wave-particle paradox:* The behaviour of particles is such that they appear to transform themselves into waves, and waves into particles, depending on whether we are spying on them or not. Thus:

> In a celebrated experiment, photons (that is subatomic particles of light) are shot at a screen containing two slits. If only one of these slits is open, the pattern that falls on the wall behind the screen is a strip of light with a fuzzy edge around it. Then both slits are opened. One would naturally expect two strips of light with fuzzy edges to be cast upon the wall. In fact this is not the case. Instead of two such images, the pattern alters fundamentally, and we see instead a sequence of regular stripes both dark and light. This is what we might expect if the photons were not particles but behave in a collective fashion, as waves do. And the pattern of regular stripes is readily interpretable as wave interference.
>
> Now comes the really curious thing. Suppose that we turn the beam down until only one particle at a time passes through the double-slit apparatus. One would suppose that, since the individual photons are being shot off separately, at intervals, they can no longer interfere with each other, and therefore that the pattern of wave interference will disappear. This is not so, however. No matter how long the interval between the projection of one photon-bullet and the next, the pattern that gradually builds up is exactly the same as that

> produced when enormous numbers of photons were pouring through the slits together. The photons are still interfering with each other, even though there is a considerable lapse of time between each firing. It is as if they 'know' what their fellow-photons have done, and what yet more are shortly going to do.
>
> Moreover, even if the experiment is performed in different laboratories, hundred of miles apart, when the different patterns set up in these different laboratories are put together, they show the same pattern of wave interference. It is as if, even separated by prodigious distances of space and time, the photons still 'know' what their distant fellows are doing.[5]

If one introduces into this experiment a method of seeing through which hole each particle goes, then this interferes with the experiment in such a way that the wave pattern is destroyed. Thus the experimenter's behaviour is relevant to the outcome of the experiment, which is not indifferent to his presence. None of this (it is evident) accords with the famed 'objectivity' of nineteenth century positivism. It introduces troubling questions as to the function of an observing consciousness and as to the very nature of space and time.

(j) *Planck length (space, time):* I am particularly fond of Max Planck's establishment of the fact of there being an ultimate minimum length. This is true both in time and in space. The minimum spatial length is roughly 10^{-33} cm. The minimum temporal length is 10^{-43} seconds. Of course we can *imagine* smaller spatial distances — and if we could not, then we could not measure Planck's distance.[6] It is perhaps questionable on the other hand whether we can perceive or visualize small temporal distances with the accuracy we can small lengths of space. We can of course build clocks of various kinds which do so, but it is then the clocks which mark off time, not ourselves.

There may however be an exception to the above. Human beings love rhythmic music and dancing, and by this means one can enable oneself to *perceive* the passage of small lengths of time. It is a mystery of a particularly strange kind that 'living' these segments of time may provide immense excitement.

(k) *nonlocality:* Einstein was very unhappy about the paradoxes which quantum physics presented. In particular he was unhappy about the Copenhagen Interpretation of Quantum Physics, proposed by Nils Bohr, and which became scientific orthodoxy. For the Copenhagen Interpretation believes that, in the context of quantum events, the conscious observer has a part in creating reality. Einstein preferred to think that the Universe exists independently of our observations.

One of the arguments he (along with Podolsky and Rosen) put forward was the following (known as the EPR Paradox): Quantum Physics predicts that a pair of particles having been put into a certain relationship, will remain in that paired relationship until a further measurement is performed. This is so even if the pair have moved a long distance apart and are now separated by metres, even by miles. The situation would then be that when you inverted the spin of one particle, and then tested the spin of the other, you would find that the other had 'magically' altered its spin to correspond with its 'twin' This Einstein and his colleagues pronounced to be absurd.

A large number of experiments have however been performed by Alain Aspect and his team, which show that this 'absurdity' does indeed occur. Moreover it occurs instantaneously, that is it happens faster than the speed of light. Now relativity asserts that the speed of light is the ultimate speed. Thus, the instantaneous change observed in Aspect's experiments runs counter to one of the Universe's fundamental laws. We appear to have action at a distance — or 'nonlocality' as this is termed.

The only similar phenomena which come readily to mind are magical spells such as the killing of a foe at a distance by sticking pins into his image — or the Scottish witches who allegedly could drown an enemy by stirring water in a teacup and thereby causing a storm out at sea.— and Psi phenomena such as telepathy, telekinesis and clairvoyance.

This finding is connected with Bell's Inequality Theorem, developed by the Northern Irish physicist John Bell in the mid-1960s. He shows that we inhabit a Universe in which certain correlations take place instantaneously, regardless of how great the distance is between their elements. John Gribbin comments on this theorem that it makes three assumptions: (1) 'that there are real things in the Universe, which exist whether or not we observe them;' (2) that the world is generally consistent in its behaviour; (3) 'that no signal can travel faster than light.' Since Bell's Inequality is violated by the Aspect experiments, at least one of these assumptions must be wrong.

Gribbin then argues that:

> if the second assumption is wrong, there is no point in trying to understand the world anyway, so if we want to understand the world we have to keep that one. If the first assumption is wrong, it is still possible to construct a logically self-consistent description of the way the world works ... But if you want to believe in a real world that exists independently of your observations, and ... operates logically, then you have to accept that it also operates nonlocally.[7]

(l) *'field:'* Particles / wavicles are not 'free-standing' entities independent of their surroundings and of each other. They are far from having the independence of, say, cricket balls in the macroscopic world. It has been said that this electron here shivers with the influence of that other electron a million light years out in space. (Nonetheless, even within a field, the way forces operate between particles is subject to the limitations of the speed of light.) The Universe is a vast field of interacting influences. Never at any point — despite the vast extents of which we are talking — do these far-distant influences become null. The Universe is one, and physicists often argue that the basic quantum reality is not to be seen in terms of particles or waves, but in terms of fields.[8]

(m) *the quantum vacuum / zero-point energies.* As Gribbin writes:

> In quantum physics, the vacuum is not nothing at all, but seethes with activity.

However, not only is the vacuum not nothing, it is a practical infinity. The vast energies of the quantum vacuum have only recently been taken seriously. In popular accounts of science until not long ago, such issues tended to be suppressed. It is true of course that the vacuum cannot be directly observed. Nonetheless some of its effects can be; and in recent years unmistakeable evidence has been provided.

When scientists attempt to measure the forces involved with elementary particles, their calculations keep coming up with unwelcome and unmanageable infinities. They usually resort to 'renormalization,' which keeps their calculations on the straight and narrow. Nonetheless the process is somewhat arbitrary or *ad hoc*, and some physicists have always been suspicious of it. These measures of the forces involved are indeed measures of something, namely of the vast energies hidden 'outside' and, as it were, 'behind' the Universe.

In fact any area of the Universe, however small, is constantly subject to quantum fluctuations. These produce particles which appear 'out of nowhere,' and vanish back into 'nowhere.' This 'nowhere' is not 'in our Universe' but constantly communicates with it, as a kind of background or underlying *ground.* At the back of the Universe (as it were) there lies a vast field of energy. This reservoir cannot be directly observed, yet its effects can be observed. Thus Bohm writes:

> If one computes the amount of energy that would be in one cubic centimetre of space ... it turns out to be very far beyond the total energy of all the matter in the known universe. What is implied by this ... is that what we call empty space contains an immense background of energy, and that matter as we know it is a small, 'quantized' wavelike excitation on top of this background, rather like a tiny ripple on a vast sea ... I suggest then that what we perceive through the senses as empty space is actually the plenum, which is the ground for the existence of everything, including ourselves. The things that appear to our senses are derivative forms and their true meaning can be seen only when we consider the plenum, in which they are generated and sustained, and into which they must ultimately vanish.[9]

The reality of these forces within the quantum vacuum is certain. It is proved by such experiments as the Casimir effect. In this, two metal plates are placed close together. Virtual photons emerge from the vacuum in the gap between the plates. Since only photons with a small enough wavelength can fit between the plates, there will be fewer in the vacuum between the plates than in the vacuum outside them. Consequently the plates are pushed together.[10] Apparently, the sticky effects of certain modern paints — the reason they don't flow off the wall — are due to the intermolecular forces produced by these vacuum fluctuations.[11]

As Laszlo observes, neglecting the Quantum Vacuum (or ψ-field, as he calls it) would be like 'disregarding the depths of the high seas while studying the dynamics of the ripples that play on its surface.'[12] He quite reasonably wonders whether many of the mysteries which still challenge us will not ultimately be resolved by paying attention to the quantum vacuum.[13] This is a point to which we must return.

The Copenhagen interpretation

The orthodox interpretation of Quantum Physics was for a long time (and perhaps still is) the Copenhagen interpretation, so called because it was originally proposed by the Danish physicist Nils Bohr (though Max Born, John von Neumann and others also made vital contributions). It arose out of the following facts. (1) The answers we obtain from a quantum system depend on the questions we ask. (2) Not only we cannot know what quons [14] (quantum entities or events) are doing in between our observations, for the reason that our attempting to make an observation alters their behaviour; but (3) also it seems that (between observations) they are in no definite state at all, but rather in a state of overlapping and paradoxical probabilities. The Copenhagen interpretation proposes that the act of observing (or measurement, as we may also call it) creates reality out of what had, previously, been a state of interlocking probabilities.

We must emphasize how strange this theory is. It looks as if it puts 'objectivity' for ever out of reach.

We must emphasize also its difficulties. It is not at all clear *when* it can be said that 'an observation has been made.' It cannot be the case that such an observation can be made mechanically, since the machine, being itself made of quons, enters into complex superposition with the quantum phenomenon being measured. It would seem that only when a conscious observer observes, can we say that the measurement has been made. But *at what precise point* does the making of the observation cause wave-collapse? Worse still, *by what means* does an observation influence the outcome? *How* does it cause wave-collapse? By what apparently invisible means does the quon 'leap from uncertainty into actuality'?

These questions seem at present unanswerable.

Nonetheless the theory suggests that consciousness may be an entity as fundamental as the fields of quantum physics or the light of photons. As Nick Herbert points out, there are many illustrious supporters for the view that consciousness creates reality: he names Fritz London, Edmond

Bauer, Henry Stapp, E. Wigner, John von Neumann, among others. According to Werner Heisenberg, the world does not exist except as a 'shimmering potentiality' until it is observed. Von Neumann claimed that, if Quantum Theory is correct, the world cannot be made of 'ordinary objects,' that is of objects that have totally independent existence. Neumann suggested that 'physical objects would have no attributes if a conscious observer were not watching them':

> According to [von Neumann], all quons and their static attributes enjoy an absolute existence whether they are observed or not. Only a quon's dynamic attributes, including the major external attributes position and momentum, are mind-created. Thus all [entities] do certainly *exist* ... but until someone actually looks at them, these entities possess no definite place or motion.'[15]

Alternative interpretations

Naturally therefore the biggest question confronting the materialist kind of quantum physicist is 'How may we avoid going to Copenhagen?' It is doubtless because of its spectacular imaginative qualities that the most famous of these alternative solutions is the many worlds hypothesis.

The Many Worlds Hypothesis

This was proposed by Hugh Everett in the early 1950s.[16] It is immensely well thought of by many physicists. David Deutsch explains the whole of Quantum Physics through it.[17] Perhaps we should look at the famous paradox of Schrödinger's cat, to clarify what is involved. In this celebrated thought-experiment, a cat is placed in a box, and the box is sealed. Inside the box is a phial containing poison gas. Whether it is released, thus killing the cat, is determined by a trigger, namely a radioactive atom with a half-life of ten minutes, so that there is a fifty-fifty chance that the cat may be dead within ten minutes. We wait ten minutes, then open the box. According to orthodox quantum theory, during this ten-minute period the cat is in a contradictory state — both alive and dead — until the observation is made. This paradox has occasioned the spilling of much ink, and many are the questions that may be asked about it, for instance 'Is the cat not itself an observer?'

If we have one world only, then the cat is in a state of superposition — both dead and alive until we open the box. Our observation makes the wave-function collapse — the cat, emerging from a state of suspended uncertainty, suddenly becomes either dead or alive. This underlines, as it is meant to, just how paradoxical the Copenhagen interpretation is.

Everett therefore seeks to avoid the intervention of consciousness by proposing that, every time a quantum event occurs, the Universe splits into two: in onc of thesc twin universes, the cat is alive, in the other it is dead. There is thus no need for the deciding factor of consciousness. Our uncertainty then becomes, not whether the cat is dead or alive, but in which of the two worlds we are. But this will be non-paradoxically resolved by opening the box.

This theory is certainly imaginative: it proposes that, every time a superposition is resolved into an observation, the Universe has split, and that in each new Universe a different outcome is perceived.

Note that there is no way of knowing whether Everett's theory is true. It is strictly untestable, for the reason that we cannot visit any of those hypothetical other universes. It presents, however, for those who prefer to suppose that consciousness has no function in the Universe, the wonderful gift of its not being a conscious observation that is involved in causing the cat's death or life. Consciousness is no longer active; it is at the mercy of the universe in which it finds itself.[18]

However, as Hodgson points out:

> Just as the Copenhagen interpretation cannot define (in quantum physical terms) the circumstances in which there is a reduction of the quantum state, so also the many worlds interpretation cannot define (in quantum physical terms) the circumstances in which worlds split.[19]

Moreover, it is not clear that this theory does indeed 'dispose' of consciousness in the desired way. For one could equally well say that (1) it is the act of observation which splits the worlds, and that (2) it is the conscious observation which decides in which world we are.

There are a number of other objections to the Many Worlds Hypothesis. *Firstly,* we must note that it is only in a strictly limited number of cases that the Universe might split into two. In the cat's case we are taking a simplified example, in which there is a fifty percent chance either way, and the cat ends up either alive or dead. But the possible outcomes of the collapse of a superposition could be multiple. There might be ten possible outcomes, or twenty, or even (according to some serious proponents of the theory) an infinity of universes produced.[20] Are we therefore to suppose that the Universe is in the habit of splitting into a vast number of copies of itself on every occasion that a quantum event occurs? But a quasi-infinity of quantum events are occurring every second. Or does it split only when a quantum event is *observed* to occur? But that brings back the observer once more. Let us look at further objections.

Secondly, Occam's Razor: When we are making a scientific hypothesis or judging its validity, this famous philosophical principle commands us: 'Do not introduce additional entities beyond the minimum necessary number.' Thus, as between two hypotheses which both explain a phenomenon, that which posits three entities is preferable to that which posits four; that which posits five is preferable to that which posits six, and so on. I fear that, in the case of the Many Universes Hypothesis, the theorists have transgressed against the principle, 'Do not introduce additional *universes* beyond the minimum necessary number.' This is a much more monstrous infraction of theory than adding a principle or two. Not merely have an infinite number of entities been conjured into existence, not only is it alleged that vast numbers of them burst into existence at every moment, but the entities in question are each of them as big as the whole Universe itself — which is perhaps itself infinite.[21]

One must note the curious inconsistency of the Many-Worlds theorists. They posit multiple universes so as to avoid the improbability of consciousness being real, or having any power over reality. Yet what could be more improbable than an infinity of worlds continually splitting into ever greater infinities? In asserting that consciousness is an 'unnecessary hypothesis,' they appeal to Occam's Razor — a principle which says, 'Thou shalt be as economical as possible with entities.' Yet was anyone ever so prodigal with universes? And if universes are not entities, whatever can qualify as an entity? Moreover if one argues that a universe is not an entity, then it must *contain* entities. These must be many more in number than the universes that contain them. These theorists prefer to be economical with abstractions such as causality, but are prodigal with realities such as universes. They are so economical with consciousness that they would prefer it not to exist.

I conclude that Occam's Razor has never been violated as blatantly as by the Many Worlds Theory, and we should therefore reject the latter. There are however still further profound objections. Thus

Thirdly, Goswami points out that, if Everett is right, an infringement of the law of conservation of energy is involved. For the amount of matter and energy would double each time the Universe bifurcates.[22] Moreover, as I have just remarked, it is not a simple matter of bifurcation. The amount of matter and energy might triple, quadruple, or centuple depending on the quantum process.[23] Now, that matter and energy remain constant is one of the fundamental principles of science.

Fourthly, how many new universes are produced, according to Everett, every second? Surely every time an observation is made, anywhere in the Universe, by anyone, a wave-function is collapsed. How many times during a single second — to restrict ourselves even to our own world — do conscious beings observe something? The question seems strictly incalculable. Is it the case that, every time I cast my eyes around the room, countless millions of universes are instantly born?

I think not. The theory is *impossible to believe* — though needless to say, it lends itself to excellent science fiction, and has been so used by countless writers, including Greg Egan and (I admit) myself.[24]

But there are harder questions still, which few except Chris Clarke seem to have noticed. For Quantum Physics is such, that the outcomes of wave collapse may be indeterminate in number. Since the number of outcomes depends upon the extraordinary calculations of higher mathematics, they often involve irrational numbers:

> Suppose, for example, a vertically polarized photon — a 'particle' of light which has passed through a piece of Polaroid filter — falls on another such filter rotated at an angle of 50°. It will pass through with a probability of $(\cos 50°)^2$, an irrational number, apparently requiring an irrational proportion of branches.

An irrational number, I would remind you, is one which is not commensurate with the rational numbers, such as for instance π which when calculated numerically confronts us with a row of decimals to an infinite and never terminating quantity. In which case we would be claiming that the number of new universes which are being created is an irrational number — or perhaps an imaginary number, that is a number multiplied by the square root of -1. Such numbers are essential to quantum calculations. But how could they relate to the number of 'real' universes?[25]

The Many Universes hypothesis started life as a brilliant idea. It has become popular for at least four reasons: a) to discount the function of consciousness in Quantum Physics; b) to discount the function of free will in human society; c) to discount arguments from design in our Universe; d) it makes a splendid basis for science fiction plots.

It has also further difficulties. One should object to its arbitrary sweeping away of all interesting problems. Indeed the difficulty with the Many Worlds hypothesis is that it sweeps away *all problems whatever*. For it has a single response to all questions (including why the Universe is here at all). This universal response is simply: 'Everything that can happen will happen.' It makes the Universe so big that, although everything is purely accidental, nonetheless everything *must* happen. In such a Universe, nothing has meaning, and there is no point in anything. The Many Worlds hypothesis substitues fatalism for scientific explanation.

The situation is much the same, in fact, as with a universe that is infinite in time. If there is such a universe everything possible must have happened already. However, even what is impossible in our universe may well be possible among an infinite number of universes, so that in principle all problems can be met by this single answer — that possibility is infinite. In which case, nothing makes sense any more.

But if this is so, surely then there are many universes where consciousness is real, operative and fundamental. The Multiverse theory thereby confutes itself.

Moreover, there is therefore one sense in which it is after all possible to test the Many Worlds Theory. For it states that, in the infinity of universes as a whole, anything and everything must happen, and must be happening all the time. But this flies in the face of experience. Since everything must happen, why is it that very improbable outcomes are not seen to happen in our world all the time? Why is it that every day we do not witness showers of blood from Heaven, or rivers running uphill? How is it that we can see regularities in the world's behaviour, and find many of them utterly dependable? How is that, because of all these regularities, we have been able to establish scientific laws, rely upon likelihoods, predict the outcomes of experiments?

We must conclude that it is, after all, possible to test the Many Worlds Theory; that it is so tested every hour of the day; and that empirical observation declares it infinitely unlikely.

Other interpretations

There are other interpretations (apart from the Copenhagen) but only the Transactional Interpretation seems to threaten the reality of consciousness.[26] This is, as far as I can see, the one remaining candidate for refuting the importance of consciousness. It states that particles influence each other across space by interacting 'at once' both forwards in time and backwards in time. This is indeed suggested by the Wheeler-Feynman Absorber Theory, and also by the way that the mathematics of quantum probabilities strongly suggests that we may take account of waves that are travelling not only forward but also backward in time.[27]

The problem here is, philosophically, a grave one. For the resulting picture is of a Universe in which every event is fixed and frozen in advance (or, as one might equally well put it, 'fixed in both directions'). We would thus be inhabitants of a 'block Universe,' a fine phrase — for it suggests our status in such a Universe as merely immobile particles, totally fixed and incapable of free movement. This conflicts with our experience of Free Will; and *therefore* we may well say that it makes it incomprehensible why we should be conscious at all. Now, as we saw in Chapter 5, there are powerful philosophical reasons for the reality of Free Will. The thinkers who have discussed the block Universe have tended to take these philosophical issues seriously. Gribbin attempts to counter them by suggesting that 'in my time frame, decisions are made with genuine free will and with no certain knowledge of the outcomes.'[28] I'm afraid this statement does not solve the problem at all. For it is a necessary attribute of Free Will, not that it is merely *ignorant* of the outcome, but that it can actually affect the outcome or bring it about.

One way of reintroducing Free Will into such a picture would be as follows. Let us suggest that (a) everything within our Universe is indeed fixed in advance, but that (b) consciousness and the will reside outside this Universe but are able (as it were) to 'lean into it' and influence it. A suitable image of this situation would be to say that the Universe is like a vast machine rattling and banging away, whose operation has been entirely fixed in advance so that (unless someone intervenes) it will continue for ever upon its preestablished path. We however are like an operator standing outside the machine, but who can occasionally intervene so as to slightly alter its functioning.

Thus, the future of the Universe would not be fixed after all, but could be 'adjusted' from 'outside.' We shall see in due course that such a picture of our relationship to the world (though one among several possibilities) is a thoroughly plausible one.

Stapp's interpretation

It is however comforting to report that the supporters of Copenhagen are still vocal. Thus a completely contemporary figure, Henry Stapp, writes:

> It is ... simply wrong to proclaim that the findings of science entail that our intuitions about the nature of our thoughts are necessarily illusory or false. Rather, it is completely in line with contemporary science to hold our thoughts to be causally efficacious, and reducible neither to the local deterministic Schrödinger process, nor to that process combined with stochastic Dirac choices on the part of nature.[29]
>
> Most efforts to improve upon the original Copenhagen quantum theory are based on Von Neumann's formulation. This includes the present work. However, almost every other effort to modify the Copenhagen formulation aims to improve it by removing the consciousness of the observer from quantum theory: they seek to bring quantum theory in line with the basic philosophy of the superseded classical theory, in which consciousness is imagined to be a disconnected passive witness. I see no rationale for this retrograde step.[30]

Stapp's view is that the Universe contains two interlocking causal systems, namely what we may loosely term (1) the physical quantum system (2) the mental system, involving consciousness, expectation and will. The first is a quantum state which proceeds blindly forward, governed by the deterministic Schrödinger equation. The second makes choices, at which point reality leaps out of potentiality. There can be no doubt that choices are made, no doubt that human beings are involved in this process. Indeed, *only* an observer can specify a choice, and without such an observer the deterministic Schrödinger process would continue for ever as an increasingly complex potentiality, without ever emerging into reality.[31] We human beings are an integral part of the quantum universe, and are in constant interaction with the universe through our stream of consciousness unfolding through the passage of time.

Stapp points out that minds can indeed influence the 'dynamical evolution' of a physical system, and that this can be the case not only at the quantum level, but at the macroscopic level of normal reality. 'The most striking example of this is the Quantum Zeno Effect.' To explain this, take a quantum system. Ask it a 'question' as to whether it is in state A or not-A. If the answer is A, put the same question again to it very rapidly. It will be found that it continues to be in state A. This is unexpected, for normally the system is subject to fluctuation, would develop, change, reach a different state. Our posing it this rapid series of questions ensures that it remains in a stable state. Thus its state can be controlled by human action, and we can see that the laws of quantum physics thereby allow us to affect even a macroscopic system.[32]

Among quantum phenomena which have been found to operate at the macro level, are the following:

(1) the superconductor;
(2) the laser;
(3) the 'freezing' of light;[33]
(4) the quantum Zeno effect;
(5) a beryllium atom in a superposition state, that is in two incompatible states at the same time.[34]
(6) quantum tunnelling.[35]
(7) It is reported that the research group of Anton Zeilinger of the University of Vienna 'has managed to fire a fullerene molecule, which contains sixty carbon atoms, through two separate apertures at once, demonstrating quantum superposition at a surprisingly large scale.'[36] His ambition is to put bacteria into superpositions. Well indeed, what a wonderful idea! It seems as if Schrödinger's cat — or rather Schrödinger's bacterium — might indeed turn out as paradoxically as its author thought.

Stapp's two types of causes resemble quite traditional views of physical causality and conscious will. One is encouraged however to see him arguing that the Universe cannot be understood except in terms of two opposite but interlocking forces: (a) one, blind but in a sense 'backward-looking,' which is entirely the deterministic (though intensely complex) result of past events; and (b) one, purposeful, conscious and forward-looking, which can exercise will and affect outcomes, and which can transform the potentialities of blind matter into actuality. We still cannot quite see 'how it's done,' but this certainly accords with our instincts, and the picture that Stapp proposes gives somehow a refreshing angle on our problem.

Does this theory create problems for the situation in the Universe before the emergence of consciousness? Stapp replies that his purposeful, forward-seeking force is a part of nature, and that it therefore existed before the appearance of life.[37] Such a picture recalls the dynamic 'life force' of thinkers like Bergson.

Hide & seek

Let us now take a closer look at some of the strangenesses of quantum physics, and ask the question: Is the Universe playing hide and seek with us?

Nick Herbert's 1985 book *Quantum Reality* presents eight different conceptions or interpretations of Quantum Theory. He argues that (with the exception of the Many Worlds Hypothesis, in which Bell's theorem cannot be proved, because all outcomes occur, and therefore reality 'chooses' no definite result) in all of these versions nonlocality must operate.[38]

Herbert's sixth point is as follows:

> Bell's theorem shows that ... any model of reality which fits the quantum facts must possess some means of exchanging information faster than light. [Thus] Bell's theorem requires our quantum knowledge to be non-local. [The Aspect experiments] show that Bell's inequality is violated by the facts. This means that even if quantum theory should some day fail, its successor theory must likewise violate Bell's inequality ... Because it's based on facts, Bell's theorem is here to stay.[39]

This is quite correct. We should note that certain facts seem to be proved, even if the theories within which they 'sit' are always up for grabs. Now let us inquire more deeply. Nonlocality suggests that the Universe is so set up that it is concealing certain facts from us. There is a veil over reality, indeed several veils. For, as Herbert argues in his discussion of nonlocal events (see Point k, page 141), it is as if the occurrence of such events is being 'deliberately' concealed:

> If all the world's phenomena are strictly local, what need is there to support local phenomena with a nonlocal fabric? Here we confront an alien design sense bizarre by human standards: the world seems strangely overbuilt. In addition the world's superluminal underpinning[40] is almost completely concealed — nonlocality would have been discovered long ago if it were more evident ...

We should note that we cannot use field theory to explain why nonlocal events occur, because the propagation of influences within fields cannot travel quicker than light either.[41]

Heinz Pagels has a similar point to make. He points out that only a small number of quantum particle interactions are renormalizable. These are the ones that we actually observe. Could it be that nature is here again hiding its mechanisms from us?[42]

Over seventy years ago, Eddington asked: 'Surely it is absurd to suppose that the Universe is planned in such a way as to conceal its plan.' That he posed this question at all shows that there may be something in it. As he himself observed later in the same book: 'I think it might be said that Nature has been caught using rather unfair dodges to prevent our discovering primary law ...' He then goes on to say, 'I believe that Nature is honest at heart ...'[43] But this is rather wishful thinking than literal report.

Hodgson asks, similarly, why Nature provides faster-than-light quantum connexions in order to maintain light-speed appearances. He connects this with the very existence of consciousness, as we shall see in a moment. He writes:

> I suspect there is a 'conspiracy of nature' which prevents signalling into one's own past; and which, in so doing, prevents any faster-than-light communication *and* any disclosure (at the macro level) of absolute simultaneity.[44]

I shall paraphrase his argument here. (a) According to special relativity, different observers have different time-frames. (b) However, according to Aspect's findings, spatial separation between correlated quons is irrelevant, and thus absolute simultaneity exists at the quantum level.

Nonetheless — very oddly, considering Finding (b) — we cannot use nonlocality to *signal* with. Thus, *signals* must travel no faster than the speed of light, and cannot be transmitted to our own past. As he writes:

> ... According to quantum mechanics all systems which have interacted have correlations, so that generally the whole universe will be a system [evincing] simultaneity of distant events, and so a preferred frame of reference.
>
> This does not mean that faster-than-light signals are possible: if they were, we could signal to our own past, and this seems unacceptable; and there are proofs by Philippe Eberhard and others that according to quantum mechanics any *measurable* influence must travel at the speed of light or slower. It would seem that the instantaneous correlations shown by Bell's theorem and the Aspect experiments are, in the words of Nick Herbert, 'private lines accessible to Nature alone.'

Thus there are two systems present in the cosmos: (a) the underlying quantum system, in which nonlocal and simultaneous influences occur, and (b) the macro-reality, in which influences can occur only at the speed of light. The latter 'conceals' the former.

This thought leads Hodgson to ask the question:

> Why does Nature need to deploy a faster-than-light subatomic reality to keep up merely light-speed macroscopic appearances?[45]

Hodgson's answer to this is remarkable. Perhaps it is (a) so as to permit the existence of consciousness; or, even more strikingly, perhaps it is (b) due to the *necessity* to permit consciousness.

For nonlocality could help to explain one of the great mysteries about consciousness — namely the way it is experienced as a unity.[46] This is the so-called 'binding problem': the mystery how countless disparate events involving many different areas of the brain, are nonetheless all perceived in consciousness *at the same time* and apprehended *as a single total picture*. Hodgson's suggestion is that quantum nonlocality might be involved in the creation of what we in fact experience — namely a holistic consciousness.

There is however a further and equally fundamental point to make. Signalling into the past must be ruled out for conscious beings who have free will (whose function is to enable us to intervene in an otherwise self-standing series of causes). It must be ruled out *because of* the famous paradoxes involved in time-travel, and equally in reverse-time-signalling (RTS). For otherwise I could signal backwards through time saying, 'Things are thus and thus now. This is awful. It is due to A having done *xy* at point *t* in time. *Stop him!'* The person signalled to could then act, and change a course of events which (for him) had not yet happened, but which (for me) had already happened — with what additional consequences it would be impossible to predict.

Now, if RTS is possible, surely there is nothing to prevent such apparently paradoxical actions happening. If they did, then history would become a chaos of alternatives, constantly changing, and consciousnesses would themselves be being continually being wiped out, created 'out of nowhere,' etc. I would refer the reader to those countless Science Fiction stories in which such events occur; and to the two popular series of films involving time-travel known as *Terminator* and *Back to the Future*. As Roger Newton argues:

> The reason nature arranges no causes to occur after their effects has to be sought in the existence of order. If some causes happened before their effects and some after, ... a causal chain of events could be set up that would prevent the occurrence of the very cause that was assumed to start it. The existence of such self-contradictory causal cycles would inevitably lead to chaos.[47]

Consciousness must be defended against the freedom to destroy itself before it is created.[48]

If God or some equivalent power exists, then we might well wonder whether even He is not limited by this consideration. Perhaps a unidirectional temporal flow (though not present in Nature as seen from an atemporal scientific point of view) has to be imposed the moment consciousness appears on the scene. It must be necessary so as to permit the existence of a consciousness which possesses free will. Hence the association of the Present with Consciousness, hence the unidirectional motion of Time.

We must return to such issues. For now let me confine myself to the current discussion. There would be no need to forbid RTS if the world were the mere inevitable succession of a chain of purely mechanical causes, leading as irresistibly from future to past as they do from past to future, because no alternative paths would be possible, and therefore no returning to a previous time would change things. Or if it were possible to change things (for an additional element from the future would be fed in at a certain point) then changing things would not matter, for there would be no consciousness there to observe it. It suggests therefore that RTS is impossible precisely because the Will, and therefore Consciousness, is real.[49]

Naturally therefore this implies that consciousness is an ontological fundamental.

While on the subject of Nature's playing hide and seek with human scientists, one must add that there have been a number of attempts by quantum physicists to avoid the Copenhagen interpretation by seeking a theory of Hidden Variables. Theories of this kind were long ignored by physicists because von Neumann had seemed to 'prove' that such theories cannot work *in principle*. However John Bell more recently showed that at least one of von Neumann's assumptions is unfounded, and David Bohm's is now probably the best known hidden variables theory. As David Chalmers remarks:

> Perhaps the most basic reason to be suspicious of these interpretations ... is that they postulate *complexity behind simplicity*. ... These interpretations make it look [as if] the world was constructed by Descartes's evil demon, [since the latter leads] us to believe that the world is one way when really it is another. ... The God of the Bohm view does not play dice, but he has a malicious sense of humor.[50]

If Bohm (or indeed any other hidden-variables theorist) is right, then we again appear to be faced with deliberate concealment. Trickster gods are well known in world mythology, and it is not merely our ancestors but also ourselves who may justifiably have the impression that all is not transparently clear. But then, if the Universe had no secrets, would it be an interesting place to inhabit?

Quon & consciousness in harmony?

The fascinations of quantum theory are many. Over the last few years it has been repeatedly called upon to *explain* consciousness. Thus, a much discussed recent theory is that of Penrose's Microtubules. Here a quantum process is hypothesized in the brain, and it is suggested that if this process is confirmed, then consciousness would cease to be mysterious.[51] Rather similarly Danah Zohar and her husband Ian Marshall have proposed that brain processes may resemble (or be an unfamiliar form of) those quantum processes known as Bose-Einstein condensates. In such states, whole masses of particles act together as a single quon. This (she suggests) would explain a number of things, such as the binding problem in consciousness, our sympathy with others, telepathy or pre-telepathic intuitions, and so forth. It must however be objected that the usual conditions under which such condensates occur are those of very low temperatures. They may therefore be impossible in living systems, and indeed nothing of this kind has been observed in the latter.[52]

All theories of this sort, however, suffer from a fundamental fallacy. As David Chalmers (perhaps the most important philosopher of our time) points out:

> But why should quantum processes in microtubules give rise to consciousness? The question here is just as hard as the corresponding question about classical processes in a classical brain.[53]
>
> At best, these theories tell us something about a physical role that consciousness may play. They tell us nothing about how [consciousness] arises.[54]

Penrose's theory may be new, but it cannot bridge the gulf between objective events and subjective experience, any more than older physical theories did.[55] Similarly we may ask where consciousness emerges from in Zohar and Marshall's theory. Bose-Einstein condensates are purely physical. The mere fact of unconscious objects acting together in harmony does not make them conscious. We are left with the same old insoluble mystery: the magical appearance of consciousness out of unconscious mechanism. Chalmers is quite right.

Conclusion

The Copenhagen Interpretation presumes a basic ontological necessity for consciousness. Recent developments (such as the Quantum Zeno effect) suggest that this is indeed the case. It is therefore part of the Universe. We have seen however that it is impossible to locate it within what is normally thought of as 'the physical universe.' Does this create an insuperable problem? No, for, as the next chapter will show, there are several plausible theories as to the whereabouts of consciousness.

9. Where Is Consciousness Located?

> You can march up and down the brain as long as you like, you'll never catch sight of the soul.
>
> Paul Valéry

> The way to do research is to attack the facts at the point of greatest astonishment.[1]
>
> Celia Green

Where is consciousness? It has often been argued that it is unlocated, that it is outside space. Here I shall argue that it is located, though still being outside normal space.

Let us look at four twentieth century theories which offer a radical solution of these issues. We shall see that these are much more interesting than merely to identify consciousness with the brain.

Charon's complex relativity

Jean-Émile Charon (whose surname so strangely echoes the name of Death's ferryman) is a French nuclear physicist who worked on a unitary theory of physics, that is one of a number of attempts to reconcile Einsteinian relativity with quantum mechanics.[2] In his later life he was given a chair in psychoscience at Stanford University, California. He is an admirer of Teilhard de Chardin, and believes he has identified Teilhard's 'radial energy.'[3]

Before we start, let's define entropy and negentropy. According to the Second Law of Thermodynamics, the amount of energy in the Universe is continually degraded into heat, is then less able to do work, and the amount of disorder in the Universe increases. A useful illustration would be an abandoned church. As time goes by, the roof will fall off, the woodwork rot away, the walls collapse, the floor split and crumble. Clothes and tools wear out, clockwork runs down, people age, mountains get worn away. In a closed system entropy always increases, that is available energy decreases; and the Cosmos will (many aeons from now) end up in a state of 'Heat Death,' where all energy is smoothed out over the whole Universe: *nothing will ever happen again*. This is, incidentally, the only principle in science which allows the scientist to distinguish the future from the past.

For several years our family has owned a cat whose name is Entropy, because its claws have an invincible compulsion to destroy things such as chairs, upholstery, curtains, wallpaper. It is a living illustration of the laws of time.

Negentropy is simply the reverse of entropy. In negentropy, things build up in cumulative fashion, energy increases. It has often been observed that living things behave like this during their periods of growth. They do so by ingesting energy from their surroundings and building upon it. These however are temporary victories over the Laws of Physics, for ageing takes over in the end. Teilhard made great play with entropy and negentropy, proposing that the destiny of life was the opposite of that of the material world — for life would build for ever towards higher levels of mental energy.

Now let us turn to Charon's theory. Its imaginative sources seem to be as follows:

(1) As in Teilhard, matter is entropic, life is negentropic. Memory, learning, experience, these augment, they don't crumble. Life runs contrary to entropy. Charon says neatly:

> 'Reasoning' ... takes the collected information memorized by our minds and leads it towards a higher 'order.' Reason is without doubt a negentropic phenomenon.[4]

(2) The electron has mass, but takes up no space — for it is a *point*. This is puzzling and counterintuitive. Though the need for an explanation has been denied, nonetheless Charon writes, 'How can we possibly [confine] a physical quantity which, by its very definition, must necessarily occupy a non-zero volume in space, [within] a mathematical point which, by definition, is zero volume?'[5] Does it therefore (he asks) exist as a point of physical energy in this world, but its mass is on the other side of a 'curtain,' as it were?

(3) What other objects in the Universe could be said to be 'on the other side' of such a curtain? Answer, a black hole. Here

anything that enters the object is locked off from the Universe.[6] Inside it, the Universe's time and space are reversed. It lives in its own time and space. It is like a soap-bubble, a polder, a locked sanctuary.

(4) Is the electron, then, a mini black hole? In black holes time takes on spatial characteristics, that is it runs in both directions, and space takes on temporal characteristics, that is it can be traversed in only one direction. In black holes time is negentropic. One would not need, like Proust, to go in search of lost time. It would not run through one's fingers like water, but accumulate like interest.

Thus (as Charon explains) once inside the Black Hole, one would perceive space moving past in the inexorable manner of time. One would be trapped within the vehicle of space, like a prisoner in an ever-moving car. On the other hand, time would not be permanently lost but would be available in the same way as space is in our normal world — simply by turning round and returning to it.[7]

(5) If the hypothesis is correct, then, we might have found the location of living mind — namely inside the black holes of electrons. An advantage of this theory is that electrons are a type of particle which are practically immortal, as we would doubtless wish our consciousness to be.

On the basis of these intuitions Charon developed a theory that he dubbed 'Complex Relativity.' It is one of many modern attempts to reconcile Einsteinian relativity with quantum theory. The Universe, he suggests, consists indeed of Einstein's three dimensions of space and one of time. This space-time is, however, 'complex' *in the mathematical sense:* thus, the four dimensions are doubled, presenting a 'real' and an 'imaginary' aspect (again in the mathematical sense). There are thus eight dimensions in the Universe, two of time and six of space. The 'imaginary' dimensions are those of our mental world, the 'real' dimensions belong to the world of matter.

There are thus two sets of time and space, one being material, the other mental. We might, to imagine this, visualize a 'wall or curtain' between the two. In mathematical terms, the former dimensions are 'real,' the latter 'imaginary.' In one, time travels entropically, in the other negentropically. In one, everything is lost, in the other, nothing is not conserved.[8]

Electrons communicate with each other by the exchange of virtual particles, namely photons. Since the interior of electrons is (by hypothesis) negentropic, none of this information is lost.

Charon pictures his Universe as follows:

> If we want a ... representation of the Universe without the use of any mathematical language, we can risk the following analogy. The Universe resembles a vast ocean consisting of water and of air above its surface. This surface has a 'right side' in the water and a 'reverse side' in the air. The space-time located in the water is the space-time of matter; the space-time located in the air is the space-time of Spirit.
>
> ... On this vast ocean of matter, minute bubbles of air, each enclosed in a minute film of water, are drifting; these are the electrons. At times we see them floating on the walls of large and small whirlpools. This is Spirit floating on matter ....[9]

This gives perhaps a reasonably clear 'picture' of Charon's universe.

I am not sufficiently competent in mathematics to judge his account of physics, whether to approve or to pick holes in it. All I can do is point to his claim that, in working out his model for the leptons,[10] he found a 'natural' pattern of quantities emerging. As we shall see in Chapter 10, the quantities involved in the fundamental constants of physics are very strange in their mutual relationships. They have to be the way they are to permit the existence of a Universe like ours. But in abstract terms, the quantities they constitute seem arbitrary, absurd, unconnected. The detection of a non-random pattern in these quantities would be an impressive achievement.

To be more precise, Charon claims that the following fundamental constants can be derived from his theory:

c (velocity of light)
h (Planck's constant)
e (elementary electrical charge)
g (coefficient of the strong interaction)
m (proper mass of the electron)
π (proper mass of the muon)
τ (proper mass of the heavy lepton)
M (proper mass of the nucleon)[11]

If in fact these quantities emerge naturally from the eight-dimensional structure of his Universe, this could be striking confirmation of Charon's approach.[12]

The great advantage of Charon's theory is that the objective and the subjective, mind and matter, are embedded in an eight-dimensional matrix which is mutually supportive. Mind and matter are complementary, mutually necessary;[13] and without both of them the world and all conscious beings within it, would instantly vanish.

As I have remarked, I hesitate to comment on the physical aspects of this theory. On the other hand there are serious difficulties with certain of its spiritual aspects: (a) There is a grave problem about the unity of consciousness (including the Binding Problem). How can the millions of electrons contained in our bodies provide such a unity?

Charon claims that electrons *literally constitute* our consciousness. As he himself calculates, a man of sixty kilos contains four followed by 28 zeros of electrons. As he himself asks, where is the 'I' among all this? Unable to see how electrons could form a totality among themselves, Charon suggests that each has the whole 'I,' though he seems uncertain whether *all* the electrons in our bodies 'contain the I' or whether it is merely some of them. He goes on to suppose that, at death, as the body decays, all these electrons separate, and that therefore our multibillion selves commence separate existences. This is counterintuitive. Am I seriously expected to suppose that, at death, I shall survive, not as a single awareness, but in forty octillions of identical copies of my consciousness?

(b) Moreover, the consequence (as Charon himself takes pains to observe)[14] must be that there are thousands of electrons present in our bodies from the lives of past human beings. Now, if these electrons carry the soul, where is our awareness of this infinitely varied past? I am not aware of harbouring Julius Caesar's memories in any part of my being — nor indeed those of any of the other myriad lives whose electrons exist within me, according to Charon.

Adjustments to the theory, or further proposals, might render these aspects of it more plausible. For the moment however we are left with grave difficulties.

Some systems collapse to dust the moment one glimpses a hole in them. But Charon's theory remains stimulating. As a brilliant example of unorthodox thinking, it should challenge us to further speculation.

The intuitive feel of consciousness

One of the virtues of commencing with Charon is that his speculations familiarize us with the notion of consciousness's being on 'this' side of a screen, and of the physical world being on 'the other' side. Before moving on to our next speculation as to its whereabouts, let us pause and consider how consciousness naturally appears to us.

From as early as I remember,[15] my own view of this (the relationship of my personal awareness to the outer world) has been as follows.

My consciousness with all its contents, visual, aural, spatial, etc, is set back from the world on *this* side of a 'window,' in *this* set of dimensions. The 'window' of course is entirely invisible, but nonetheless this is how it feels, and in all logic it is there. It is clear that I am looking through this window — which consists of my senses and of the modalities in which I 'receive' them — onto an outer world ('*that* world') which is four-dimensional. My consciousness, on this side of the window, seems in some respects four-dimensional, in some respects non-dimensional. As for *that* world, the deep contemplation of many philosophers throughout history has suggested that — argued out to the end — it cannot ultimately be distinguished from a virtual reality. There is a chapter in Iain Banks' s novel *Walking on Glass* where one of the two protagonists discovers such a window.[16] This is Plato's Cave, a notion invented two and a half thousand years before Aldous Huxley's Feelies, or our modern virtual reality.

I do certainly feel myself to be my body — but more often it is rather that I feel myself to be operating through my body. I know of course that I am intimately attached to it. Nonetheless, there is the obvious analogy of one's feeling the ground with a stick, or feeling the road through one's driving of a car — one does literally *feel* the ground, though it is really a stick that is doing it, and my proprioception is operating when I guide a car along a road. Tools and motorcars are simply extensions of one's senses and are felt to be such. This sense of attachment to my body is therefore not conclusive evidence of my simply *being* my body. On the contrary, the situation is exactly like that of virtual reality: my unmistakeable feeling is that my real self is located in a three-dimensional 'room' or space which is attached to the earthly world of 'reality' *by* this window. The window *is* the attachment.

As for time, nothing could be more ambiguous. What is time? Is it my consciousness moving onwards? In which case it is I who move. Or is it the world, seen through the window, moving past me? In which case I am eternally motionless — like the Eternal himself watching the display of onward-moving evanescence. The explanation of this double relationship between consciousness and the present is to be found in a luminous and profound observation by Schopenhauer:

> The *present* has two halves: an *objective* and a *subjective*. The objective half alone has the intuition of time as its form and thus streams irresistibly away; the subjective half stands firm and thus is always the same. ... Whenever we may live we always stand, with our consciousness, at the central point of time, never at its termini, and we may deduce from this that each of us bears within him the unmoving midpoint of the whole of endless time. ... Through this consciousness of the identity of all present moments one apprehends that which is most fleeting of all, the moment, as that alone which persists. And he who ... becomes aware that the *present*, which is in the strictest sense the sole form of reality, has its source *in us*, and thus arises from within and not from without, cannot doubt the indestructibility of his own being. ...

He further writes:

> The more clearly you become conscious of the frailty, vanity and dream-like quality of all things, the more clearly will you also become conscious of the eternity of your own inner being; because it is only in contrast to this that the aforesaid quality of things becomes evident, just as you perceive the speed at which a ship is going only when looking at the motionless shore, not when looking into the ship itself.

The conclusion must be that we are immortal, though this immortality consists in a very different state:

> All this means, to be sure, that life can be regarded as a dream and death as the awakening from it: but it must be remembered that the personality, the individual, belongs to the dreaming and not to the awakened consciousness, which is why death appears to the individual as annihilation ...[17]

Our individual consciousness is destroyed at death, but the producer of consciousness, its source and ground, is not destroyed. We shall not end up unconscious, but rather conscious in a new way, in 'a state in which the antithesis of subject and object falls away.'

This insight of Schopenhauer's — this beautiful piece of analysis — reminds me of Meister Eckhart's striking words:

> The soul has two eyes, one inward and one outward. The soul's inner eye is that which sees into being, and derives its being without any mediation from God. The soul's outer eye is that which is turned towards all creatures, observing them as images and through the 'powers.'[18]

The *inner* present which we live *is*, for Schopenhauer, the everlasting and changeless experience of eternity, and is our assurance of immortality.

As for the transient passing moment, modern technology has produced a fairly close reproduction of this situation, namely those virtual reality 'environments' where one dons a helmet, and is thrust into a *simulation* : for instance driving an aeroplane, or steering a car.

Plato, back in the fourth century BC, had a similar vision of things. The world, he thought, is a pseudo-space, and we are like prisoners locked in a cavern, perceiving only poor imitations of a superior reality. St Paul in *I Corinthians* makes the same remark:

> At present all we see is the baffling reflection of reality; we are like men looking at a landscape in a small mirror. The time will come when we will see reality whole and face to face.[19]

A striking parallel is given by something we *know* about the insufficiency of our senses. Thus, if Einstein's theory of relativity is correct, we live in a four-dimensional space-time world; but, as Fritjof Capra says:

> [we] can only observe its three-dimensional 'images.' These images have different aspects in different frames of reference: moving objects look different from objects at rest, and moving clocks run at a different rate. These effects will seem paradoxical if we do not realize that they are only the projections of four-dimensional phenomena [onto a three-dimensional world], just as shadows are projections of three-dimensional objects [onto a two-dimensional visual space].[20]

What we take to be reality is a drama of shadows cast by the light of a more complex world.

If this is a correct view, and therefore the world we see is not entirely trustworthy, we nonetheless know that our own consciousness is real, being the ground of all experience. Therefore other consciousnesses are real too. It is plain that you, my present reader, and that I, your present author, partake of the reality behind appearances. For it is we who are questioning those appearances.

As for Schopenhauer's second aspect of the present, that is its unceasing transience, many have claimed that this too gives an essential importance to consciousness. The reason is that, although every minute of our lives time moves ineluctably forward, yet, astonishingly, science has not succeeded in identifying any fundamental feature of physics which would dictate that forward movement. Thus Lucas reminds us:

> The laws of Newtonian mechanics and electromagnetic theory are indifferent to the direction of time. If at a certain instant we were to reverse all the velocities of all the constituents of a Newtonian system, the system would proceed to 'unwind' and run backwards, and would be in exactly the same position at date *t* after the reversal as it had been at the date *-t* before reversal. If we were shown a film of a Newtonian system we could not tell whether the film was being run forwards or backwards. This contrasts ... with films of human activities, biological processes or the phenomena

> of thermodynamics. If we see men walking backwards, or plants growing smaller and smaller and contracting into seeds, or a cup of warm tea separating itself into hot raw tea and cold milk, we know that we are seeing the film the wrong way round. But if we saw the planets all going backwards in elliptical orbits, there would be nothing to indicate that anything was amiss. ... There is no direction of time implicit in Newtonian mechanics, as there is in human activity, in biological process or in thermodynamics.[21]

Now that the reigning theories are Quantum Physics and Relativity, the situation remains the same. Physical science is at a loss, for though it has invented the term 'entropy,' it has not detected any cause of it in physical processes. The principle of entropy is thus unique within science. It is observed to occur, and to occur without fail; but we have no physical process to point to as its motive force. *Time is not a force.* John Gribbin writes 'One of the greatest mysteries in science is the distinction between the past and the future.'[22]

Yet the subjective sense of the passage of time, as John Smythies writes:

> is a basic phenomenal *fact* that cannot be spirited away by any amount of analysis. Since contemporary physics cannot account for it, it must be mind-dependent. In which case mind cannot be reduced to contemporary physics, so we need to expand physics to include it ...[23]

Perhaps consciousness is the source and cause of passing time.

One thing however does seem clear. Time always has a direction, only one direction moreover, unlike space. It is thus not only monodimensional but also monodirectional. It would seem reasonable therefore *to suggest that time,* as we in our world experience it, *is only half a dimension.*

The notion of 'half a dimension' is entirely clear. In any *one* spatial dimension there are only *two* directions. In all spatial dimensions, one can travel freely in both directions — down and up, to and fro, forward and back. In time alone is one confined to a single direction, from past to future. Clearly, as opposed to spatial dimensions, in the temporal dimension *there is a directional lock.*

Smythies' 'theory of extension'

One of the most unorthodox theories of the nature of consciousness is that developed over a number of years by the psychologist and neurologist John R. Smythies.

He notes that the basic visual field has a centre, a periphery and a boundary. It is roughly circular or oval. It is certainly not rectangular or triangular. We can confirm these facts for ourselves, and it is possible to do so in conditions of little or no light.[24] For instance it 'may be studied in the *ganzfeld* situation in which the visual stimulus is an entirely homogeneous field of light, or when we are in the complete dark.' Subjects will then report that they experience 'a uniform but spatially extended blackness.' This visual field is about two inches away.[25]

The visual field thus has a *geometrical form.* This at once raises the question of whether the mind is spatial. Descartes of course asserted that matter was spatial and mind non-spatial, and many philosophers have followed him ever since. However the question is not so simple. It is certain that many mental experiences are not spatial. Thus one does not 'place' feelings such as anger or joy, and notions like democracy and guilt appear to have no spatial relationships. Nor does the Self seem to possess extension. However other mental activities may well be spatial. It may seriously be wondered whether the mind could grasp spatial relationships in the outside world if it did not, in its own inside world, have dimensionality. My visual field is, for example, laid out spatially; and *this is the one of the main reasons why I have an understanding of space at all.* How could we have any notion of spatiality in the outside world if we had no experience of it in our inner world? We could not comprehend extension if we did not experience it in consciousness.

As Smythies himself writes:

> It is impossible for us to imagine a non-spatial entity — we cannot form a mental image of it — and this is because mental images themselves are spatial entities ...[26]

The philosopher Ted Honderich has also suggested that mental events occupy space, that is a special mental space.[27] Perhaps a part of our resistance to this idea may be our confusion between body and body-image.[28]

As Smythies says, our awareness of our body is not direct. It comes to us *entirely* through the communication of the senses to the brain, including vision, touch, pain, pleasure, proprioception, etc:

> Naïve common sense identifies the body-image with the physical body, but this is a mistake. [For] the somatic sensory field ... is ... a construction of the nervous system. Jonathan Harrison's well-known account of Ludwig, the brain in the vat, whose entire conscious experience is programmed by the illustrious Dr Smythson by means of neurocybernetic stimulators, drives this point forcibly home. Ludwig has a perfectly normal body-image but no physical body (except his brain).[29]

Smythies therefore roundly declares that 'Descartes made a fundamental error' in believing that mind has no spatial extension. Of course it is true that, unlike visual sensations, 'a thought does not have sides' or edges. But we must therefore conclude that:

> the extended / unextended dichotomy really represents a division within consciousness itself ... rather than a basic distinction between mind and brain.

This is the natural conclusion, if the mind is to understand *both* the spatial *and* the non-spatial, as it does. As Smythies notes, contemporaries of Descartes, including Princess Elizabeth of Bohemia, remarked on his mistake.[30] And, in an interesting recent discussion, Colin McGinn suggests that:

> our entire structure of thought is based upon a conception of space in which objects are severally arrayed ...[31]

The logical implication which tempts us at this point is obvious: *could the mind have dimensionality?* Now, it is quite clear that these mental dimensions cannot be found among the normal four Einsteinian dimensions of the material Universe. There is 'no place' for them. Much as there is no place for Heaven in the physical four-dimensional Universe, there is no place for Mind either. But, though we do not know whether there is a Heaven, we do know there is a Mind.

Now, others have proposed multidimensional Universes.[32] Smythies mentions C.D. Broad, H.H. Price, and the cosmologist Andrei Linde.[33] However it is essential to add to this list a variety of cosmological theories, intensely popular among contemporary scientists, including ten-dimensional string theory, eleven-dimensional supergravity, and eight-dimensional supersymmetry. Let me emphasize that these are speculations, none of which has been proven. Now if physics may speculate multi-dimensionally, so may we all.

The logic of our argument is that we must propose further dimensions. Our opponents will bitterly oppose this move, for the reason that conclusions, unwelcome to them, but welcome to us, will follow. Frank Jackson for instance writes:

> I am sometimes asked why I do not follow the lead of those who locate mental objects in a special private space. To me this is like saying 'I find it mysterious that mental objects are in normal space, so I will locate them in mysterious space.'[34]

It is nonsense on Jackson's part to claim that mental objects are in normal space. It is evident that they are *either* not in normal space *or* not in space at all. Nor is mental space any more 'mysterious' than so-called 'normal' space, which, as Kant showed two centuries ago, is a category or parameter of our perceptions and understanding, *and cannot be shown to be anything more.*[35]

Let us therefore put Smythies' proposal on the table. It is both logical and extraordinary. Briefly and simply he proposes that the mind is located in a three or four-dimensional space which interlocks with the other more 'familiar' four-dimensional material space.[36] Such an additional space forms, of course, part of the Universe as a whole. For the sake of clarity I shall refer in what follows to Einsteinian space (that is the four dimensions of spacetime), to hyperspace (that is the hypothetical extra dimensions of mental space) and to omnispace (that is the two considered in combination). Smythies dubs his hypothesis 'The Theory of Extension':

> If we want to maintain that the brain is the organ of mind we can suggest that the brain has a missing lobe, hidden in a fold in hyperspace, that we can call the cryptic lobe.[37]

It is not so far clear how many dimensions we need for our mind-containing Universe. We may not for instance need an additional time-dimension, but at the very least we need more than the four posited by Einstein. We cannot detect these extra dimensions, except internally, because our senses bring us information only from the familiar physical universe. We can witness our own inner hyperspace. This is why it is 'our own.'

There is great resistance to seeing things in this kind of way. It is due at least partly to our tendency to confuse phenomenal space with physical space, that is our inner images of the outer world with that actual outer world.[38] Honderich makes the same observation.[39] We naturally think we see the outer world directly. We don't. It's a fundamental error, widely recognized and entirely demonstrable, but we go on making it.

Smythies' theory solves many problems. For instance:

> Why should brains, and indeed only small areas of brains, [possess conscious experience? For] the only feature that distinguishes the brain from other physical objects is its electrochemical complexity. Yet the cerebellum is as complex as the cerebrum, but plays no direct role in phenomenal consciousness.

That is those parts of the brain which participate in consciousness are no different in any physical way from those which do not. So they provide no physical explanation of consciousness. The problem could be solved by the suggestion that, interlocking with these parts of the brain, is Smythies' mental hyperspace.

It may be wondered why — supposing there is indeed a hyperspace which intersects with the Einsteinian space we are familiar with — our awareness of these extra dimensions is limited to our own individual consciousness. That is *why* is it that our personal mental space has, as it were, 'walls,' which prevent us seeing (a) into other people's mental spaces, (b) into whatever else, outside the small 'locked rooms' of these personal mental spaces, might lie in hyperspace? As Smythies puts it, why are 'the walls of Plato's cave opaque,'[40] why do they form a screen, and why do we see nothing on them except the images brought in by our senses from the outer world and cast by them upon that screen?

The answer to this question is that, for us to operate successfully in Einsteinian space, our awareness of our inner space must be reduced to a minimum. We cannot afford to be distracted from 'the real world.' If it were common for such distracting visions to occur, when crossing the road we would be mown down, when descending the stairs we would infallibly break our necks. In the interests of our survival, evolution has to suppress any such tendency. Let us term this principle 'The Law of Mundane Attention.'

A logical exception to this would be during sleep. At such times our bodily movements are deactivated, and there is little need to suppress messages from elsewhere than the 'real world.' Another exception is parapsychological messages which — for those who accept their reality — constitute a temporary folding back of the screens around our inner awareness. In the light of the Law of Mundane Attention, this must be only a rare event; and indeed the majority of reports of telepathy suggest that these occur only when something of great human importance is being communicated, as for instance the death of, or danger to, a loved one. Smythies does speculate that other areas of psychic space are perhaps concealed behind the visual field.[41]

If the reader is not alarmed already by his previous suggestions, s/he will be perhaps by these latter ones. For further speculations follow naturally. Thus, if our internal awareness of the outside world is situated in hyperspace, individual consciousness could pre-exist human life, and could post-exist it too.[42] If one seeks a theoretical basis for survival after death, Smythies' hypothesis provides it.

Despite the Law of Mundane Attention, do people sometimes catch a glimpse of the unreality of the 'real world'? This is certainly the case. Christopher Langton, a theorist in the new science known as 'complexity,' had a grave hang-gliding accident in the autumn of 1975, in which he suffered damage to his brain. Of what kind? The medics, at a loss, vaguely described it as 'generalized trauma.' After this he had no 'sense of my presence in the world':

> ... Chris felt he was living in the middle of a cube, the sides of which were cinema screens with pictures projected on them. 'It's hard to describe,' he told me. 'It was as if I could see the world, but somehow I wasn't in it, no emotional presence. Like looking at a picture of something rather than seeing the real thing and reacting to it as a person. I was aware of what I was missing, but I couldn't conjure it up. It distressed me a lot. Then it came back, just like that.'[43]

He notes the difficulty of communicating this experience. Perhaps Langton was seeing things as they really are. But his experience also illustrates one of the reasons for the Law of Mundane Attention: it is acutely uncomfortable to be thus 'locked out' from the 'real world.'

Is Smythies's theory testable, and thereby 'scientific' according to Popper's definition? He claims that it might be, and offers such a proposal in the *Walls of Plato's Cave*.[44] The phenomenon he points to is as yet unexplained, and this is the kind of direction in which we should be looking.

The Quantum Vacuum

In Chapter 8 mention was made of the Quantum Vacuum (QV), that huge reservoir of quasi-infinite energy which has been compared to a vast ocean upon which our tiny Universe floats as a mere surface. It is the orthodox opinion that an accidental fluctuation in the Quantum Vacuum caused the entire Universe to emerge from it. Thus our Universe is the creation of the QV, which underpins and is in continuous interaction with it through the exchange of virtual particles. (In this respect it resembles the Next World of the Celts, which was held to interlock and interact with This World.) It must therefore have structure, since our Universe depends upon the continuous exchange of energy between ourselves and the Quantum Vacuum.

The energies locked up in the QV are so immense that:

> If [they] were ordinary positive energies, the universe would instantly collapse to a size smaller than the head of a pin.

Thus God, in the Kabbalah, had to remove himself from a space in the Universe so as to create the World. Our material Universe is a mere insubstantial figment, tenuous and incorporeal compared to the density and energy of the QV.

The QV, however, is very hard to explore, and almost nothing is as yet known about its structure. It is *in itself* unobservable, and can only be studied through its observable *effects*. In this respect it resembles Being, which cannot be observed, but only the outer appearances of Being.

We may well ask such questions as:

Firstly:

(1) How does the QV 'keep its distance' from the Universe, so allowing the latter to exist?

(2) Does time function differently in the QV? Could it be timeless, or outside time in some sense? Is time in the QV a complete dimension rather than a mere half-dimension?

(3) Does the QV explain nonlocality? Is it itself intrinsically nonlocal?

(4) Alternatively, could the situation be as Kant proposes — namely that space is a category of the understanding — that is actually a figment or fabrication due to the limitations of the human mind? In this case the extended spatial nature of our Universe would be a mere appearance. 'Real' extension might be limited to the QV, but the non-extension of the familiar Universe would be sufficient to explain nonlocality.

The above questions are highly speculative. Those which follow are more closely connected with the present state of knowledge:

Secondly:

(5) Are the phenomena we observe in our Universe not the result of activity and structure within the QV? Thus Andrei Sakharov suggested back in the 1960s that gravitation may be due to processes in the QV; and the Hungarian physicist Lajos Jánossy has suggested that Einsteinian relativistic effects such as the slowing of clocks or the increase in mass of objects when accelerated towards the speed of light — that these phenomena may be due to interaction with the QV.

(6) Inertia may be derived from the QV. Ervin Laszlo quotes work by Paul Davies, William Unruh, Bernhard Haisch, Alfonso Rueda and Harold Puthoff to this effect. Similarly, these researchers have suggested that:

> the concept of mass is neither fundamental nor even necessary in physics. When the massless electric charges of the vacuum ... interact with the electromagnetic field ... mass is effectively 'created.' Thus ... mass may be a structure condensed from vacuum energy ...

But if mass is the creation of the QV, then so is gravity, for it is always associated with it.

(7) Are long-term structures present in the QV? Can we experimentally produce such structures ourselves? Recent experiments by Russian physicists would suggest that the answer to both these questions is Yes.[45]

We should be cautious with these theories, for they are at present speculative. I cannot however resist making a philosophical point, namely that if such thinking is correct, then the QV is both (a) the creative source of the Universe and (b) by virtue of that fact an appearance-producing mechanism. I am reminded of the term *Maya* in Indian philosophy, which signifies the deceptive nature of the Universe, and meant originally the magical and delusive charm spread over reality by a divine being.

Thirdly:

The answers to *other* urgent questions may well be found in the QV:

(8) How was our Universe so precisely delineated at its outset as to produce life?

(9) How was life created in the first place?

(10) How were the necessary features of life developed? — enzymes, proteins, intelligent behaviours?

(11) What is the ultimate nature of things? What is consciousness and its relation to the Universe?

Let us suppose for the moment that materialism is correct. Then, as a matter of simple logic, the answer to such questions must lie in the QV, from which, after all, as materialists agree, our Universe emerged. Our questions about dead matter as opposed to life, about brain as opposed to mind, might find some answer there. Is it not in fact suggestive that the mystics in all religions have claimed to have experience of a fount of vast energy, the source of the Universe? What is the relationship of the QV, not merely to time, space and matter, life and evolution, but also to mind, consciousness and purpose? Is the essential being of the QV 'material' in any meaningful sense?

Such questions show unmistakably that our materialists have jumped the gun. They seek to explain our Universe on the basis of what we know about it *so far*, whereas explanations must await our future understanding of the QV, which is (as they themselves admit) the source, fountainhead and support of the phenomenal Cosmos. They have refused to turn their heads and observe that the vast glittering immensities of outer space are a veil drawn upon a further hidden darkness, the latter being of almost boundless size and energy.

Of course this is unsatisfying. It is frustrating to be told that almost all possibilities may be out there in the 'too-muchness' beyond outer space. Yet the impatience of materialists must be resisted. We *must wait till we know more*.

But the QV is not only out there in the space beyond outer space. On the contrary it exists within the very configurations of this room, interacting with the physical Universe that we think so familiar. It is right here right now, and it is what prevents your house from collapsing, the view from your window becoming radioactive, and the very atoms in your street from turning into something indistinguishable from *both* everything *and* nothing.

One thing however is very clear. In its nature and likely function the QV bears a close resemblance to the Ground of All Being in the Perennial Philosophy. Thus in the Tao Te Ching we read:

> The Way is like an empty vessel
> That may yet be drawn from
> Without ever needing to be filled.
> It is bottomless, the very progenitor of all things
> in the world.[46]

And in the Mundaka Upanishad:

> What cannot be seen, what cannot be grasped,
> without colour, without sight or hearing ...
> What is eternal and all-pervading, extremely minute, present
> everywhere —
> That is the immutable,
> which the wise fully perceive.[47]

And in Plotinus, where the One, which is the origin of all things, appears as a vast Nothing to us. This absence, this void resembling the inscrutable vacuum of quantum physics, is in fact the plenum. It is beyond the reach of human thought or language. It is a boundless source of energy, a timeless, spontaneous pouring-forth.

Ervin Laszlo is among the most eloquent of those who are at present proposing the QV as the probable location of Mind. By way of further illustration however, as also for its intrinsically great interest, I must mention the views of the English cybernetics expert, Peter Marcer.[48]

I met him by perfect accident one Edinburgh morning back in 1996 and briefly we had coffee in Waverley Station before he returned south. We had both been revolving around the same street seeking a conference on Mind and Computers — but it had been cancelled — I forget for what reason.

Marcer distinguishes between brain and mind, and between neural and mental events. He denies that mind is simply 'a useful metaphor for describing the state or action of the brain.' He suggests that 'the brain is the classical wavefield apparatus, and the mind is the dynamic quantum vacuum (or non-classical medium) ... with which the classical apparatus can be said to interact.' [Thus] 'the mind is indeed a true ghost in the machine.' He mentions Karl Pribram, whose theory of the mind is that it functions in the manner of a hologram.[49]

Consciousness is real. It contains: a) the arrow of time; (b) a fixed unalterable past and advancing present; (c) three-dimensional objects in motion or development; (d) a future which is often unpredictable; (e) a brain / mind picture of the outside world which corresponds to it.

He notes our impression that we see, hear and sense events in the 'outside world' as being 'in the places they are in.' This is because our brain-mind images do indeed coincide *spatially* with the outside world. 'Snap your fingers,' he told me. I confessed I'd never learnt to do this, so he snapped his. The point is that we hear the sound 'at the distance' it occurs from our ears and that, for Marcer, this is no mere appearance. The sound does come from outside, but we are inside this outside, for our minds are in the QV. He does not accept the delusory nature of the body-image, or rather he thinks the body-image is in the QV, which has spatial extension into the Einsteinian universe.

He further assumes 'a complete historical record of the totality of the brain / mind's experience in the form of mental events quite separate from any corresponding record kept in the brain in neural form.' Thus, he argues that:

> if the brain / mind is a quantum system ... the phase of this system called the Berry or geometric phase allows us to say that the mind ... consists of a complete historical record of the totality of the brain / mind's experience in the form of mental events ... quite separate from any corresponding record kept in the brain in neural form.[50]

That is memory is not dependent on the neural system of the brain. Mind is a quantum phenomenon, and has the long-lived memory appropriate to its nature. Memory does not depend on neural processes, but on quantum processes embedded in the QV.

Here we must recall Wilder Penfield's claim that memory appears to contain, in great detail, every event that has occurred throughout a person's life; and that there is no room in the brain for such detailed memory. In Marcer and Laszlo, such total recall is explicable by the fact that memory is not in the brain, but in the mind, whose location is in the Quantum Vacuum.

Moreover Marcer's claims are even larger. Not only do we as human beings have total recall. But a complete record of the past is a feature of quantum systems, that is there is no loss of information in the Universe as a whole. The QV sustains a complete record or memory — an Akashic record as some Hindus have called it[51] — of all events. Here again Laszlo would concur, for he too sees the QV as containing a complete holographic record.[52] That the Universe preserves a perfect memory of its own past is exactly the claim that Bergson made in 1896 in his *Matière et Mémoire*.

Summary

In this chapter I have presented three contemporary theories of consciousness, each of which locates it in a hyper-dimensional space outside the normal four-dimensional universe. Charon proposes a vast amendment to Einstein, in which there are eight dimensions (two sets of four, there being a kind of 'curtain' between them), thus providing an extra four dimensions for the location of consciousness and the Universe's 'spiritual' side. Smythies, in his extremely attractive Theory of Extension, proposes an additional three or four dimensions to accommodate the mind. Laszlo and Marcer have proposed the

Quantum Vacuum as the likely location of mental and spiritual events. As far as I can see, the general drift and structure of Smythies' and Marcer's theories might be made quite consistent with each other.

Finally, all the theories discussed in this chapter bring with them as a likely, or sometimes *necessary* corollary, the feasibility of consciousness's survival after death. For if consciousness is located elsewhere than in the physical brain, it will not necessarily be subject to the laws of mortality.

Everything we have discussed so far underlines the vast importance of consciousness, both in ourselves and as an element of Nature. This leads us to the subject of the next chapter. Is there evidence of purposive design in the Universe? The arguments for it are, at this opening of the twenty-first century, more persuasive than ever.

10. Design

> Not all the aeons of time can produce something out of nothing.
>
> Seyyed Hossein Nasr[1]

All modern discussions of design seem to begin by quoting a famous passage written by an Anglican clergyman William Paley in the early nineteenth century. It is quoted for instance by Dawkins, as by his opponent Behe. I shall be no exception.

> In crossing a heath, suppose I pitched my foot against a *stone*, and were asked how the stone came to be there; I might possibly answer, that for any thing I knew to the contrary it had lain there for ever .... But suppose I had found a *watch* upon the ground ... I should hardly think of the answer which I had before given ... For this reason and for no other, viz. that when we come to inspect the watch, we perceive (what we could not discover in the stone) that its several parts are framed and put together for a purpose, for instance that they are so formed and adjusted as to produce motion, and that motion so regulated as to point out the hour of the day; that, if the different parts had been differently shaped from what they are, of a different size from which they are, or placed after any other manner or in any other order than that in which they are placed, either no motion at all would have been carried on in the machine, or none which would have answered the use that is now served by it. To reckon up a few of the plainest of these parts and of their offices, all tending to one result: We see a cylindrical box containing a coiled elastic spring, which, by its endeavour to relax itself, turns round the box. We next observe a flexible chain ... connecting the action of

> the spring from the box to the fusee. We then find a series of wheels, the teeth of which catch in, and apply to, each other, conducting the motion from the fusee to the balance, and from the balance to the pointer ... We take notice that ... over the face of the watch there is placed a glass, a material employed in no other part of the work, but in the room of which, if there had been any other than a transparent substance, the hour could not be seen without opening the case. This mechanism ... being once ... observed and understood, the inference we think is inevitable, that the watch must have had a maker ... who comprehended its construction and designed its use.
>
> ... Neither ... would it invalidate our conclusion, that the watch sometimes went wrong, or that it seldom went exactly right. ... It is not necessary that a machine be perfect, in order to show with what design it was made ....[2]

This gives us the subject of our present chapter. Does the Universe have, like the watch, a complexity so great that only one conclusion is possible, namely that it must have had a designer? William Dembski claims in his article 'Naturalism and Design' that scientists and mathematicians are now able to detect design within a given universe, because we have made a breakthrough, that is we have discovered a rigorous criterion for distinguishing intelligently designed objects from ones that are accidentally produced. We can detect, to use a metaphor, the 'fingerprint of God.'

For instance, we have an organization called SETI (the Search for Extra-Terrestrial Intelligence). How do these scientists set about their task? What criteria do they demand from the phenomena they observe in outer space? They require complexity and 'specification' (the latter means purposive structure). The greater the complexity the greater the probability that its source is some extra-terrestrial intelligence.

Take the experimental case where (a) we randomly toss a number of coins, and note down the sequence of heads and tails, and (b) ask a human subject to *simulate* such a random sequence. Is it possible to tell which is the true random sequence, and which is the product of the human mind? A statistics professor can immediately spot the difference. The reason is that a true random sequence produces the unexpected: strangely longer strings of heads or tails. But the human being expects too little of the unexpected, and fails to simulate the wilder irregularities of chance.[3]

In Dembski's book *The Design Inference* we have a closely argued investigation of probability, and of what odds we should accept in making judgments about design or random emergence. He argues:

> Within the known physical universe there are estimated to be no more than 10^{80} elementary particles. Moreover, the properties of matter are such that transformations from one physical state to another cannot occur at a rate faster than 10^{45} times per sec. [This is because of the Planck time, which places an absolute lower limit on the speed of events.] Finally the universe itself is about a billion times younger than 10^{25} seconds (assuming the universe is around ten to twenty billion years old).[4] If we now assume that any subject that ever specifies an event within the known physical universe must comprise at least one elementary particle, then these cosmological constraints imply that the total number of specified events throughout cosmic history cannot exceed:
>
> $10^{80} \times 10^{45} \times 10^{25} = 10^{150}$
>
> ... Technically, 10^{150} is the total number of state changes that all the elementary particles in the Universe can undergo throughout the duration of the Universe.[5]

If the odds against something happening are as large as 10^{150} we may reasonably say that it will never occur by chance. Moreover this calculation draws upon present scientific estimates as to the total size and duration of the Universe. We may assume that everything has been factored into Dembski's calculation of 10^{150} — at least unless scientists were to adopt an immensely longer time-scale.[6]

Now, in the light of figures such as these, what are the odds in favour of life emerging in the way most scientists claim it did, namely by pure accident? First let us consider what features a universe must necessarily possess, if life is to develop within it.

The design of the universe

In the past, science often held that the Universe had existed for ever. Indéed, until quite recently Hoyle's theory of continuous creation was regarded as one of two equally plausible theories. For some time now, however, most cosmologists have preferred to think that the Universe was created at a certain moment in time, at the so-called Big Bang. This (currently orthodox) theory holds that our universe occurred as a quantum fluctuation in the quantum vacuum — a suggestion first made by E.P. Tryon in 1973.[7]

If on the other hand the Universe is uncreated and has existed for ever, there being no beginning to time, then there would have been time for everything possible to happen already. The whole notion of eternity is deeply problematic — as we shall see shortly. If, however, the Universe was indeed created at a particular moment (it has been lately calculated that this would have been between ten and twenty aeons ago, that is between ten and twenty billion[8] years ago) then there are interesting conclusions to be drawn.

For of course we are not considering the creation of 'just any old universe,' but of one which is capable of producing life. It turns out that in almost every conceivable universe life would have been impossible. Thus the conditions on the creation of a universe such as our own turn out to be surprisingly tight. The way our Universe is constructed is so improbable that — as John Leslie in his book *Universes* concludes — *either* there is a Creator *or* there exist vastly many very varied universes.

Some of the most remarkable problems are as follows:

(1) The 'Smoothness problem': 'Large regions coming out of a Big Bang could be expected to be uncoordinated since even influences travelling at the speed of light would not have had time to link them.'[9] If the Universe had begun in this way, life could never have appeared.

(2) The 'Flatness problem': The cosmos would either collapse or expand too fast for galaxies to form, unless its rate of expansion is 'flat' enough. Fine tuning for this would be necessary to a figure of 10^{55} — a hugely improbable sum.

(3) 'Inflation' is also needed. Fine tuning is necessary for this too, and a similar improbability emerges: 10^{50}.

(4) Had the Nuclear Weak Force been only slightly stronger, then the Big Bang would have burnt all the hydrogen to helium. As a result the Universe could not have supported life.
(5) If the Nuclear Strong Force were increased by two percent, this would result in no protons, and therefore no atoms, or else it would make stellar fires too rapid. If it were decreased by five percent, stars would burn too slowly.
(6) If electromagnetism were very slightly stronger, 'stellar luminescence would fall sharply. Main sequence stars would then all of them be red stars' and therefore probably too cold for life to develop. In any case they would be unable to explode — and the explosion of supernovae is necessary for the creation of elements heavier than iron. All quarks would become leptons, and therefore atoms could not exist. If electromagnetism on the other hand were only slightly weaker, all stars would be blue, and therefore too hot and too short-lived for life to develop.
(7) Gravity needs fine tuning for stars and planets to form.
(8) Particle masses need to be much as they are. For instance, the neutron / proton mass difference, superheavy particles, electrons (which must be much less massive than the proton), also the masses of many other scalar particles. If for instance 'the strong force that binds the nucleons in the atom were merely a fraction weaker than it is, deuteron could not exist, and the sun and other stars could not shine. If the strong force were slightly stronger than it is, the sun and other active stars would inflate and possibly explode.'[10]
(9) Moreover, the strengths of the various fundamental forces have a very odd range, this being surprisingly wide and puzzlingly irregular. The Nuclear Strong Force is 100 times stronger than Electromagnetism, which in turn is 10,000 times the Nuclear Weak Force, which in turn is ten thousand billion billion billion times Gravity. This renders the very narrow ranges of their *precision* even stranger. The behaviour of the Nuclear Strong Force is bizarre. At a very short range it repels; at a slightly greater range it attracts; then it disappears entirely.[11]
(10) The quantity of massive particles (baryons) in the Universe has to be very precisely 'judged' for life to exist. 'In terms

> of energy they account for only about one-billionth of radiation. But this thin layer happens to be precisely the right thickness to permit the evolution of life,' since, if it were not so exactly 'judged,' planets would freeze, vaporize, or be knocked out of their orbits by the higher density of the stars.[12]

Had even *one* of the above features not been present in our Universe, it would have been incapable of producing life. It can at once be seen that for a universe of our sort to occur by accident is vastly improbable. Roger Penrose calculates that, for a designer to create our universe, he would have had to make a bafflingly precise initial move:

> This now tells us how precise the Creator's aim [that is his 'aim,' as one aims at a target] must have been: namely to an accuracy of one part in $10^{10^{123}}$. [Penrose continues:] This is an extraordinary figure. One could not possibly even write the number down in full, in the ordinary denary notation: it would be '1' followed by 10^{123} successive '0's! Even if we were to write a '0' on each separate proton and on each separate neutron in the entire universe — and we could throw in all the other particles as well for good measure — we should fall far short of writing down the figure needed.[13]

We should pause for a moment and consider the scale of this figure. Later in the chapter we shall meet another, fairly like it. Surely it is too immense for there to be any doubt. If the odds against a universe being created by chance are of the scale of (on the one hand) one to (on the other hand) the total of particles it contains, then plainly it is not the product of chance.

The oddness of this situation is only increased by the fact that 'the Universe has to be as big as it is in order to support just one lonely outpost of life,' that is there might well not be any other civilizations anyway, despite the Universe's size. This is because of the vast lengths of time it takes to produce, and in sufficient quantity, the atoms necessary for life. 'Noone should be surprised to find the Universe to be as large as it is. We could not exist in one that was significantly smaller.'[14]

With his inimitable irony, the physicist Andrei Linde writes:

> One might suspect that if God knew theoretical physics, he would not even attempt to create the Universe. Too many problems: the monopole problem, singularity problem, flatness problem, isotropy problem, gravitino problem ... One should think before starting on this work! [15]

Many contemporary scientists profess themselves unworried by the gigantic improbabilities involved in the creation of the Universe. The reason for their unconcern is that they believe there is a way out, namely the Many Worlds Hypothesis. This, however, is popular largely because it allows materialists to avoid looking facts in the face. The arguments put forward in Chapter 8 are more than enough to refute it.

The design of life

Let us now move from the vast canvas of the Universe to the features of our own little Earth, or rather of the living beings which inhabit it. Before we take a glance at the design of even the simplest animals, it is worth having a look at one of the preconditions for life, namely water.

H_2O is a molecule whose behaviour, resembling no other, is outrageously odd. Yet without these many oddnesses, life could never have emerged:

> [Water's] specific heat, its surface tension, and most of its other physical properties have values anomalously higher than those of any other known material. The fact that its solid phase is less dense than its liquid phase (ice floats) is virtually a unique property.

Water has unusually high specific heat. This enables it to act as a store of heat and to stabilize the temperature of the environment, indeed of the Earth at large. Its expansion as it freezes is essential for life. Fish survive under a floating roof of ice, below which warmth and liquidity are conserved. If water did not expand as it freezes, then ice would be heavier than liquid water. Therefore the ice would sink to the bottoms of the oceans, all lakes and oceans would freeze from the bottom up, and this would have rendered the development and survival of life impossible.

Barrow & Tipler discuss several other remarkable features of water.[16] There can be no doubt that these qualities together make water *uniquely* suited for life. Such a concatenation is a most lucky 'coincidence' — if such it can be presumed to be.

Before moving on from water to the complexities of living creatures, I wish, first, to say that until two or three years ago, I had always regarded Darwin's theory as invincible common sense. When I started reading the new research, I was astonished by what I found, and at first disbelieving.

Darwin will always remain one of the great men of science. For a long time, however, it was uncertain how evolution might work. Then Gregor Mendel (all his life obscure) was discovered, and suddenly there was an explanation: a mechanism had been found for genetic inheritance.

We must remember that, according to the orthodox neo-Darwinian theory of evolution:

> of course nature does not have goals, purposes or intentions ...[17]
>
> The mechanisms of evolution do not possess foresight, [nor are they purposive].[18]

Though there is room in nature for bower birds, bombardier beetles and bat radar, there is no place in the theory of evolution for such exotic creatures as a *purpose*. The giraffe did not obtain a long neck by stretching it in an effort to reach higher leaves, nor did some unconscious process in the giraffe's brain affect the relevant genes and thereby alter its genetic 'hand of cards.' It was merely because (1) by accident some giraffes had taller necks, (2) the location of high leaves favoured these taller giraffes, and (3) these had thus a survival advantage over shorter giraffes which (4) they passed on through genetic inheritance to their offspring, that (5) we now have long-necked giraffes. The change in the gene pool of giraffes was brought about solely by chance mutations. The orthodox theory absolutely denies any intervention by 'nature,' by the 'unconscious,' by the strivings of the animal itself, or by any other purposeful process, known or unknown. The Nobel prize-winner Jacques Monod claims that 'the Postulate of Objectivity' in science consists in:

> the systematic or axiomatic denial that scientific knowledge can be obtained on the basis of theories that involve, explicitly or not, a teleological principle.[19]

That is, according to this eminent evolutionist, science is not science unless it rejects all notion of purpose.

Talking with my student classes made me aware that almost no educated person (except, I assume, in the sciences) understands this fact — namely that *evolution denies purpose*. Mind you, it is hardly surprising that my students felt like this, for evolutionists themselves find it impossible to avoid the language of purposes, goals, and intentions — those very things that their theory denies. Thus we find phrases such as:

> Brains make it easier to *keep* the [lucky] break *going* ... It is surprising that on the whole the invertebrates have not *exploited* their individual intelligence to *get* the next generation off to a good start. ... Many different kinds of animal have *invented* winged flight ... [My italics] [20]

Or is this sleight of hand? Do some writers seek, by a disingenuous choice of words, to give the appearance of having already 'explained' purpose? At any rate the incautious are often deceived by such language.

There can be no doubt whatever that Darwinian evolution is a constantly occurring event, and that it does explain many adaptive changes. It is likely to provide the explanation for the giraffe's neck. However, it has never been clear how some of the major developments could be due to sheer chance. Biochemistry has recently injected into the theory of evolution the gravest of doubts.

Before I proceed I shall issue a warning. The moment Darwin's theory is touched, the cry is 'blasphemy!' In the old days people like poor Giordano Bruno were burned for speculating. These days you might lose your job, or the scientific reviews might reject your articles. You would be discussed in hushed tones behind your back ('His early work looked so promising.') There is no need for such a reaction. Why should Darwin be regarded by scientism with the awe reserved in the old days for dogmas about the wine of communion? To point out the holes in Darwinian theory, as serious scholars like Behe and Dembski have done, is to advance the cause of science. It is not to revert to the superstitions of two-hundred years ago, and to assert, with Archbishop Ussher, that the World was created at 6 p.m. one evening in the autumn of 4004 BC. Nor is it to revert to a ridiculous literalism vis-à-vis the Bible.

No assertion will be made in this chapter except that there must be a designer *of some sort*. For the *fact* of design does not specify the *nature* of the designer. As Dembski says: 'Who or what is the Designer? Not necessarily the God of Scripture!'[21] As Behe says, 'Inferences to design do not require that we have a candidate for the role of designer.' There is no implication that this must be a perfect being with absolute foreknowledge and absolute power, as in orthodox Christianity. However, as Behe says:

> The philosophical commitment of some people to the principle that nothing beyond nature exists should not be allowed to interfere with a theory that flows naturally from observable scientific data.[22]

The presence of design shows nature to be *more than nature.*

Intuitively, it has always been hard to see how certain sorts of animal behaviour could ever have emerged by pure accident. One might take as examples the orchid whose flowers resemble a female wasp, with eyes, antennae, wings and even the odour of a wasp on heat; or the tropical caterpillar which makes itself a tent, so it can eat its leaf peacefully inside it without being gobbled up. It cuts a leaf one way, then cuts it another, then folds it over, then eats away happily inside its 'shield,' unseen by predatory birds:

> There is a parasitic flatworm that spends part of its life inside an ant, while its reproductive stage is inside a cow. The technique that it has evolved to affect the transfer from one animal to the other shows just how subtle the effects of 'blind' evolution can be. The parasite infects the ant, and presses on a particular part of its brain. This interferes with the normal behaviour of the brain, which causes the ant to climb a grass stem, grasp it with its jaws, and hang there, permanently attached. So when a cow comes along and eats the grass, the parasite enters the cow.[23]

One should emphasize here that (1) I have not described the full complications of the parasite's growth inside either cow or ant, (2) ants do not sit on the top of grass stems waiting for cows to come and eat them. Such behaviour is quite anomalous, and the parasite has to press on a particular part of the ant's brain to cause it to act in this way. How does the parasite know it must do this? How does one calculate the likelihood of such behaviour developing by sheer chance?

We shall have a shot at this kind of calculation in a minute. Before we do so, let us have a brief look at the number of necessary steps in the development of life. Barrow and Tipler list ten essential steps — each of which is absolutely crucial — without which humankind could not have evolved. These are:

(1) the development of the DNA-based genetic code;
(2) the development of aerobic respiration;
(3) the 'invention' of glucose fermentation to pyruvic acid;
(4) photosynthesis. This trait is not in the human lineage, but it is essential if oxygen is to be put into the atmosphere;
(5) the origination of mitochondria. Without them, cell efficiency would be too low to permit higher forms of life;
(6) the formation of the cendriole complex, for this is essential to the reproductive system of eukaryotes and of nerve cells;
(7) the evolution of an eye precursor;
(8) the development of the endoskeleton, since this seems essential to large terrestrial animals;
(9) the development of chordates, since these are the only terrestrial lineage which could develop a complex central nervous system;
(10) the evolution of *Homo Sapiens.*

The above list (they explain) is not exhaustive. Besides, each is essential to the development of *any* intelligent form of life. It may be that Lovejoy is right in suggesting that the traits essential to intelligence are so unique to human beings 'that the probability of the evolution of *any* intelligent species is equal to the probability of the evolution of ... *Homo sapiens*.'

What are the odds against each of these complex developments occurring? Let us take just one. De Ley estimates that the odds against assembling a single gene are so great that:

> an enzyme arises only once during evolution. There simply has not been sufficient time since the formation of the Earth to try a number of nucleotide base combinations

> even remotely comparable to these numbers. The number of bacteria on Earth today is estimated to be the order of 10^{27}; assuming a bacterial reproduction time of one hour, there have been at the most about 10^{40} bacteria in the entire past history of the Earth. [It would have been] possible to try some 10^{47} nucleotide combinations in the past, [but this is] 52 orders of magnitude too few.

Barrow and Tipler continue: 'The odds against assembling the human genome spontaneously are even more enormous.' They are so enormous indeed that they go on to say that our species will evolve on the average on earthlike planets between 10^{400} and 10^{800} light years apart. Now the visible Universe has an extent of approximately 2×10^{10} light years. Thus, Barrow and Tipler's calculation suggests that it is impossible for there to be man-like creatures anywhere else in the visible Universe. And this is a fairly general consensus among evolutionists.[24]

So much for Science Fiction. It is after all not surprising that our attempts to find intelligent life elsewhere in the Universe have so far met with a total blank.[25]

Life's building blocks

Until about forty years ago very little was known of the secrets of the living cell. It was in effect a 'black box,' manifestly active, but its inner functioning remained a mystery. Now, over these last forty years, many of its secrets have been unlocked. In Darwin's time nothing was known about the biological and chemical underpinnings of living processes, for biochemistry did not yet exist. It was hoped that the unknown underpinnings of life were simple enough to permit Darwin's theory to work. The picture that has been built up over the last forty years is, however, one of bewildering complexity. The biochemical systems which Michael Behe studies in *Darwin's Black Box* make Paley's famous watch look childishly simple. Even conscious human designers had not invented mechanisms of such convoluted ingenuity until very recently in our history.

This complexity is of the sort that is termed 'irreducible.' This is no mere emotive adjective chosen for rhetorical effect, but has a precise significance. Let us allow Behe to explain:

> By irreducibly complex I mean a single system composed of several well-matched, interacting parts that contribute to the basic function, wherein the removal of any one of the parts causes the system to effectively cease functioning. An irreducibly complex system cannot be produced ... by continuously improving the initial function ... by slight successive modifications ..., because any precursor to an irreducibly complex system that is missing a part is by definition nonfunctional. ... *Natural selection can only choose systems that are already working*, [so] if a biological system cannot be produced gradually it would have to arise as an integrated unit, in one fell swoop, for natural selection to have anything to act on.[26]

Behe employs a large number of examples in his book. On pages 18–20 he discusses the functioning of the eye, which he sketches over five paragraphs. Behe's description comprises some thirty-four sentences. According to my count (which is certainly an underestimate) at least twenty-five different functioning elements / events occur in this complex machine called 'vision.' Each of these processes has to be activated in the correct order for vision to occur. The odds against such a process occurring by chance (as neo-Darwinians would have us believe) are astronomical.

Dawkins and his fellows of course disagree. Dawkins prefers to tell the old Darwinian story of gradual development from one stage to the next. He takes the emergence of each of the many features of vision for granted.[27] He does not mention the extraordinary complexity which lies behind each of them — behind light-sensitivity, for instance. He glosses over these facts for he needs to present them as 'simple.'

Behe aptly quotes Darwin himself at this point:

> If it could be demonstrated that any complex organ existed which could not possibly have been formed by numerous, successive, slight modifications, my theory would absolutely break down.[28]

Darwin himself would have rejected neo-Darwinism.

Another of Behe's many examples is the clotting of the blood. This is essential to life, and any animal whose blood fails to coagulate will infallibly die. It is therefore vital to Darwinian survival — which is ironic since it is impossible to see how Darwinian survival can explain its appearance. The processes involved in this apparently 'simple' process are of mind-bending complexity. Twenty or so proteins are involved. Behe's brief description contains over eighty sentences, most of which describe some essential protein, some essential process, or both. It is hard to judge just how many interacting factors there are, but I will take the rough calculation of eighty necessary factors, every single one of which has to occur in the right order, otherwise the blood will not clot. The appearance from sheer chance of such a system is of *astronomical improbability*.

To make the neo-Darwinian story convincing, we would need a detailed account of just how each of these several scores of processes (including the complexities of the proteins themselves) could have developed gradually, by small steps. Moreover, we would need an explanation of why, in the case of every small step, the process survived through generations — an explanation of why each small step by itself conferred a survival advantage. But how could any such small step (S) confer such an advantage, in the absence of many other equally complex functionings each of which is essential to S's own functioning? As modern medicine makes clear, a single failure in a single process can cause instant death.[29] How can an advantageous (indeed essential) function such as coagulation be produced when none of that advantage can be conferred until the *final step* is arrived at?[30]

We need therefore to issue a challenge to the neo-Darwinians to explain themselves. Behe claims that there is an extraordinary silence from them. Though thousands of papers have been published on the flagellum, no scientist has ever published an evolutionary account suggesting how the flagellum might have developed. Only two attempts have been made to publish an evolutionary account of the cilium. Both are very fuzzy and imprecise, and avoid the harder issues. Vesicular transport-pathways (the bodily system which takes proteins from A to B) have been much studied, and in detail. But there is no literature which speculates how such processes might have evolved. 'Molecular evolution,' writes Behe:

> is not based on scientific authority. There is no publication in the scientific literature — in prestigious journals, speciality journals, or books — that describes how molecular evolution

> of any real, complex, biochemical system either did occur or even might have occurred. There are assertions that such evolution occurred, but absolutely none are supported by pertinent experiments or calculations.[31]

What sort of improbabilities are we dealing with here? Some years ago, Fred Hoyle tried to calculate the likelihood of creating the set of enzymes (there are about 2,000) needed for the duplication of one simple bacterium.[32] He came up with the figure of 1 in $10^{40,000}$ (= 1 followed by 40,000 zeros). Hoyle says that this compares to the likelihood that 'a tornado sweeping through a junkyard might assemble a Boeing 747 from the materials therein.'[33] We are — again — dealing with figures which exceed by many magnitudes the total number of fundamental particles in the entire observable Universe. And it will be seen that Dembski's calculation, quoted above, as to the maximum 'permitted' improbabilities is here grossly exceeded.

'But,' says Shapiro in his book *Origins*, 'in fact things are much worse' than in Hoyle's calculation. In Harold Morowitz's calculation: the odds are 1 in $10^{100,000,000,000}$. 'The improbability involved in generating even one bacterium is so large that it reduces all considerations of time and space to nothingness.'[34]

As he says, this is no reason to believe in creationism — which, in the usual sense, is the naïve presumption that the world was created in 4004 BC. We can state quite flatly that we *know* it wasn't, and we know this for quite other reasons than that of evolution. Other theories however which inject purpose or purposive beings into the Universe might be acceptable, and seem to be needed.

What is the response of the neo-Darwinists to these points? Elliott Sober, Michael Ruse and Daniel Dennett are among the people who have resorted to the same argument that Dawkins uses in his nicely entitled book *The Blind Watchmaker.* Dawkins writes:

> A haemoglobin molecule consists of four chains of amino acids twisted together. Let us think about just one of those four chains. It consists of 146 amino acids. There are 20 different kinds of amino acids commonly found in living things. The number of possible ways of arranging 20 kinds of thing in chains 146 links long is an inconceivably large number, which Asimov calls the 'haemoglobin number.'

Dawkins comes up with the number 1 in 10^{190}. These are the chances against ever producing haemoglobin by the random processes of evolution. It is plain that such a figure is quite outside the bounds of possibility. 'And,' adds Dawkins, 'a haemoglobin molecule has only a minute fraction of the complexity of a living body.'

Dawkins, it would seem, agrees with our calculations. But wait! He has a neat side-step to show us. Another couple of paragraphs and he will, like some scientific Houdini, be free of our logic.

There is one law for objects, he proposes, and another for living things. For living things are subject to evolution. That is to say that any element in their makeup which does not contribute to survival will be 'sieved out' as he puts it, by the rise and fall of generations. The mindless process of sheer random chance he refers to as 'single-step selection.' He agrees that this will *never* produce our haemoglobin, still less the totality of our physical processes. The other kind of selection will do so, however: he terms this 'cumulative selection.' He illustrates this by calculating how long it would take, by chance, to type the words METHINKS IT IS LIKE A WEASEL.

How does cumulative selection work? Why, Dawkins inserts into the process an observer (!) which 'examines the mutant nonsense phrases, the "progeny" of the original phrase, and chooses the one which, however slightly, most resembles the target phrase ...' Then, instead of taking a longer period than the Universe has yet existed, he can get his result within quite a brief time.[35]

But wait a moment! Isn't the process of evolution supposed to be mindless? In a mindless evolutionary process, only those mutations in the animal which turned out to be of *immediate* survival value could possibly survive for long.[36] How is evolution supposed to know in advance that it must retain certain letters in certain positions and which others to reject? Dawkins has inserted a purposive observer into his process — that very purpose which he denies is present in Darwinian evolution. He performs this sleight-of-hand so as to substitute a manageable number (27×43 or some such similar figure) for the true calculation of random chances, which is 27^{28} (that is 27 multiplied by itself 28 times) and which Dawkins admits would take more than a million million million times longer than the Universe has so far existed.[37] Back in 1986, Shapiro, in his book *Origins*, was already complaining about this type of swindle.[38] While still *claiming* that his process is purposeless and unconscious, Dawkins has inserted a purposeful and conscious intention into it.

As Behe points out:

> Instead of an analogy for natural selection acting on random mutation, the Dawkins scenario is actually an example of the very opposite: an intelligent agent directing the construction of an irreducibly complex system.[39]

Fred Hoyle has an excellent image which will very precisely illustrate the reason why Dawkins's view of chance is grossly over-optimistic:

> Suppose, said Hoyle, that a blind man is trying to order the scrambled faces of a Rubik cube. As the experience of anyone who has tried it shows, matching the colours on all six faces of the cube can be a lengthy process; even a bright and physically non-handicapped person can spend hours groping a way towards the solution. A blind man would take much longer, since he is handicapped by not knowing whether any twist he is giving the cube brings him closer to or further from his goal. In Hoyle's calculation his chances of achieving a simultaneous colour matching of the six faces of the cube are of the order of 1 to 5×10^{18}. Consequently a blind man is not likely to live to see success; if he works at the rate of one move per second, he will need 5×10^{18} seconds to work through all the possibilities. This length of time, however, is not only more than his life expectancy; it is more than the age of the universe.
>
> The situation changes radically if the blind man receives prompting during his efforts. If he receives a correct 'yes ' or 'no' prompt at each move, he will unscramble the cube on the average in 120 moves. Working at the rate of one move per second, he will need two minutes, rather than 126 billion years, to reach his goal.[40]

Dawkins presumes that random chance — which is blind — is not blind. That it is purposive. For he must do so — for he assumes that every time a right square is put in a right place, it is *known* to be in a right place. But this is a contradiction of his own position, which is that evolution is blind, random, unaware, unconscious, and devoid of purpose.

Dawkins' writing is exceptional. He expresses himself with beautiful clarity. His wit is devastating. His clarity of expression is so luminous that it has dazzled him.

It is plain that we must return to Dawkins' own original calculation. The odds against haemoglobin having arisen by the purely random processes of neo-Darwinism are indeed 1 in 10^{190}, a figure which (as we saw Dembski calculating above) is greater than the total number of state changes that it has been *possible* for the Universe to undergo throughout its history. Evolution, as an explanation of such complex phenomena as haemoglobin, must be declared to be a non-starter.

The statistics seem overwhelming. There is one way out, and this again is the claim that our Universe is only one of many. However, as Hodgson notes, those who argue for the Many Worlds Hypothesis require close to an infinity of worlds to make their argument plausible. But in that case, absurdly improbable events — frogs falling from the sky, blood issuing from rivers — must be part of many people's experiences. But they are not.[41]

In the light of the above arguments here and in Chapter 8, it is quite unreasonable to accept the Many Worlds Hypothesis, exciting and imaginative though it is.

It may seem at first sight that a further way out is offered in a series of books by Fred Hoyle and N.C. Wickramasinghe in which they eloquently argue for the seeds of life, in the form of bacteria (developed in outer space) being present everywhere in the Universe. Carried by comets, these would seed planets in every quarter of the Cosmos. This would give us perhaps about ten more aeons of time for such development to occur. However, (1) this is still not a long enough period; and (2) there is still not enough time for later developments (*after* the supposed seeding of the Earth) such as the creation of further enzymes, of organs like the eye, etc. For this reason Hoyle and his associate are still arguing for a universe (a) which did not begin at a Big Bang some fifteen aeons ago, (b) in which continuous creation exists, and (c) whose history stretches back over possibly an infinite past. Despite all this, they nonetheless hold that the difficulties with design are so enormous that there must be a cosmic intelligence directing the affairs of the Universe.[42]

If indeed the Universe is quasi-eternal, then a little thought shows that it is logical to accept the existence of such a hyper-intelligence. In a quasi-eternal Universe there is necessarily enough time for almost anything to emerge, including beings with quasi-supernatural powers.

This shows that the 'way out' I spoke of above, offered to reductionists by Hoyle, is not in fact a way out at all. It too entails the *likelihood of a designer*, of a controlling being or beings of immense power.

Defects in design & other puzzles

One problem about intelligent design is the following, pointed out in a letter in *Philosophy Now* by Rui Vieira. Irreducible complexity bespeaks Intelligent Design (ID). Yes, says Vieira, but where does the intelligence come from in the first place?

> Since all intelligent designers of complexity (including deities) must themselves possess at least as much complexity as their creations (for instance humans), then, according to the above premise, all intelligent designers must also bespeak further intelligent design, and their intelligent designers before them, *ad infinitum*. ... Any recourse to Aquinas's First Cause argument doesn't help. If a particular intelligent designer in our regress is claimed to be a First Cause, then there is no reason why the Universe itself cannot be (since both would still possess unexplained complexity). ... If the infinite regress problem isn't effectively addressed by ID's proponents, then ID ... will remain a non-starter.[43]

This is a point worth discussion. However, the Universe is hardly a candidate for intelligent designer unless it is itself conscious and purposeful, since consciousness is needed for intelligence, and since design entails purpose. The Universe therefore does not provide Vieira with the creative, but unconscious and purposeless, machinery he prefers. On the contrary a creative universe of the kind that is needed would have to possess as much intelligent purpose and power as a divine creative spirit. It would therefore *be* that spirit. Aquinas's argument therefore does not fall.

Two of the most common objections to the existence of a designer are (a) the imperfections in the design of the world, and (b) the cruelties involved in it. This book, however, is not a defence of any established viewpoint; it is an investigation. I am not committed to *either* the moral *or* the technical perfection of any supernatural designer.

The biologist Kenneth Miller has claimed that we can detect in living systems 'errors that no intelligent designer would have committed.'[44] But we do not know who or what the designer is, still less his intentions. Did he desire perfection? Human designers do not always seek perfection. Moreover it is a fallacy to suppose that there is such thing as perfect design, for all conceivable designs can be improved.

One suspects that most thinkers are obsessed by the Christian God, that allegedly perfect and infallible being, as the only possible candidate for a designer. They suppose that it is Christian fundamentalists who are their opponents. But why should the Designer be perfect? Why should he be the Christian God? We have not the remotest idea what limitations there were on the Creator, nor on the materials with which he had to work.

Moreover, some of these imperfections could be held to cut both ways, and are just as good an argument against evolution as they are against design. Jaron Lanier tells us:

> I once asked Richard Dawkins (in a dialogue that appeared in *Psychology Today* magazine) what he thought the best explanation was for the vulnerable placement of many mammalian testicles, including those of humans. I compared them to a soldier who must pilot a well-armoured tank through a war zone while he himself is protected only by a balloon attached to the outside of the vehicle. Neither the tank nor the driver would get very far, however effective the armour was. The testicles ought to be better protected than the brain, by vernacular evolutionary reasoning.[45] He replied with a variety of 'just so' stories to explain testicles, but conceded that they all have serious problems. While it is true that the testicles are helpfully cooled by their position, evolution holds all the cards of the game, and could have evolved air conditioners, or different chemistry. After all, testicles are *the* jewels she is protecting.[46]

If evolution can be so incredibly ingenious in the case of the Bombardier beetle,[47] the cow's liver fluke, the tent-building caterpillar, etc., why have its mechanisms not produced a secure and well-protected site for mammalian testicles? If neo-Darwinian evolution is such an all-powerful mechanism, why these extraordinary lapses? At the very point where the whole driving force of evolution should be centred, we find an anomaly. Evolution is sometimes too good to be true, sometimes too bad to be true. Evolutionary mechanisms, though indubitably part of the truth, are not enough to constitute the whole truth.

Conclusion

Supposing the Universe was created at a particular point in time, its features are, mathematically, so improbable that we must assume a purposeful act of creation so as to enable life to occur within it. Moreover there has not been sufficient time since the creation of the Earth — nor even since the Big Bang — for life to have evolved by random, orthodox, Darwinian pathways. There must therefore be a designer or designers.

11. Creation and Eternity

> In 1961 Yuri Gagarin circled the earth in a spaceship and pronounced that God did not exist because he did not see him out of his little window.
>
> Peterson 1991, p. 68

We have seen that, provided the Universe began at some point, it requires a designer. We therefore need to ask: 'Did the Universe begin at all?' For if its history in past time has been infinite, then logic demands that every single possibility will already have been fulfilled. Even the *almost impossible* will have happened, and will moreover have occurred *already*. Moreover, since infinity knows no limit to repetition — it will have occurred an infinite number of times. It follows that, if the Universe has existed through infinite time, no designer is needed. On the other hand, and by an equal logic, since everything possible must already have happened, every possible designer would inevitably have evolved — and that an infinite length of time ago.

This picture of infinite repetition is dizzying. Can it be refuted? Let us work out what the likelihoods are. *Did the Universe have a beginning?*

Was there a creation?

There are a number of traditional arguments which are supposed to 'prove' the existence of a divine being. These include:

(1) Anselm's Ontological Argument. St Anselm (1033–1109) argued that we can conceive of God as 'a being than which none greater can be conceived.' Yet, if we conceive of such a being as existing only in the understanding, a greater being could be conceived, namely one that exists also in reality. For existence in reality is greater than existence in the understanding alone. Therefore the greatest conceivable being must exist.

This argument I find intractable, inscrutable and slippery. Why anyone should assent to it, baffles my understanding. It was already attacked by Anselm's contemporary Gaunilo.[1]

(2) Aquinas's Cosmological Argument: when we look at movement / change in our world, we see that it is always caused by a previous movement. But this process involves an infinite regress into the past, which is impossible. Thus a halt in this backward movement must be found at some point. This is the unmoved mover, that is God.

(3) The Kalâm Cosmological Argument. This is drawn from medieval Islamic philosophy, and has a particularly attractive clarity.

It starts by stating that (a) the Universe either had a beginning or it did not. (b) If it had a beginning, then this was either caused or not caused. (c) If the beginning was caused, then this cause was either a conscious being or it was not. Thus the argument seeks to establish, step by step, that the Universe had to have a beginning, that this had to be caused, and that this cause had to be a conscious Creator.

We have already estimated the likelihood of points (b) and (c). The immense precision of the Universe's many complex and unexpected features make a Designer an unavoidable conclusion. This leaves us to consider point 1 (whether the Universe had a beginning).

How may we address this problem? As we know, the present view among scientists is that the Universe commenced with a Big Bang. This offers strong support to the proposition. But science is always changing, and who knows what will be believed in another twenty years? It remains a theoretical possibility that the Universe has existed for ever, as many used to believe.

Here I intend to rely heavily on the arguments of William Lane Craig.[2] Craig's way of attacking this problem is as follows. He states, as his first premiss:

(1) though *potential* infinites may exist, no *actual* infinite can exist;

as his second premiss:

(2) An infinite temporal regress of events is an actual infinite. But actual infinites are impossible. He deduces therefore:

(3) *The Universe must have had a beginning.*

Proposition number 1 depends on our intuitions about infinity, and in particular about (a) number and (b) infinite time. It will readily be admitted that the set of numbers 1, 2, 3 ... stretches out infinitely and has no end ... for however enormous the number one mentions, we only have to add another 1 to it, or indeed any other number we like. The series of numbers stretches towards infinity, yet no actual number possesses infinity.

Secondly, we seem to live in a Universe which, potentially, might stretch infinitely into the future. But at any given point we are not 'at' the infinite, which cannot be located at any point upon the line of time, but is rather an ever-receding *principle* of beyondness and unreachability. One may endlessly add additional numbers or days ... but at no point does one reach the actual infinite. For no actual infinite can, *by virtue of its own definition*, be reached. It is generally admitted therefore that we live in a world of *potential* infinites, but that none of these is actual.

Actual infinity had throughout philosophy been generally regarded as impossible. This distinction between potential and actual infinities was a masterly idea thought up by Aristotle in the fourth century BC, and most thinkers have agreed with him — until the nineteenth century.

Then there came the revolutionary work of the mathematicians Bolzano, Dedekind and Cantor. They convincingly demonstrated that notions such as infinity, and indeed an infinity of infinities, could be ingeniously dealt with by mathematics. However, most mathematicians say that their work is concerned with the mathematical, not the real, world, and some (the intuitionists) go so far as to assert that 'even the conceptual existence of the actual infinite is impossible.'

Maybe indeed it is unimaginable. If actual infinities did exist, then a number of paradoxes and absurdities would follow, and some of these are listed in Craig & Smith's *Theism, Atheism and Big Bang Cosmology*[3] including that famous hostelry Hilbert's Hotel. Hilbert was another of those mathematical geniuses who played with the infinite, to the dazzlement of their peers. I am not sure I would like to visit Hilbert's Hotel, but it has at least one advantage over ordinary hotels. It has an infinite number of rooms, all of which are full ... when an additional guest arrives. All the landlord has to do to accommodate this extra guest is to move the occupant of Room 1 into Room 2, the occupant of Room 2 into Room 3, and so on. Hey Presto! For one of the features of infinity is that, even when it is complete, it is still incomplete. By its very definition, it is endless incompleteness.

Whether such a picture has anything to do with the 'real world' may be doubted. Does the Quantum Vacuum operate like this? (But we cannot answer questions about the Quantum Vacuum.) These ideas are most entertainingly set out in the mathematician Rudy Rucker's *Infinity and the Mind* and in his novel *White Light*.[4] Nonetheless, Hilbert's Hotel does not prove anything more than that the sequence of numbers may always be added to, and added to infinitely — which we knew already. It does not demonstrate an *actual* infinity, but rather the logic of *potential* infinities.

Let us take a case cited by Craig:

> Imagine a library with an actually infinite number of books. Suppose further that there is an infinite number of red books and an infinite number of black books in the library. Does it really make sense to say that there are as many black books in the library as there are red and black books together? Surely not. Furthermore, I could withdraw all the black books and not change the total holdings in the library. Let us also assume that each book has an actual infinite number of pages. There would be just as many pages in the first book in the library as there are in the entire, infinite collection. If someone read the first book, she would read just as many pages as someone who read every page of every book in the library![5]

In contradiction to this, some have argued that infinite set theory exists within mathematics, and that therefore the infinite must be taken seriously. However, as Moreland says, 'the mere presence of a generally accepted theory in mathematics says nothing, by itself, about anything in the real world ....' Which, for instance, of several theoretical geometries actually fits the real world? Not necessarily all of them. Indeed, 'no one geometry is true as a matter of logical necessity.'[6] Thus the mere existence of a consistent mathematical theory does not mean that it necessarily corresponds to anything real.

In this context, we should listen to Hilbert himself:

> Nowhere is the Infinite realized; it is neither present in nature nor admissible as foundation in our rational thinking ... The role that remains to the infinite is, rather, merely that of an Idea ...[7]

Here the term 'Idea' has to be understood in Kantian terms, as one of the fundamental categories of human understanding. We need to have the notion of the infinite so as to have a notion of the finite. Thus even the great theorist of the Infinite, Hilbert, did not assert its *actuality*.

Now future time, we admit, may be 'infinite.' (It is hard to imagine its not being so.) But we do not mean by this that it is an 'actual infinite,' for it is not infinite yet, nor could it in practice ever become so. Indeed, if it ever became so, then it would cease to be infinite. For a 'complete infinite' is a contradiction in terms, for infinity signifies 'infinite incompleteness.' One of Aristotle's most clear-sighted arguments was to describe the infinite (το απειρον) — as 'untraversable' — and draw the consequences.[8] For since the Infinite has no bounds, therefore one can never get to thc end of it. Or one might say that, no matter how far one goes, the 'outer edge' of the Infinite is always further on. — Since the Infinite is that whose outer boundary can never be reached, the whole notion of its ever being complete is contradictory, and the whole notion of an actual infinity is paradoxical.[9]

We must turn now from the Future to the Past. Plainly, to state that the Universe has always existed, is to state that the past is an actual infinite.

But this creates extraordinary logical problems. For instance, in Sterne's novel *Tristram Shandy*, the eponymous fictional author spends a year writing the events of one day. If therefore he were given enough time to write down his whole life, he would have to be given an infinite time, and would be continually falling behind at the rate of 365 to 1. Let us therefore grant Tristram Shandy an eternity in which to write, and say that an infinite amount of time separates us from his beginning to write. Thus, (on the one hand), because he requires an eternity in which to write, he would be writing throughout eternity. On the other hand, since he has had an infinite time in which to complete his book, he must already have completed it, and moreover at any given time in the past at which one examined the situation, one would find that hc had completed it. Paradoxes such as this make it impossible for us to accept infinite regress into the past as real.[10]

This view was firmly held by the majority of philosophers until recently. Kant for instance maintains that 'an elapsed infinity of successive events is a self-contradictory concept.' Consequently, the Universe cannot be infinite in time, for nothing could ever have got to where it is now.[11]

In his excellent book on *The Infinite*, Moore quotes Aquinas:

> Even if the world had existed for infinitely many days, no one of these days would be infinitely far away. ...[12]

Anything that takes a finite time to occur would already have occurred had the Universe begun an infinite time ago. Therefore it is inexplicable that the Earth still exists. Therefore the Universe must have *begun* at some time in the past.

Moreover, if the past has existed for ever, everything possible must have happened already. It must therefore be the case that what we are doing now has been done an infinite number of times before. Which of this infinite number of times are we doing this? Neither we nor Time can tell. Is this not to make a nonsense of reality?

Furthermore, if the past is an infinite regress, how do we reach the present moment? We cannot. If the infinity of past time is true, then it follows that *no moment in time can ever be reached.* For reaching it is like jumping out of a bottomless pit.[13] As John Hospers remarks:

> If an infinite series of events has preceded the present moment, how did we get to the present moment?'[14]

The paradoxes are extreme. Everything must have happened already. Nonetheless the present moment could never have been reached. So nothing of our present reality can have happened already. Imagining actual infinites is fine, so long as these are mathematical or conceptual. But they cannot be applicable to the history of the Universe.

Many scientists have also argued against an infinite universe on much the same grounds. Barrow & Tipler argue against an infinite past that 'any event which could have happened by now would have already happened by now.' Therefore universal heat-death would have already occurred. Davies writes:

> The ... universe cannot have existed for ever, otherwise it would have reached its equilibrium end state an infinite time ago. Conclusion: the universe did not always exist.[15]

Craig also concludes that the universe must have had a beginning in time. It 'began to exist.'[16]

Smith's 'chance creation' refuted

Astronomers were initially most disquieted about the Big Bang. The last thing they wished to believe was that the Universe had had a beginning:

> This is an exceedingly strange development, unexpected by all but the theologians. They have always accepted the word of the Bible: In the beginning God created heaven and earth. ... For the scientist who has lived by his faith in the power of reason, the story ends like a bad dream. He has scaled the mountains of ignorance, he is about to conquer the highest peak; as he pulls himself over the final rock, he is greeted by a band of theologians who have been sitting there for centuries.[17]

The apostles of materialism therefore, while accepting that the Universe did have a beginning, seek to *avoid the consequences* of this probable fact. Quentin Smith argues that a singularity[18] is 'a point beyond which spacetime curves cannot be extended, and thus which cannot have causal antecedents,' However, what justifies the belief that causes can exist only within a spacetime of our kind? A 'point outside' our spacetime could perfectly well provide a 'location' for such a cause. (God is not spatio-temporally located, according to orthodox Christianity.)

Smith's argument that the universe could be a vacuum fluctuation fails as an argument against cause, because:

> Virtual particles do not literally come into existence spontaneously out of nothing. Rather the energy locked up in the vacuum fluctuates spontaneously in such a way as to convert into evanescent particles that return almost immediately to the vacuum.

Thus vacuum fluctuations are not an exception to the principle that 'whatever begins to exist has a cause.' There is continual causal interaction between the Vacuum and our own Universe.

Smith also claims that 'uncaused means "in principle unpredictable."' Now, an event 'caused by a well-understood material process' does indeed imply predictability. However, 'caused by some conscious decision' often *does* imply unpredictability. Hence Craig comments:

> What is ironic about this conclusion is that it is one with which the theist is in whole-hearted agreement. For since according to classical theism creation is a freely willed act of God, it follows necessarily that the beginning and structure of the universe were in principle unpredictable even though they were caused by God.[19]

If we add the unpredictability of Creation to the complexity of it, we may well conclude that this shows it to be *freely* produced and *willed* as opposed to either deterministically caused or produced by blind accident.

Smith's conclusion is counter-intuitive, namely that:

> ... our universe exists without cause and without explanation. The universe (including, in Smith's view, the initial singularity) simply sprang into being out of nothing without a cause, endowed with a set of complex initial conditions so fantastically improbable as to defy comprehension, and as it evolved through each symmetry-breaking phase cosmological constants and quantities continued to fall out wholly by accident so as to accord with this delicate balance of life-permitting conditions. Such an interpretation seems implausible, if not ridiculous. The metaphysician can hardly be regarded as irrational if he reposes more confidence in the principle *ex nihilo nihil fit*[20] than in Smith's [dubious assumptions].

As Craig says, one may ask:

> ... whether the whole of being could come out of non-being; and here a negative answer seems obvious. ... If there were absolutely nothing, then it seems unintelligible to say that something should spring into existence[21]

In the Upanishads over two and a half thousand years ago, the sage Uddalaka had the same insight: 'How could being be produced from non-being?'[22] As Barrow writes:

> Complete Nothingness is inconceivable. Nothing *at all* is unimaginable for us because it would mean [that] no facts could exist — not even a fact like the statement that 'nothing exists, in fact.'[23]

We must conclude that this kind of argument does not succeed, and that the Universe did indeed have a beginning.

Hawking's beginningless universe

One recent attack on the necessity for a Creator is to be found in the works of Stephen Hawking. The mathematics is subtle, the vision imaginative. He asserts that there is no need for a creation, because the Universe is, as it were, wrapped up in a bubble, safely locking within itself the processes of time, which do not occur outside it, but which are existent only within it. By this he does not mean that the Universe swims in a universal timelessness which exists outside its boundaries — but rather that there are no such boundaries. There is nothing but the Universe, it has no temporal boundary or edge whatever. It is 'completely self-contained.'

So far so good. Images of this kind are astonishing, no doubt, but valid in the world of modern science. Hawking, however, goes on to argue that:

> So long as the Universe had a beginning, we could suppose it had a creator. But if the Universe is really completely self-contained, having no boundary or edge, it would have neither beginning nor end: it would simply be. What place, then for a creator?[24]

As Keith Ward decisively replies:

> It is very odd to suppose that, if the Universe had such properties as those of having four basic forces, acting according to invariable laws, being mathematically structured, and having a first temporal moment, then God might explain its existence, whereas if it had all those properties except for having a first temporal moment, God would be superfluous.[25]

As we have seen, the Universe's amazing concatenation of properties *requires* conscious design. That the Universe might be 'self-contained' and 'have no beginning' does not abolish its need for an explanation.

The curious thing is that Hawking's argument depends on a suggestion -— namely that of shutting off all time and space inside a closed Universe— which closely resembles that of traditional theology. The notion of God's being outside time, beginningless, was mooted centuries ago,[26] and was precisely Boethius's view of the matter (a theologian who was put to death by Theodoric the Ostrogoth). According to Boethius, the solution to these problems was that God was eternal in the sense of being beyond the destructive dimension of forward-moving time. Thus the very notion of 'beginning' itself was created when the Universe was created. Time did not exist 'before' that. This was also the view of the ninth century Hindu philosopher Shankara:

> Though One, Brahman is the cause of the many. There is no other cause. And yet Brahman is independent of the law of causation. Such is Brahman, and 'thou art That.'[27]

Hawking has given mathematical expression to this notion; he has offered one account of how a temporal universe might exist inside a fundamentally non-temporal Hypercosmos. The one difference between himself and traditional theology is this: that he denies the need for a Hypercosmos or a God.[28]

Ward, however, wins the argument.

Breaking the infinite regress

The problem of the infinite regress of causes is, perhaps, more puzzling. Every intelligent child, asking 'Who made the World?' and hearing the response 'God,' immediately asks, 'Who made God?' An answer being given to this, the question 'Who made this even greater God?' immediately surfaces. Here we are faced by an infinite regress of causes, one divine spirit being caused in turn by another *ad infinitum*. The child's logic is excellent.[29] We are again faced by a temporal infinite. This is to say that if the chain of causes stretches back into infinity, then we have the same problem we have just disposed of.

Craig neatly answers this (it is more or less Aquinas's answer). Anything that began had a cause of its beginning. But perhaps before all beginnings — before the first beginning of all — there is a 'first cause.' The causer of this first cause (by this argument) must have had no beginning. The problem is that this sounds like an artificial and arbitrary let-out: 'Let's call a halt where it's convenient for us to do so.'

These issues are difficult — they lie *at the outer edges of* our rational intuitions. Nonetheless the reply to the above objection is quite simple. The argument against infinity shows that an infinite regression of causes is impossible. We need therefore to find a plausible point where this backward recession must halt.

However, materialists are in no better situation. They equally cannot admit an infinite regression of causes. They also need to call a halt at some point. They simply prefer to do so *before* (or rather just after) a conscious Creator might be called upon. The question therefore becomes, not, Is it illegitimate to call a halt? But rather, As between ultimate causes (behind which there is no further cause), is a mindless cause, or an absence of cause more likely than a mindful, conscious one? We have already seen the answer to this question. The extraordinary unlikelihood of our Universe shows that a purposeful cause is the only likely possibility.

The vicious circle solution

What alternative can we propose to the need to deny an eternal regression of causes? The answer is, I fear, equally paradoxical, for it is *the vicious circle*. Circles have much the same nature as infinite regressions, for one can traverse them for ever, though in the case of circles one gets dizzy as one does so. However, this is the physicist John Wheeler's proposal. He suggests that the Universe is a vast consciousness regarding itself as in a mirror — that mirror being the physical universe. He draws a picture to this effect. This wonderful image is in fact ancient, and perhaps its most striking instance occurs on the final pages of the twelfth century Persian poet Attar's *Conference of the Birds*. Here a number of birds, led by a hoopoe, seek God. After enduring countless travels and listening to countless parables, they are confronted with the majesty of the One. He however is a mirror of themselves. For they are the One, the One is themselves, and it proclaims to them: 'The sun of my majesty is a mirror.'[30]

The fact that the image of the self-reflecting Universe is ancient does not prevent it being absolutely modern. Creation, according to Wheeler, is a mutually-supporting paradox. Consciousness creates matter — which is the former's mirror and enables it to regard itself; while matter equally creates consciousness.

But is this (a) an image of how the Universe, *once created*, supports itself, by being self-regarding? But then creation is not explained. Therefore if Wheeler's idea is to answer our question, it must be (b) an image of origination. But in that case origination is explained as follows: 'The Universe regards itself. That is it *decides* to regard itself.' Thus there must be an act of will at the outset. Again, this act of will — this act of creation — must be outside the normal causal and temporal sequence — otherwise we shall be sunk once more in endless regression.

There is no non-paradoxical solution to the problem of ultimate creation — except to (as it were) step *outside* the paradox.

This is very Gödelian.

According to Gödel, all mathematical and logical systems involve at least one inconsistency. To resolve this inconsistency, it is necessary to step outside the system into a higher system. This however will in its turn involve at least one other inconsistency, which will make it necessary to step outside into a higher system once again. Though the human mind can perfectly well see what the problem is, this is nonetheless an ever-receding process, an ineradicable paradox, at the heart of logical systems. In the same way as a halt has to be called at some point, by stepping outside the whole system of systems to a stance where the whole paradoxical situation can be seen and judged from above; so we must step outside the ever-receding or else circular locating of beginnings within normal time-space, into an eternity-space of a quite different order of being.

For, as we now see, it is highly arguable that the logic which has led us to reject the possibility of there being an *actual infinite* — demands that there should be such an eternity-space, in which the laws of time are not the same as in our own Universe.

With this in mind, let us return to the cause of creation — the Universe's need to know itself and see itself. The littlest book to contain the biggest statement is the *Laws of Form* by G. Spencer Brown who argues (I paraphrase):

(1) The real, as science itself agrees, merely conceals a deeper reality. So the universe is an expression of a reality deeper than itself.
(2) All the particles of the universe are, ultimately, indistinguishable from each other. Thus the observer consists of what s/he observes. S/he is therefore the universe observing itself.
(3) So as to observe itself, the universe must obviously cut itself up into (a) the observed and (b) the observer.
(4) This gives us a possible reason for the universe having divided itself up and thus 'come to form.' Perhaps its motive for its own creation is so as to perceive itself.
(5) But in cutting itself up, it partly falsifies itself. It therefore partly eludes itself.
(6) To continue to be observed, it must continue to be partly falsified and to partly elude the observer. 'Thus the world, whenever it appears as the physical universe, must always seem to us, its representatives, to be playing a kind of hide-and-seek with itself.'[31]

This corresponds with remarkable closeness to several very ancient myths. Thus, in the Gnostic writings attributed to Hermes Trismegistus, it is said that creation began because God 'fell in love with his own form'; and Proclus relates that Dionysos, 'led astray' by his own image in a mirror, created all things.[32] In myths of this kind, the source of creation is the wish of the Divine to know itself. But — as Quantum Theory made us suspect in Chapter 8 — the Universe seems so constructed as to disguise its own nature.

If the cosmic impulse behind creation is to see and know oneself, consciousness must be a fundamental element of the universe. Otherwise no such process as Spencer Brown describes could occur. Consciousness is a precondition of Creation. And thus we return full circle to the primacy of consciousness

Conclusion

In this chapter we have confirmed that there must be a Creator, by establishing the validity of the Kalâm Cosmological Argument. We see that the Creator must reside 'outside' the causal processes of time. More speculatively, we surmise that his motive in creating the Cosmos and the living beings within it is *to understand*. If so, we see again that consciousness is more fundamental than the created Universe.

Is there any *knowledge* to be had of this fundamental creative consciousness? Can it be experienced, or must it remain for ever speculative?

12. Scientists of the Soul

Tortoise

The Minister of the Interior is inside;
Shyly he pokes his head outside.

Humble. He has no rival for lordly humility:
Snooty. He sniffs at the down-to-earth with his
twitchy snout.

Now and then, he can't help it, he makes a
bid for freedom.
Lumberingly galloping from this plant to the next,
He aspires to heaven, seven plants further on ...

He fails to escape, for neither tortoise nor Minister
of the Interior
Nor we, none of us, can get to the outside.

Armand Robin[1]

The sensation of the mystical ... is the source of all true science. He to whom this emotion is a stranger, who can no longer wonder and stand wrapped in awe, is as good as dead. To know that what is impenetrable to us really exists, manifesting itself as the highest wisdom and the most radiant beauty ... — this knowledge, this feeling, is at the centre of true religion.

Einstein[2]

What *evidence* is there of a universal consciousness, and how might it be inquired into? To answer this, we must first ask, 'What is the fundamental method of discovery in science?' It is *empiricism*, namely the obtaining of knowledge through observation and experiment. The term comes from the Greek word for 'experience.'

The empirical method is often contrasted with hypotheses obtained through reasoning. A much quoted example of this contrast is the ancient belief that heavy objects fall faster than light objects. This belief seemed on the face of things 'reasonable.' Galileo however showed that, surprisingly, objects of differing weights fall at the same rate. For it is a plain fact that reasoning may be faulty, and does not necessarily correspond with the real world. (Indeed, reasoning may on occasion be unreasonable.) Observation and experiment (preferably repeated and thereby verified) are therefore the final test of hypotheses, and no theory can claim to be scientific if it cannot undergo the test of experiment.

But here comes a serious problem. If consciousness is of such central importance, how can it be inquired into? It is a private phenomenon. My consciousness is inaccessible to anyone else, and so my reports of my experiences cannot be confirmed by independent observers. The successes of science are due to its use of the empirical method. But how may we investigate private experience? The answer is present in the words. 'Empirical' means 'what is experienced,' and science began to progress only when humankind ceased to assume how the physical world 'must' behave and instead began to *observe* how, to their surprise, it *actually* behaves.

Observation, then, is the secret. But every observation, even of an 'objective event,' is a private observation. To say that such observations are 'publicly demonstrable' merely means that A, B and C appear to observe themselves agreeing that X happened at time Z.[3] Most people think there is a radical distinction between objective public facts and subjective private facts. But this is not so, for there is no such thing as a public fact. Any so-called 'public fact' is always (first) observed privately by a number of individuals who (secondly) agree as to what they have witnessed.[4] The phrase 'an accepted scientific truth' is both frank and exact. What science claims to be truth is what most scientists in that particular field agree upon for the time being. *Objectivity is the product of agreement between subjectivities.*[5]

Every observation without exception is private. It is agreement about them which makes them 'public.' When an apple is seen falling from a tree, we may all agree that 'We experienced it.' Equally when different experiences of loss cause different people suffering, we can all agree that 'We experienced it.' Private experiences repeat themselves in similar form in many different consciousnesses, and this constitutes the basis of agreement. Why then should *an apple* be regarded as more objective than *suffering?*

As the neurologist Antonio Damasio writes:

> The idea that subjective experiences are not scientifically accessible is nonsense. Subjective entities require, as do

> objective ones, that enough observers undertake rigorous observations [and that these] be checked for consistency across observers .... Moreover, knowledge gathered from subjective observations, for instance introspective insights, can inspire objective experiments ...[6]

Clearly therefore there is no problem about the objectivity of the phenomena of consciousness *or at least about those on which agreement can be reached.* We need to describe and discuss them and seek such agreement.

It does not detract from these observations that, just as many areas of scientific investigation can only be undertaken by certain gifted individuals, so some have a special talent in exploring the inner worlds of consciousness. Again, where they agree, the evidence must be regarded as good. Because they are a minority, there is no more reason to reject their findings than in the case of scientists, who are equally a minority. We may truly call them 'the scientists of the soul.'

The testimony of experience

Normal experience argues strongly for the centrality of consciousness. Owing to the law of Mundane Attention we easily overlook many simple facts of experience which we test out in our lives every day. It will be helpful therefore to pay particular attention to some of these.

Firstly, as John Searle says:

> Consciousness is not just an important feature of reality. There is a sense in which it is *the* most important feature of reality because all other things have value, importance, merit, or worth only in relation to consciousness. If we value life, justice, beauty, survival, reproduction, it is only as conscious beings that we value them.[7]

Searle's point is self-evident. Let us add to his list compassion, truth, knowledge and love. Consciousness is the unique source of all values.

Secondly, we saw in Chapters 1 and 2 that certain experiences are ineffable, that is they cannot be defined in words, but are themselves the basis of all verbal definitions. Thus, 'red,' 'hot,' 'consciousness,' 'time,' 'space,' etc, can be defined only by appealing to other people's experience of them. They are indefinable because they are basic, and hence it is upon them that all other meanings depend. To deny the existence of qualia and of consciousness itself is simply to cut away the very foundation on which all knowledge and all meanings rest. Again we see the *fundamental* role of consciousness and its contents.

Thirdly, as in the amusing, touching and wise poem by Armand Robin, we cannot emerge from our consciousness to see how things 'really are' on the outside. We are locked within our own individual consciousness like the tortoise in its shell, we are isolated from each other, we cannot feel each other's pain, we cannot feel each other's joy. It would be accurate to say that we are in prison, and to specify it as solitary confinement.

There is however a more positive side to this. Unlike our bodies, which are at the mercy of the external world, our minds are, in John Clute's terminology, 'polders,' that is microcosms defended against encroachment from outside. (Polders are reclaimed Dutch land defended by dams against the North Sea.)

This situation has two aspects. Nobody else's consciousness can see into mine and perceive what my senses are perceiving or my mind is imagining. Marc Hauser tellingly illustrates this in *Wild Minds*, when he explores the (quite striking) evidence for compassion on the part of wild animals. Unfortunately, as he then argues, we cannot be sure that any of these animals *feel* compassion — for two reasons: (1) they have no language, and (2) we cannot enter into their minds.[8]

Secondly (and this is clearly positive) since no outside person can 'peer into' our consciousness, therefore our consciousness cannot be tampered with, manipulated, reprogrammed like machinery. Murderers and torturers can assail our bodies, by intrusion, mutilation etc. But they cannot directly intrude into our consciousnesses. Brainwashing may effect a breakdown of the structures of the mind, but it is achieved by external manipulation, not *via* a direct entry into consciousness. There is a fundamental ontological difference between the accessibility or vulnerability of bodies as opposed to minds. One cannot gain access into anyone's consciousness 'from behind.' This one must regard as fortunate, for — though the violence some people exercise on others' bodies is bad enough, a violence even more appalling could be exercised if *mind-entry* were possible. This indeed would be a world even worse than the one we live in.

The contemporary philosopher Parfit, in his interesting *Reasons and Persons*, argues that 'psychological continuity' may be destroyed by a surgeon's 'tampering with the brain.' For he argues that we might progressively have bits of ourselves taken away, until we could not say if we were the same person or not.[9] This famous argument stems from Ancient Greece, where it was asked whether Jason's *Argo* was still the *Argo*, although over the centuries every timber in the boat had rotted and been replaced.

However, this is exactly what happens in the case of ourselves, since every seven years or so our physical cells are completely replaced without any difference resulting to our sense of self. Parfit's argument depends on the mistaken view that the perceiving consciousness can be identified with its contents, with brain machinery, and with that all too convincing fabrication, the 'person' and his characteristics.

We have just seen that, as far as consciousness *itself* is concerned, such tampering is impossible. Consciousness is invulnerable, for its physical basis and location cannot be found. It sits *behind* the physical world, and observes it. Parfit's argument therefore falls to the ground.

Are there exceptions to this general rule? It was long held that a mind could be possessed by supernatural beings. Aldous Huxley made the case of the Devils of Loudun famous by his book of that title. But, strange though the phenomena were, these were cases of psychological illness rather than possession. Then again one could draw the reader's attention to a celebrated twentieth-century case — the personal report of Voodoo possession by the anthropologist Maya Deren.[10] She herself however became unconscious during the whole period of the possession, and hence this is not an exception to the rule.

Do apparent exceptions occur under hypnosis, in which the will and the perceptions appear to be directly under the hypnotist's control? No, since the hypnotist never enters into the subject's consciousness as such. Thus, the subject may taste a peppermint which the hypnotist has in his mouth; or may be successfully commanded by the latter *not to see a table*. Clearly such cases do not interfere directly with the centres of consciousness, but only with the content of perceptions — though admittedly with rather many of the latter. Moreover — and this is the main point — neither hypnotist nor hypnotee can enter each other's consciousness.

There thus seem to be no real life cases such as appear in the literature of Science Fiction — namely the absolute mind control described in my novel *The Soul Master*, and in works by other authors. Consciousness is indeed 'inaccessible from the rear'; and this strongly suggests that Mind is prior to Matter, since it is 'behind' Matter. As a medical and physical fact, Matter can be accessed by Mind, but the inverse is impossible. Mind is 'outside' matter (perhaps as in Smythies' theory): this means that there *is* a mental universe.

Fourthly, consciousness has access to various rather puzzling 'places,' such as memory, imagination, dreams, lucid dreams, Out-of-Body Experiences (which undoubtedly happen, though what precisely they are we have no space to discuss here). This has always suggested to human beings, perhaps rightly, that there are other 'worlds'; and perhaps it is *so as to* suggest this to us.

Fifthly, we have already mentioned Schopenhauer's observation about time, namely that consciousness, witnessing the passing moment yet stably positioned in eternity, appears to guarantee the latter.

Sixthly, and lastly, we must make an observation which may be conclusive. We have discussed two varieties of knowing, namely the tacit and the explicit. There is however a third way of knowing (which is, as everyone's experience shows, perfectly commonplace). *This is knowledge-by-identity.*[11] We know ourselves directly, from the inside. At the same time, the outside of this inside is invisible to us (which is why science will never be able to probe into our consciousness through anything physical such as the brain). But then *is* there such an 'outside'? Perhaps consciousness is like the disc of Odin, which according to Borges 'is the only thing in the world which has only one side.'[12] In this it resembles another thing closely related to consciousness, namely time, the only dimension which *has only one direction*.

Someone might ask whether 'knowing-by-identity' is not merely a form of 'knowing-by-acquaintance'? But knowing-by-acquaintance is knowing something else from the outside; whereas knowing-by-identity is knowing yourself from the inside. Plainly the two are different.

There are thus three modes of knowing, at differing degrees of distance. Knowing by identity is closest. Knowing by acquaintance is the next closest. Knowing by abstraction is at arm's length. The first and second share the quality that neither is known by abstraction; the second and third have in common the fact that neither is known from the inside.

This solves the reductionist's problem about how my identity and my consciousness are associated. It is by virtue of my knowing-by-identity that I experience unbroken identity throughout my life. The philosophical problem of identity is not to be solved by argument. Identity is an experience, and experiences are the foundations of arguments, not their outcome.

My true 'I' is therefore my consciousness itself. It is the deepest, most essential, of myself, that without which no aspects of personality or character, of experience or even memory, could possibly 'be mine.' For, just as I have (first) to be in the world so as (second) to have worldly possessions, so my consciousness has (first) to exist, before it can be ascribed any psychological features. My personality and all its attachments are secondary, contingent accidents of my 'being thrown into the world,' at this time, at this place, in this brain and in this body. We always ask 'Why here, why now, why me?' and this always appears to us as a great mystery. This puzzlement of ours shows, not the contingency of my consciousness as such, but the contingency of its present worldly context, finding itself here, now, and 'dressed up as myself.'

Now — and here is the crux — consciousness is the *only thing* which knows itself, that is it is the only thing which, by being a self-knowing identity, resolves the fundamental philosophical problem, enunciated by Berkeley, namely that of *percipi* and *percipere*, that is the incomprehensible gulf between the perceiver and the perceived. We may reasonably surmise therefore that *consciousness, since it in practice every moment of our lives resolves this fundamental split in the Universe, must be of the Universe's original and basic nature.*

This is remarkable. Is it possible that the nature of the Universe is revealed by the most simple everyday fact of experience?

Empirical inquiry into consciousness

So much for the evidence of self-inquiry to the extent that most of us are able to conduct it.

There is, however, still other, stronger evidence; and 'evidence' it should indeed be termed. Throughout history many different witnesses have confirmed it, from many different eras, societies and religions, yet their observations (making due allowance for differences of terminology, cultures and audiences) are strikingly similar. The experience is of a transformation of consciousness. Though the subject feels he is no longer himself, he has found his true self; and that true self is identical in nature with the universal spirit. These experiences are most usually unsought, indeed totally unexpected: they befall the lucky experiencer without warning and for no apparent reason. Alternatively many have found it possible to train themselves by meditation.

I refer of course to what is usually termed mystical experience.

The term 'mystical' is confusing, and such is the misuse of words that my students always imagined it meant either 'mysterious' or 'religious.' In reality, however, the word is unusually precise. Mystical experiences come in two kinds: (1) where the world is felt to be infused with divine unity and reality, and (2) where the world vanishes, to be replaced by inner consciousness which is felt to be identical with the divine.[13] Mystical experience is felt to be of a *supremely different order* from ordinary life. It is felt as sublimely blissful and revelatory of ultimate truth. I should add that such experiences have *nothing whatever to do* with visions, whether of angels, devils, or any other hallucinatory events. The Eastern tradition warns us against such visions, for they are deceptive and illusory.

Mystical knowledge (1) is not based upon dogma, scripture, nor on abstract speculation, but upon experience, that is it is empirical, as (in principle) is science;

(2) it is not a matter of feeling, but of perception: that is, it is not the addition of a particular quality to experience (for instance feeling an ordinary event with special joy); it is *other*, and during it the world shines with a radically different light;

(3) it appears to provide direct insight into the deep nature of the Universe;

(4) it obtains verification from the fact that mystics have had similar experiences in all societies and at all periods;

(5) and from the fact that it carries with it a sense of absolute conviction. Consciousness is overwhelmed by its self-evident truth;

(6) it is the evidential ground for the Perennial Philosophy, a set of beliefs which are exemplified in all societies and from all periods, and which have been held by many of the world's greatest philosophers.

What is such a revelation like? Here a man remembers the experience he had as a schoolboy:

> The thing happened one summer afternoon, on the school cricket field, while I was sitting on the grass, waiting my turn to bat. I was thinking about nothing in particular, merely

> enjoying the pleasures of midsummer idleness. Suddenly, and without warning, something invisible seemed to be drawn across the sky, transforming the world about me into a kind of tent of concentrated and enhanced significance. What had been merely an outside became an inside. The objective was somehow transformed into a completely subjective fact, which was experienced as 'mine,' but on a level where the word had no meaning; for 'I' was no longer the familiar ego. ...

F.C. Happold's first experience was also quite unexpected:

> It happened in my room in Peterhouse on the evening of 1 February 1913, when I was an undergraduate at Cambridge. ... There was ... no sensible vision. There was just the room, with its shabby furniture and the fire burning in the grate and the red-shaded lamp on the table. But the room was filled by a Presence, which in a strange way was both about me and within me, like light or warmth. I was overwhelmingly possessed by Someone who was not myself, and yet I felt I was more myself than I had ever been before. I was filled with an intense happiness, and almost unbearable joy, such as I had never known before and have never known since. And over all was a deep sense of peace and security and certainty. ...
>
> Though I now recognize the experience as of the kind described by the mystics, at the time I knew nothing of mysticism ...[14]

In the above examples, the self is expanded. In the next, it expands so as to feel itself in unity with a universal spirit:

> I had wonderful experiences which lasted for about ten minutes at a time as a rule. I would be walking along the street when things would suddenly change before my eyes, to become unbelievably beautiful and *real*. Things science tell us about light and sound waves, gravity and atoms and so on were clear and understandable. ... Everything had significance and *everything and everybody was one*. Not only every human being, but all animals, plants, atoms, everything was one in unity, making nonsense of the view that only human

beings have souls. There is no such thing as time as we know it. Everything that is, has been, is and always will be ... And we are *here and now* in eternity.[15]

Here our informant not only experienced universal unity, but received a special understanding. Such events do not strike only at peaceful moments, as the following case shows:

> Major Bernard W. Haswell, during the Second World War, was moving his section of six 25-pounders from near Brussels towards Dunkirk. They were under very heavy fire and, as he was about to pray, his men asked him to include them. This he did. His account continues: 'I then gave the order to jump out of the slit trench and, at this moment, as I led the men out, the noise ceased completely, although I could see the smoke and flame from the exploding shells. ... Suddenly my eyes were attracted to a white cabbage butterfly fluttering on the dung-heap. The astounding thing was that I was now conscious of every movement of its wings — it seemed I knew how many times they were moving, the very pulsation of its body. My attention was suddenly diverted to the grass ... and again — astonished — I was aware of every single blade of grass and of a vital dynamic life-force, and still the moving butterfly wings were being consciously recorded in my mind. As suddenly as it came, the experience ended ... We moved down to the other guns ...' He concluded, 'This gives me the clearest indication of life beyond this life-on-earth and which, had any of us been killed, we should have experienced for a brief moment before moving onwards to our destiny.'[16]

Here the experience was seen as proving survival after death. In Warner Allen's *Timeless Moment*, we find the following description:

> Rapt in Beethoven's music, I closed my eyes and watched a silver glow which shaped itself into a circle with a central focus brighter than the rest. The circle became a tunnel of light proceeding from some distant sun in the heart of the Self. Swiftly and smoothly I was borne through the tunnel

> and as I went the light turned from silver to gold. There was a sense of drawing strength from a limitless sea of power and a sense of deepening peace. ... I came to a point where time and motion ceased. In my recollection it took the shape of a flat-topped rock, surrounded by a summer sea, with a sandy pool at its foot. The dream scene vanished and I am absorbed in the Light of the Universe, in Reality glowing like fire with the knowledge of itself, without ceasing to be one and myself, merged like a drop of quicksilver in the Whole, yet still separate as a grain of sand in the desert. The peace that passeth all understanding and the pulsating energy of creation are one in the centre in the midst of conditions where all opposites are reconciled.[17]

Here our informant sees himself being drawn through the centre of his own consciousness into the ultimate Consciousness which lies 'behind' it. He passes beyond time and change to become not only one with, but also still distinct from, that ultimate Consciousness, and comprehends the latter as ever-creating Creator and as reconciler of all contradictions. As in Hindu mysticism, Atman (the individual soul) *is* fundamentally Brahman (God). As in all these accounts, the sense of peace and bliss is such that the Ultimate is *felt and perceived* to be utterly benevolent.

The experiences I have quoted were all spontaneous. Ken Wilber points out in *A Sociable God* that, in the West, mystical events were regarded as unusual ' peak experiences,' and were originally:

> assumed to occur rarely and involuntarily. However, certain Eastern psychologies and religious disciplines were subsequently found to contain not only detailed descriptions of such states but also instructions and technologies for attaining them at will.[18]

Thus, we must now conclude that these transpersonal peak experiences are part of the panoply of human abilities. *Pace* the prejudice of Freud and others, there is nothing pathological about them, and indeed they often befall the most eminent and level-headed people, as for example Richard M. Bucke (1837–1902), an adventurous youth who became in maturity an eminent doctor, President of the American

Medico-Psychological Association and of the Psychology Section of the British Medical Association. He summed up the import and weight of a mystical experience as follows:

> Like a flash there is presented to his consciousness a conception (a vision) of the meaning and drift of the universe. He does not come to believe merely; but he sees and knows that the cosmos, which to the self-conscious mind seems made up of dead matter, is in fact far otherwise — is in truth a living presence. He sees that the life which is in man is eternal ... that the foundation principle of the world is what we call love ... Especially does he obtain such a conception of the whole — as makes the old attempts mentally to grasp the universe and its meaning petty and ridiculous.[19]

Countless of our contemporaries have had mystical experiences. There are records of them from ancient India, ancient China, Medieval Europe and Islam, and indeed from all the epochs of human history. They are common to human nature, and one may learn to achieve them.

As evidence of the truth of their experience, mystics often refer to its being 'more real' than anything previously experienced. They are making a serious point. For why do we deny reality to dreams? Above all because, on waking, we are conscious of a stronger sense of reality in the waking world than in the dream world. *At least one* of the criteria for what is real is sheer intensity, that 'sense of overwhelming reality' provided by certain conscious experiences. And as experienced dwellers in our world, we are practised and skilful in making such judgments.

Mystical meditation is an *empirical* practice. It is a method of observation and discovery. It is, like science, a search for truth, only its object of investigation is, not the world as perceived, but consciousness as perceiver. Since it cannot be chopped up and dissected by physical methods, consciousness must be submerged into: the shining pool of awareness must swim like a fish into its own depths.

Mysticism is thus empirical, universal, and its findings are confirmed from all periods and many societies including our own. We must take it seriously as evidence. It points to consciousness as the root of all existence.

Emotion? Drugs?

The claims of mystics are a grave threat to physicalists, and naturally have been bitterly attacked. Thus Stace notes Bertrand Russell's 'delightfully simple syllogism' in which the latter claims:

> The essence of mysticism ... is emotion. Emotions are subjective in the sense that they supply no objective truths about the extra-mental world. Therefore mysticism is subjective and supplies no objective truths about the extra-mental world. 'Mysticism is [merely] a certain intensity and depth of feeling in regard to what it believes about the universe.'[20]

Russell's assumptions are mistaken. Mysticism is not emotion but *perception.* It is an exploration of consciousness from the inside — an activity which science cannot undertake, since it can explore things only from the outside.

A second angle of attack is to claim that mystical experiences are the results of chemical processes in the brain. These, it is asserted, may be brought about by fasting or other ascetic practices; or they may be produced by 'magic mushrooms,' or their modern equivalents such as LSD or Mescaline. Perhaps the most impressive of all such effects are produced by Ayahuasca, an ancient drug from the Brazilian rain-forest, which has been used for (perhaps) thousands of years.

Drugs however are dangerous. May some conduct us to the single door of truth? More certainly many will ferry us across the several thresholds of madness.

Let us therefore listen to Allan Smith. For, to take a second objection, the critics also assume that a 'psychedelic or entheogenic experience'[21] due to drugs is as powerful as a spontaneous mystical experience. But to make this judgment we require witnesses who have undergone *both.* I have not come across any such — with one exception, namely Allan Smith's very detailed report of attaining cosmic consciousness. After this he sought to recreate the experience by taking LSD (which at the time was held to be 'mystical' in its effects). He reports that spontaneous mystical experience and LSD are incomparable, and that the former is forty times more ecstatic than the latter. He writes, 'I could be more easily convinced that the computer at which I now sit is illusory than I could be convinced that Cosmic Consciousness was.' The effects of LSD were temporary and confined to the period of the drug's presence in his bloodstream. This experience did not change his appreciation of the beauty of leaves, etc, after the event. 'On the other hand, my experience of Cosmic Consciousness changed my whole life.'[22]

It would be interesting to find testimony from others who are qualified to make similar comparisons. What, however, is abundantly clear is that the countless witnesses to mystical experience have not been at the mercy of artificial substances.

Constructivism

In recent years reductionists have also attacked the Perennial Philosophy's claim to universality. It has been asserted that the mystics of different religions have quite different experiences, and that these are governed by their quite different socio-religious expectations. Thus Katz writes that it is:

> as a result of his process of intellectual acculturation [that] the mystic brings to his experience a world of concepts, images, symbols and values which shape as well as colour the experience ...[23]

Robert Gimello writes that mysticism is 'simply the psychosomatic enhancement' of a person's beliefs, meaning that the experience is 100 percent caused, shaped and determined by his or her belief system.[24] But if Gimello is right, then it follows that such experiences cannot occur to someone whose belief system forbids it.

But this is plainly untrue. The contemporary world can show us countless individuals who had no inkling of any religious beliefs until, without warning, the sublime experience fell upon them from out of a clear blue sky. Moreover, though people do often witness visions and hallucinations, the experiences we are discussing here *are not of that kind.* They do not involve 'seeing' angels, a favourite saint, Christ on the Cross, Mary ascending into heaven, and so forth. They involve cosmic consciousness. Now, religions are largely expressed in myths and pictures. Therefore if Gimello and Katz are right, and it is religious expectations which cause the experience, then one would expect visions to occur. Since such visions are absent from mystical experience their argument fails to explain it.

These 'constructivists,' as they are termed, claim that:

> There are no human experiences except through the sociolinguistic relations which mediate them.[25]

Steven Katz claims that 'we now know' that unmediated experience is impossible. He asserts that experience is always filtered through concepts, words, etc. Mysticism would then become merely an epiphenomenon of language and culture:

> a kind of delusion fostered by the indoctrination system .... The mystic first learns about mysticism and then has the experience.

But:

> The constructivists commit the fallacy of *post hoc ergo propter hoc* when they suggest that merely because Svetaketu learned about Atman before he experienced it, his experience was therefore *caused* by that prior learning. I heard that Indian food makes people's throats burn long before I had Indian food, yet my hot throat was not caused by my prior knowledge, but by the peppers.[26]

Then again, constructivists overlook the fact that almost always people start studying mysticism as a result of a supreme experience which fell upon them out of the blue. Previously they had known nothing about it, and in most cases had never even heard of it.

Moreover, as we saw when discussing the tacit and explicit, it is a gross error to suppose that language dictates all aspects of experience, for there are many elements of the latter which are quite outside the grasp of language. One important meditational practice is to put aside language and preconceptions of all kinds so as to contemplate an enigmatic natural object, preferably one which — like a bizarrely shaped stone or tree — it is very hard to grasp *through* one's presuppositions, and which therefore resists being pigeon-holed. Thus, as Deikman says, meditation involves an 'unlearning' of learnt categories, a 'deautomatization' of customary reactions.[27] As Forman reminds us, Eastern philosophy often takes a view which is very close to constructivism. Thus in the Yogâcâra system of fourth century Buddhism, we are advised to beware of the distortion of our minds caused by our prior assumptions, our predispositions, the influence of language and society. But we are also advised that it is possible to step outside all this 'brainwashing' and reach a state beyond it — this state being precisely that of mystical 'pure consciousness.' Furthermore, in Buddhist mysticism, authors often describe themselves reaching (in the fifth *jhana*) a point of mystical experience where they have gone beyond their own belief system: 'One is to be so devoid of concepts, at least during the Pure Consciousness Experience, that even the very conceptual system which has led one to it is itself to be forgotten.'[28]

Now plainly, accounts of mystical experience by those brought up in different religions will show variation. There are several reasons for this. (1) The mystic is writing *for* readers in his own tradition, and needs to adjust his statements to their understanding. (2) These are the words he knows, those which his society offers him. (3) These experiences are very hard to express, and mystics all assert that they are ineffable. The words will necessarily be those which are 'lying about' in the current religious tradition. Fourthly (4) when describing their experiences, mystics are obliged (by the necessities of language) to interpret them.

Differences can therefore be discerned between mystical traditions. Christian mystics describe the ultimate mystical experience as 'Union with God,' but they do not interpret this as identity with God. Hindus describe it as 'Union with Brahman or the Universal Self' and do assert identity. In Buddhism there is no Supreme Being. Have we then three different experiences, with superficially similar features? Or is the basic experience the same in all three, but interpreted slightly differently?

Stace argues that it is fundamentally the same. He points to the extraordinary agreement between the authors of the Upanishads (in ancient India in the eighth or seventh century BC) and the Christian mystics Eckhart and Ruysbroeck in the Middle Ages. These authors were completely unknown to each other. The difference in their beliefs is irrelevant since, *when describing their experiences*, they use a similar language.

He then wheels on evidence showing that the swallowing up of the I in the universal self has been experienced by mystics in all the great religions. There are clear reasons why devotees of the different religions express their experience differently. Thus, for Christians, theological authority obliged them to acknowledge that the soul is separate from God. Islam and Judaism similarly objected to mere creatures asserting their identity with the Divine, and famously the Muslim mystic Mansur Al-Hallaj was crucified in AD 922 for making that claim. Nonetheless such statements are not hard to find in Sufism, for instance Mahmud Shabistari (AD 1320) wrote:

> In God there is no duality. In that Presence 'I' and 'we' and 'you' do not exist. 'I' and 'you' and 'we' become one. ... Since in the unity there is no distinction, the Quest and the Way and the Seeker become one.[29]

And in the poem 'No Room for Form' by the Persian poet Rumi (1207–73) God says:

> I am the clear consciousness-core of your being ...
> And don't look for me in a human shape.
> I am inside your looking.[30]

Similarly, Martin Buber's description of his own experience shows that he experienced unity; but then gave two inconsistent interpretations of it — doubtless for Jewish theological reasons. In Hinayana Buddhism the experience of 'undifferentiated unity' is again asserted. But (in Stace's account) Buddha refused to say if the individual consciousness has united with the universal self, or with something one might term God. Nirvana is simply ineffable. Nonetheless, this appears to be the same experience, it is simply that other religions interpret it, Buddha avoids doing so, regarding it as outside all states of mind and all descriptions.[31]

Moreover the experience of 'pure consciousness' is universal in mysticism. It is described in the Upanishads:

> That which is non-thought [yet] which stands in the midst of thought. [What remains is] the understander of understanding, the seer of seeing.

and equally in Ibn al-Arabi:

> consciousness or sheer awareness ... utter undifferentiation, pure unity, sheer consciousness.[32]

and equally in Meister Eckhart, who writes:

> Thou shalt know him without image, without semblance and without means. — 'But for me to know God thus, with nothing between, I must be all but he, he all but me.' — I say, God must be very I, I very God, so consummately one that this he and this I are one *is* ...[33]

> The eye by which I see God is the same as the eye by which God sees me. My eye and God's eye are one and the same — one in seeing, one in knowing, one in loving.[34]

Constructivists deny the existence of pure consciousness. They reject it on *a priori* grounds, since their belief is that all conscious experience is mediated by sociolinguistic experience. Logically however this cannot be true, since sociolinguistic experience cannot get going in the first place if the infant could experience nothing before society and language. Mystics assert the reality of pure consciousness, for the very good reason that many have experienced it. This again is reported by mystics from all ages and religions. Hui-Neng (the sixth and last Zen patriarch) spoke of *wu-hsin* and *wu-nien*, terms which are sometimes mistakenly translated as 'unconsciousness.' As Forman explains, taken together they signify non-intentional (that is pure) consciousness. He describes it from his own experience as follows:

> In this place beyond words, there is no content to speak of, no consciousness that stands apart, no seer to be seen, but only pure seeing ...

He quotes several modern accounts of such experiences of *samadhi*. They conform with the description to be found in the *Heart Sutra:*

> no eye, ear, nose, tongue, body, mind; no colour, smell, taste, touch phenomena. No world of sight, no world of consciousness. Because the mind has stopped functioning and the

> senses have stopped processing, there can no longer be any 'world of waking consciousness.'[35]

As the Pseudo-Dionysius wrote (probably in the fifth century AD):

> Here, renouncing all that the mind may conceive, wrapped entirely in the intangible and invisible, he belongs completely to him who is beyond everything. Here, being neither oneself nor someone else, one is supremely united by a completely unknowing inactivity of all knowledge, and knows beyond the mind by knowing nothing.[36]

Our conclusion is clear. Pure consciousness actually occurs, so that arguments purporting to show it is logically impossible are necessarily mistaken. Everything is *not* therefore subject to cultural, linguistic, conceptual factors, and pure consciousness is prior to them, lies outside them, and gives us access to an unconditioned truth.

Moreover, although mystical experience is most commonly temporary, some people may achieve permanency of transformation, as Forman attests in his own case:

> What is 'me' is now this silence; everything else seems somewhat different [from] this silence within, of a different kind or separate.

He quotes Bernadette Roberts's *Experience of No Self* in further confirmation. As he points out, people may often be mistaken about 'short-lived phenomena (viz. I thought Susan entered the room before Rob, but I was mistaken).' But individuals who live with the permanence of this inner silence, can hardly be mistaken as to its nature, for they can 'check it out' at any time they wish.[37]

How far back does the Perennial Philosophy go? The experience has been undergone by many people in many different civilizations. In the Ancient Egyptian Memphite cosmology (2700–2200 BC) 'the god who had created himself and heaven and earth, who was the maker of gods and men and animals and all that exists, was a Spirit and the Eternal Mind of the Universe.'[38] This god was named Ptah. The Upanishads date back to the eighth and seventh centuries BC. Buddhism, Taoism and the wisdom books of the Old Testament all arose around 500 BC in cultures which, as far as we know, had no contacts with each other.

As I argued above, mysticism provides reliable empirical knowledge. This is because, just as with objective knowledge, the basic experiences are confirmed by many different witnesses from an astonishing variety of eras and societies, yet their observations are strikingly similar. Mystics are a minority among humankind, but there are enough to constitute an impressive weight of evidence. Science does not require that a majority of the population confirm an experiment, but only that trained and qualified persons do so. The standard of evidence provided by mystics is at least as high as this. It is fair to conclude that mystical experience is sound evidence.

It is also *practical* knowledge in the following sense. As in science, mystical experience may be repeated, at least in many cases and for trained practitioners.

Might one even assert the *superior reality* of mystical experience over the hypotheses of science? Whiteman who, besides being a mystic, was a professor of mathematics and a musician, believed so. In science, you observe data; on the basis of data, you propose hypotheses; on the basis of hypotheses you erect a 'conceptual system.' Thus, he argues, in science *there is no direct observation*, because you are always outside the data. Nor is there any direct confirmation of the conceptual system, for you are even further outside the hypotheses, which cannot be directly verified.

In mysticism, however, you have direct observation, and perceive truths which appear self-evident, from which you work out a structure.[39] This structure again is an interpretation, but the data on which it resides are directly observed.

Paradox

What then is this direct experience? The mystic becomes aware of a vast power, which presents itself as the All. This power is of the same nature as his own consciousness, and indeed access to it is, as it were, through the back of the individual mind. It is the ever-active source of all creation, and its energy and its benevolence are inconceivable. It contains all qualities, all opposites, all negations of qualities and of opposites.

As we shall see, *logically* the All must be *paradoxical.*

This Allness is often expressed in negative terms, and we may ask how God can be described as Nothingness. Or indeed the similar Buddhist description of the ultimate as *sunyata* (emptiness)? Indeed, Ward goes so far as to explain the Jewish mystic Maimonides's negative description of God as the result of a false theory of linguistic meaning.[40] However, Maimonides wrote:

> Know that the description of God ... by means of negations is the correct description, a description that is not affected by an indulgence in facile language.[41]

For to describe Him is to falsify Him. Similarly, in Madhyamika Buddhism, all descriptions of the Ultimate are 'empty,' for human language is absurdly inadequate.

This 'emptiness' is to be identified with the absolutely unseeable, namely the uncreated creator, the unperceived perceiver, source of all things. Thus, according to the Kena Upanishad, Brahman is 'not what people here adore.' It is:

> What cannot be spoken in words, but that whereby words are spoken. Know that alone to be Brahman, the Spirit, and not what people here adore.
> What cannot be thought by the mind, but that whereby the mind can think.
> What cannot be seen by the eye, but that whereby the eye can see.
> What cannot be heard by the ear, but that whereby the ear can hear.
> What cannot be indrawn with breath, but that by which breath is indrawn.[42]

The above dates from the eighth or seventh centuries BC. It identifies consciousness with divine consciousness, which it locates *as an ontological necessity* right at the source of everything.

Mystical experience is always seen (after it has ceased) as paradoxical. During its continuance it is felt as truth, reality transcending paradox. Stace writes:

> This void, this nothing, is ... at the same time the Infinite; it is pure consciousness, pure ego, the One of Plotinus and the

> Vedanta, the Divine Unity of Eckhart and Ruysbroeck; and it is the Universal Self. It is both positive and negative, light and darkness, the 'dazzling obscurity' of Suso. I shall call this the paradox of the vacuum-plenum.

He then proceeds to analyse this 'One.' Normal this-world 'ones,' as he observes, are a combination of many different things. Thus a frog, a pond, a stone, a butterfly, my eyes watching them, and indeed my whole contingent self — all these are a combination of disparate things, all working together in disparate ways. The ultimate One is nothing like this, for once you have got as far as Oneness, there are no parts in it.

This is hard to grasp, for how can the All (which consists of all the parts in the Universe) be a One (which has no parts at all)? We are faced with the paradox that the One is both a plenum and a vacuum:

Plenum	*Vacuum*
(1) The Universal Self has all qualities.	It has no qualities.
(2) It is personal.	It is impersonal.
(3) It is dynamic, creative, active.	It is totally inactive, static, motionless.[43]

People have long strained their minds over these paradoxes. Perhaps, however, an ultimate paradox is logically unavoidable. For opposites are real, because the Universe is constructed of oppositions and differences. But these opposites must have a single source, which must logically 'contain' them, for they must emerge in all their contradictory difference from it.

Perhaps some light might be shed on these difficulties by an interesting proposal of Whiteman's — one which ties up also with my suggestion that time is, in our Universe, merely half a dimension. Whiteman takes music as his explanatory mechanism. As he points out, one can hold a whole piece of music in one's mind and contemplate it, which suggests that (since music normally happens in time) one can hold time in one's mind and contemplate it. Time-durations, tempi, etc (says Whiteman) are conceptual, that is we can grasp them:

> like features on a spatial map which can be explored backwards and forwards without in the least altering their conceptual character or the relations between them.
>
> This insight is the evident origin of statements by mystics that there is no such thing as time (that is physical time) in higher mystical states. The condition is, instead, called eternity; and what is known in it is eternal concepts, essences, or Ideas.

This, he says, is not a question of memory. We can 'stop time' while contemplating such experiences: he terms this 'primordial recollection.' He compares this with the famous letter of Mozart, in which the latter claimed that entire symphonies were often created whole and complete in his mind, as if 'outside time,' and he could survey their whole structure and duration. Whiteman's conception *explains* how Mozart might have done this.[44] From this follows the possibility that in the Quantum Vacuum, or in some other realm of the Cosmos, time's missing half-dimension might be restored.

Whiteman suggests this explains the nature of eternity — where, just as in space, the mind can travel backwards as well as forwards, visiting any part of time at will. And indeed Eckhart writes of eternity:

> Time ends when there is no before and after; when all that is is here and now, and you see at a glance all that has ever happened and shall ever happen. Here there is no before or after; everything is present, and in this immediate vision I possess all things.[45]

This casts light upon yet another apparent paradox. In space, mobility and immobility co-exist without contradiction. In time (as we know it) there is no immobility. But reinstate its other half-dimension, and both immobility and mobility can co-exist. If time, having regained its missing half, becomes whole, so that one may move *or not* through it, reversing one's direction as one wills, then in a sense *the moving and the unmoving become as one*. This sounds paradoxical, and is usually thought to be so; but, after our discussion, may well look quite rational.

Ineffability and tolerance

Mystics assert that the supreme experience is indescribable in words. Thus Dionysius wrote:

> If anyone saw God and understood what he saw, then it was not God that he saw, but something that belongs to Him.[46]

Dionysius's long list of those attributes which God does not possess (namely any that is conceivable), and how it is inadequate to describe him in any way at all, for he 'transcends all affirmation, [is] outside of every negation [and] free from every limitation,' illustrates very plainly His ineffability.[47]

Nonetheless, if these experiences are ineffable, Stace comments that they are only relatively so. For at least mystics can give some gist of their at-Onement, they can hint at its nature and point in a particular direction.

Moreover *even the most ordinary experience is ineffable*. We saw this earlier in the present book, when discussing the tacit. For words may translate experience, but all such translations are both inadequate and inaccurate. *Tradere est trahere*. To suppose that any experience can be 'effed,' is to suppose that the signpost pointing to 'Manchester' — that piece of painted metal — is the same as the town Manchester with all its houses, people, rats and cats, joys and sorrows. Besides, let us beware: *signposts sometimes point the wrong way*.[48]

To remind ourselves of the ineffability of the divine is salutary. For since what is ineffable cannot be reduced to words, it cannot by any means be reduced to the narrowness of dogma. Thus, as Wilber points out, 'false cultic beliefs' are a regression to prerational thinking. As he remarks:

> Mysticism and science have usually been historically linked, simply because both have always rejected dogmatic belief and insisted on open experience.

This was true, he claims, in ancient China; and it is certainly true of the modern inventors of Relativity and Quantum Physics, such as Einstein, Schrödinger, Von Neumann and Eddington, many of whom paid respect to the Perennial Philosophy. In true religion, one discovers 'a larger self in the spiritual dimension of creation at large,' whereas, in clan-cults, one reduces 'the self to prepersonal and passive dependence by restricting and prohibiting the free engagement of critical reflexion. The aim of *sangha* is to keep mind but transcend ego; the aim of the cult is to prohibit both.'[49]

Bliss

According to Hindu belief, the three fundamental elements from which the Universe is formed are *sat, chit* and *ânanda*, namely *being, consciousness* and *bliss*.[50] Bliss is an ever-present accompaniment of mysticism, and carries with it many messages, from which I shall pick out the following: (1) the divine is utterly benevolent: love and joy radiate from the centre of all things, we are protected and cherished. We may therefore admit that the Problem of Evil has a solution — though we cannot see what form it takes, and it too may be paradoxical. (2) Creation can be its own joyful purpose. For one may feel an ecstasy in sharing the being of a flower, or of a mountain, while being still oneself, not melting away into it, but being aware of it and with it. This could be the *why* of the whole of Creation, its *raison d'être*. The separation of the Universe from itself — its struggle with itself — its fragmentation into pieces — leads towards a paradoxical final unity. There is great intensified awareness in a separation that is also a unity, not being 'one with the mountain,' but being 'two with it.' With it, while not being subsumed in it, knowing it at the same time both from outside and from within.

But if bliss shows love, then so should the mystic on returning from his exaltation. As Eckhart wrote:

> What a man takes in contemplation he must pour out in love. ... It is better to feed the hungry than to see even such visions as Saint Paul.[51]

Meister Eckhart preaches *both* contemplation *and* action.

Conclusions

What lies outside the Walls of Plato's Cave?

(1) Without stepping outside them, we may still perceive important truths about consciousness. (a) It locks us within a tiny span of time and

space, yet is invulnerable to mind-entry on either the material or spiritual plane. Our world is tiny, but nothing can 'burrow into it from behind.' The reason for this is very simple: consciousness cannot be physically tampered with because, unlike a physical object, it cannot be located. Mind, we may therefore assume, is 'outside' matter. (b) Consciousness gives access to strange places such as dreaming which, despite a multitude of famous theories, is still in fact without explanation. (c) Self-awareness is the resolution of the problem of *percipere* and *percipi*, for it is the single and only phenomenon in nature which is not merely *seen*, or which does not merely *see*, but which *sees itself seeing*.

This perhaps already allows us a glimpse through Plato's frustrating Wall. But a second glimpse is offered when we consider with Schopenhauer (d) that half of our present moment seems stably poised in eternity.

(2) The mystic offers us further evidence from behind the Wall. In the mystical experience consciousness expands till it finds inclusive oneness with the world; the Universe is seen as a vast living unity, with which our consciousness is one; though united with the universal spirit, the individual's identity is not obliterated, for s/he still remains a 'spark' within the Whole. As for the nature of this Whole, it possesses power, bliss, wisdom, benevolence, and timelessness.

Mystics are unanimous that their sublime experience assures us of immortality. To take a down-to-earth parallel — when a man sees, touches and tastes a common or garden apple, he is quite simply sure of the fact. Equally — with as much evidential certainty — mystics have *experienced and known* their own fundamental unity with the creative source of life. Those who have seen and lived this, have been *shown* that our consciousness is of the same nature as the Ultimate, and that its timelessness must be ours too.

Conclusion

> Thus nature gets credit which should in truth be reserved for ourselves: the rose for its scent; the nightingale for his song; and the sun for his radiance. The poets [should turn their lyrics] into odes of self-congratulation on the excellence of the human mind. Nature is a dull affair, soundless, scentless, colourless; merely the hurrying of material, endlessly, meaning-lessly.
>
> A.N. Whitehead,
> *Science and the Modern World*

IN THIS BOOK I have inquired into the present state of scientific knowledge, and (despite the materialist preferences of most scientists) I have concluded that the weight of probability favours the reality of the soul and the presence of conscious intelligence in the Universe.

First, what is our likely candidate for the soul? It is consciousness, which is the root and foundation of all experience and knowledge, and without which life would be but darkness. I have asked whether consciousness might be the product of unconscious matter. Reductionists contend that one day it might be simulated by computers. In part these claims depend on a number of verbal confusions about the meanings of the words 'simulate,' 'represent' and 'information.' More profoundly still, they depend on a failure to understand the nature of conscious experience. For there are two kinds of knowing, tacit and explicit, and by the very nature of their functioning, computers are incapable even of 'simulating' the more fundamental of the two. We may dispose therefore of the claims, famed both in science fiction and in universities, for artificial consciousness.

What 'is' this matter of which materialists tell us mind is made? (1) The man-in-the-street usually claims to 'know by experience what matter is.' On investigation, however, we find that this 'knowledge' is no more than how his senses present the outside world to him, namely as hard / soft, resistant, coloured, cold / hot, etc. Thus matter is merely the way mind perceives its surroundings, that is matter is appearance. This is exactly how Indian philosophy has always seen it. (2) The physicist on the other hand does not claim to 'know what matter is.' Whatever it is, however, it provides calculations and pointer-readings, that is it is that aspect of appearance which can be quantified, reduced to measurements, and thereby manipulated. The 'true nature' of matter is absent from both these views, nor is it possible to ascertain what that 'true nature' might be. Berkeley's view of matter chimes with this. For him, there are only two elements in nature: *percipere* (what perceives and cannot by its nature be perceived) and *percipi* (what is perceived and cannot by its nature perceive). Materialists deny the former, and believe that the latter is all there is: yet they seek to derive the former from the latter.

Surely this involves them in a logical contradiction, for how could consciousness be built of unconscious bricks? How are unconscious molecules to *begin* to have conscious experience? There are many accounts in the copious literature of reductionism, but none is successful. All pretend to provide a plain demonstration of how living consciousness can emerge from dead matter — meanwhile introducing consciousness into their accounts surreptitiously, in the manner of a conjuror concealing a white rabbit up his sleeve. Every account is a conjuring trick. None satisfies Chalmers' 'hard problem.'

The raw materials of consciousness, namely its *qualia*, raise equally grave difficulties. Nature, as far as physics is concerned, is colourless, soundless and odourless. *Qualia* do not occur in nature but in the mind, and how the mechanical processes of the brain become transformed, during conscious experience, into the infinitely colourful symphony of our ten senses, no-one has ever explained. Moreover *qualia* exist in at least ten different modalities (sight, sound, smell, touch, proprioception, etc), each almost as different from the others as time is from space. How did blind matter create all of these when no ingenious professor has ever successfully described how it can produce even one?

Some have claimed that, since one could build a machine which (for instance) can distinguish colours from each other, there is no problem. This however is an elementary mistake: our problem is not (1) to set up a mechanical pigeon-holing system which can distinguish red and blue *without* sensually experiencing them, but (2) to explain how it happens that we *do* sensually experience red and blue. As for the attempt of some to dismiss consciousness as 'an illusion,' this is another glaring fallacy. For, without consciousness, no-one can have an illusion. Such claims remind one of the zany in the folktale who denied there was such a thing as light, because he couldn't catch it in his fishing-net.

Thus, on examining the explanations of materialists, we find these do not stand up. No scientist or philosopher has ever offered a convincing description of how unconscious sense data even *might be* transformed into conscious experience. It is at present philosophically impossible to see how any such explanation could be provided. It is therefore unacceptable to argue that consciousness could be the product of unconscious matter.

These facts show that materialism is untenable. It is essential therefore to look seriously at non-materialist theories.

Turning to the brain, we discovered that no physical site has been found in it for (1) consciousness, (2) tacit memory or (3) long-term memory. The argument that, because brain damage causes mind damage, the brain must be the one and only source of consciousness, was shown to be deceptive. For if a computer breaks down, it does not follow that it obliterates its user, merely that the latter has lost contact with some customary information.

Once one abandons the narrow rigidity of materialism, many more interesting possibilities open up. The mind (or some parts of it) may therefore be outside the brain; and in Chapter 9 four theories of this kind were seriously considered. Bergson's theory that the brain acts as a filter upon consciousness and upon memory for the benefit of its owner's survival may be thought highly plausible.

Even if *(per impossibile)* reductionists were able to invent an explanation for conscious experience, they would meet further difficulties. If consciousness could be reduced to unconscious processes, then what would be the point of it? Recent research has certainly not disproved the ability of consciousness to exercise free will and purpose. Besides, the arguments against it depend on a belief in absolute causal determinism. However, the source of the causal principle is actually our personal experience of active free will, which we *observe* ourselves exercizing in the world. It cannot be asserted that causal determinism disproves free will, since the experience of free will is the reason why we believe in the reality of causation. Hence determinists are caught in a logical contradiction, and free will remains untouched.

Secondly, though no-one has ever seen matter creating mind, we must ask on the other hand whether mind can create matter? Now we have all (in our dreams, for example) seen mind creating remarkable semblances of matter, which (in some circumstances) cannot be distinguished from it. Indeed, we should go further: it seems that it is of the very nature of consciousness to tirelessly create semblances of reality. When it is prevented from such creations (prevented, for instance, from dreaming) sanity starts to break down. As we saw above, it is a tenable philosophical view that matter is a stable kind of 'appearance.' Mind is on every score much more likely than matter to be the source of creation.

Much mockery has been levelled at 'Cartesian dualism,' as if it is somehow very silly to suppose that the Universe might be made out of two things and not out of one. But why this strange prejudice? Why should one principle be preferred to two? It is very odd of these materialists — all fierce opponents of metaphysics — to impose such a purely metaphysical requirement on the Universe!

Besides, Descartes's basic insight (I am conscious, therefore I am) is absolutely irrefutable. The only thing that exists without doubt is the mind; matter is a mere hypothesis — though admittedly a useful one. Since Materialism is untenable, therefore either Dualism or Idealism must be the correct position, and Mind must be as real as Matter or more so. The argument that *without consciousness nothing could exist*, is philosophically quite plausible.

What has Quantum Physics, currently one of the two basic theories of the Universe, to say about this? The Copenhagen interpretation of Quantum Physics suggests that the Universe is a vast intermeshing structure of conflicting probabilities — which requires conscious observers to resolve it into fact, actuality and event. If this is so, then as an element of the Universe, consciousness is at least as fundamental as gravity or electromagnetism — though it seems at present a mystery as to exactly *how* it transforms potentiality into actuality.

If however consciousness lies outside the physical world, then the latter might well record no traces of its action.

This aspect of Quantum Theory represents a threat to reductionists, and so there are several contemporary efforts to remove consciousness from the quantum picture by rejecting the Copenhagen Interpretation. My discussion in Chapter 8 suggests that none of these succeeds.

Moreover the Quantum Vacuum is an immense source of energy lying outside space and time, supporting our entire universe and resembling the mystical ground of all being. Thus the materialists' conception of the Cosmos is incomplete. It used to be thought naïve to believe in 'regions' other than the physical, for 'Where are they?' But it is now known that *outside* the Universe[1] as described by physicists there are regions that could be as alien to the conditions of our own world as any spiritual heaven could be.

Thirdly, does the Universe appear to be the product of consciousness? Here we approach the Anthropic Argument.

To have a universe in which physics permits life of our kind, the fundamental forces of physics need to be extraordinarily fine-tuned, so that the first moment of such a universe must have an almost inconceivable precision. Contemporary mathematicians have calculated the improbability of the creation of such a universe, that is our own. The mathematics strongly suggest that the Universe must be the product of intelligent design, and therefore of purpose.

Moreover the 'fine detail' of our Universe produces the same conclusion. Life depends on water, whose many convenient qualities are often unique in nature and, if the product of accident, hard to explain. As for life — and particularly intelligent life of our kind — contemporary biochemistry (a very recent discipline) shows that there are a vast number of fundamental processes upon which living structures depend — for instance enzymes, flagella, proteins. Many of these are of such complexity that they could not reasonably have evolved during the known time-scale of planet Earth. As for them *all* evolving over this period, this multiplies impossibility by an equally impossible quantity. Again, a designer or designers must be supposed, though we cannot at present know *either* their nature or their *modus operandi.* This is not to deny evolution, merely to show that there must be other factors too.

There are indications however that the Universe presents us with deceptive appearances. Is it by any chance concealing its own nature? Perhaps Spencer Brown is right in suggesting that the cosmic impulse behind creation is for consciousness to see and know itself — thus however creating paradoxical difficulties of self-knowledge. Alternatively, many thinkers have suggested we have been set a sort of 'intelligence test' — perhaps concerning particularly the *moral* intelligence.

I conclude that the Universe is in all likelihood the product of conscious intelligence. Is further confirmation possible of this finding? And how is our own consciousness and that (or those) of the Universe related?

Einstein famously expressed surprise that we minuscule beings on our tiny planet should be able to guess so much so truly about the nature of things. Why for instance is human mathematics such an excellent tool? He surmised that there is a natural harmony between our minds and that of the Demiurge.

The world, as Berkeley saw, consists of two modes of being and two only, namely *percipi* and *percipere*, which exist in absolute opposition. Their mutual exclusion, each of the other, finds no resolution anywhere in Nature — except within human consciousness, in the form of self-awareness or knowing by identity. It is reasonable therefore to suggest that consciousness, being the only thing that resolves this fundamental split at the root of all being, is of the Universe's original and fundamental nature.

These speculations would tend to be confirmed by the only known method of exploring the depths of inner consciousness, namely mystical experience, recorded throughout the ages by people who have felt their own consciousness expand into the Universe, in apparent unity with a divine consciousness — providing insight, bliss and a sense of eternity. Since (no matter the epoch, the religion, the belief, or indeed the absence of one) mystics bear witness to unmistakably similar experiences, the latter conform to the rules of good evidence, and deserve our credence.

To conclude, this book has been an inquiry into the reality of the soul. I have explored quantum physics, artificial intelligence, brain science, biology, mysticism, theology and philosophy (both European and Indian). On the basis of this inquiry I believe we can establish certain probabilities. We have seen that consciousness (1) has no material explanation; (2) nor can it be explained away. (3) Intelligence and purpose are required to explain the creation of the world and the development of life; and (4) there are good reasons to think that consciousness constitutes the common nature of ourselves and our Maker. At this opening of the twenty-first century, the balance of evidence supports the reality of the Soul and its participating in the existence of a Divine Spirit which created and sustains the Universe.

We have found that reductionism / materialism, though the reigning philosophy of our time, is plainly mistaken. Materialism looks at first sight plausible, since it is such an excellent *method* in science, and its achievements are outstanding. Nonetheless explanations of its kind must be regarded as applying solely to some aspects of the Universe. It is a method of approach, it is not a final explanation. We must announce the end of Materialism's pretensions to explain the World.

Endnotes

Introduction

1. Charon 1983c, p. 58.
2. Brian Magee comments on the whole philosophical climate of that time: 'Non-linguistic reality presents us with problems which are fundamental to the nature of the world and to our being in it, and are not to be explained in terms of our use of language. This being so, it cannot be the case that the problems can be solved by analysis.' Magee 1998, p. 114.
3. Wolpert 1993, p. xii.
4. Lem 1983, pp. 103f.
5. Güven Güzeldere in 'Philosophy Now,' no 36, June / July 2002, p. 14f.
6. Paine 1938, p. 3.
7. Midgley, in Cornwell 1998, p. 176.
8. Popper 1976, p. 29, quoting in part Clifford Truesdell.
9. Sartre 1949, p. 20.

Chapter 1

1. Quoted by Lanier 1995, p. 333, where he comments 'At least I'm told it's a Navajo proverb by John Perry Barlow.'
2. Recognition can these days be achieved by certain kinds of computer. This is done by chopping the face up into very tiny portions. However, this is not the way human beings operate. 'Faces are recognized in a single gestalt' by human beings. They are not recognized by breaking them down into small bits. Cytowic 1996, p. 438, referring to Farah 1990.
3. Braud & Anderson 1998, p. 49.
4. Steven Rose writes to me that 'the analogy with Polanyi is very clear.' See also Rose 1993, pp. 119f.
5. Poetry achieves this by forcing tacit memories into awareness. I discuss this in Martin 1981, Chapter 4.
6. This example is drawn from Waismann 1951, pp. 121f.
7. See her famous and moving autobiography. *Cf.* Cotterill 1998, pp. 384–8.
8. I must by no means give the impression that ignoring the tacit is a universal failing among philosophers and logicians. The logician Patrick Grim remarks that it is not too surprising 'that no formal system could model a genuinely comprehensive knowledge or a genuinely omniscient mind.' Grim 1991, p. 87.
9. I had already completed most of this book when I came upon Laura Weed's excellent *Structure of Thinking*. She seems to be unaware of Polanyi, but her insight is fundamentally identical with his. She too argues that computers can never be conscious, and the mind cannot be a computer. She calls for philosophy to recognize once more the importance of experience. It is a pity that her terminology ('x-type and y-type thinking') is so abstract and unmemorable.
10. Merrell 1991, p. 185.
11. Eddington 1928, pp. 251f.

12. Hawking 1988, p. 174.
13. Hawking, Halley Lecture, Oxford, June 1989, quoted in Ferguson 1995, p. 132.
14. Tallis 1999, pp. 109, 111.
15. Penrose 1999, pp. 96-98.
16. Ib., pp. 113ff. See also Penrose 1989 and 1994 for a much fuller discussion (ad nauseam, as Penrose says.)
17. Tipler 1995, pp. 124–7.
17. Thus, even if consciousness is 'information,' it is Information type I, whereas the information you feed into a computer is Information type II. Quoted in Tallis 1999, p. 92, from Shannon & Weaver's classic text of 1949.
19. E.J. Lowe 1995, p. 268. His italics.
20. Rose 1993, p. 91. He tells us he draws this example from H Von Foerster.
21. *Cf.* Lanier 1995, p. 340.
22. *Cf.* Tallis 1999, pp. 125–8.
23. Turing 1950.
24. Tallis 1999, pp. 125f.
25. *Cf.* the events in Chapter 21 of my novel *Half a Glass of Moonshine.*
26. *Cf.* Tallis 1999, p. 128.
27. Fodor 1998 p. 48. For accounts of the functioning of PDP machines, see for example Pinker pp. 100–111, 167f; Cotterill 1998, pp. 134 ff; Fodor 1998, pp. 204–6; Fodor 2000, pp. 48–51; Johnson-Laird 1988, pp. 174–194.
28. Pinker 1998, pp. 25, 80, 110.
29. Searle 1997, p. 11. His italics.
30. Ib. For numerous references to the controversy, see *Journal of Consciousness Studies* Vol 11, nos 5/6, 2004, pp. 156–169.
31. Searle 1997, p. 16.
32. Pinker 1998, p. 94, p. 565.
33. Searle 1997 p. 18.
34. Cotterill 1998, p. 434, p. 427.
35. Aleksander 2001. pp. 5, 161, 12, 73, 134.
36. Fodor 1998, pp. 204f.
37. Johnson-Laird 1988, pp. 189–193. Tallis 1999, p. 130.
38. See Penrose 1989, pp. 1f, & 451. Slightly altered, I fear, and done in my own words except for the Chief Designer's speech. As for 'Deep Thought,' this seems a good gesture to borrow from Douglas Adams.
39. Moravec 1988. A hilarious account is given by Regis 1992.
40. Lem 1983, pp. 173–180, 184.
41. The name Dobb is a combination (read backwards) of the English word 'God' and its Slavonic equivalent *Bog*.
42. Lem 1983, p. 196.
43. See discussion in Ruse 2002, pp. 146 f, 152. Dawkins' argument does not hold water, since it applies only to a God who is omnipotent and omniscient in the classic Christian style, and not to any other possible candidates.

Chapter 2

1. Cytowic 1996, p. 29.
2. Charman 1997, p. 11.
3. Griffin 2001, p. 242.
4. Rose 1993, pp. 122f, Rose 1999, p. 9.
5. Smythies 1994, p. 142.
6. Eddington 1928, pp. 270, 251–260.
7. Schlick in Vesey 1964, p. 302.
8. Griffin 1997, p. 111.
9. Save by itself. Self-awareness is a special mode of consciousness, which we shall discuss in Chapter 12.

10. This is also the case in Sartre's view of consciousness: 'Matter' and 'the contents of mind' are both included in *en-soi*, not in the active conscious *pour-soi*, which is 'pure consciousness.'
11. In expressing this luminous idea of Berkeley's I have used the language of Griffin 2001, p. 99.
12. Democritus of Abdera, Diels fragment 125; quoted in Schrödinger 1992, p. 163. The Greek word here translated 'ostensibly' is νόμῳ, which means 'according to the conventional way of thinking' or, as we sometimes say, 'nominally.'
13. One must presume that Democritus had an argument to put against this statement of his own. Unfortunately his reply (like so much else of the ancient world's philosophy) has been lost. Nonetheless, *what could conceivably refute his own objection to himself? Cf.* Lockwood, 1989 p. 6.
14. Fodor 1992, quoted in Hutto 1998, p. 328.
15. Griffin 2001, p. 127.
16. de Quincey 1999, p. 95.
17. de Quincey 2000a, p. 69 (his italics); p. 81.
18. Hobson 1999, p. 95.
19. Lanier 1997, p. 181.
20. Voorhees 2000 p. 57. *Cf.* also his interesting suggestion, ib., p. 67.
21. Lanier 1995, p. 334.
22. Martin 1990, p. 75.
23. Chalmers 1995, p. 200.
24. Lowe 1995.
25. A conscious animal's subjective experiences are particular to its species. See 'What is it like to be a Bat?,' Nagel 1979, pp. 165–180.
26. Chalmers 1995, pp. 201–3, 208f.
27. Chalmers writes 'Conscious experience is not logically supervenient on the physical,' which has the same meaning as my paraphrase. *Cf.* Griffin 1998, p. 220.
28. The first three points in Chalmers 1996, p. 161.

Chapter 3

1. Bertrand Russell, *The Problems of Philosophy*, quoted in Magee 1997, pp. 75f.
2. Ramachandran and Hirstein 1997, pp. 430f.
3. The naming of many qualia is conventional: 'crimson, willow green, lapis lazuli,' etc., but the names are in no way precise, and there is no guarantee that the name controls any individual experience. A name is of course not a description.
4. *Cf.* Clarke 1996, p. 119.
5. Velmans 2000, pp. 152f.
6. Sherrington 1906, pp. 335–344. For an excellent contemporary account of proprioception, see Sheets-Johnstone 1998, particularly p. 270 onwards.
7. Kripke 1980, pp. 146–155. See Wall 1977, also the interesting discussion in Chalmers 1996, pp. 146–9.
8. Dennett 1993, p. 459.
9 Dennett 1994, pp. 129f.
10. Velmans 2000, p. 84.
11. David Lewis 1983, pp. 130–2.
12. Cotterill 1998, pp. 18–20.
13. Quoted in Ridley 2001, p. 176.
14. Dawkins 1991, p. 41.
15. Tallis pp. 71–3, 84.
16. Velmans 2000, p. 41, 231.
17. Smythies 1993, pp. 215f.
18. Cytowic 2002, p. xix, p. 73.
19. Chalmers 1995, p. 209.

20. Chalmers 1996 pp. 156–8. For he would like to claim that the physical world is causally closed, ib., p. 161.
21. Wilber 1997, p. 83. Nonetheless, Wilber recognizes that Chalmers makes a number of excellent points.

Chapter 4

1. Quoted in Benor Vol 2, p. 85.
2. Stuart Sutherland, in NS Sutherland ed, *The Macmillan Dictionary of Psychology*, Macmillan, London.
3. Wallace 2000, p. 28, quoting from 'Psychology as the Behaviourist Views It,' *Psychological Review* 20, 1913, pp. 158–177.
4. Thalberg 1983 quoted in Smythies 1994, pp. 165–7.
5. Blackmore 1999, p. 237.
6. Josephson & Ramachandran 1980, pp. 27f, 9–14.
7. Olson 1998.
8. Language is not a set of unchanging quantities like the pieces in chess. Words have a superficial appearance of stability, but their meanings are multiple, they are more like living things interacting with their surroundings, and they always contain unrealized potentials for further change.
9. Sharf 2000.
10. Popper 1976, pp. 29f.
11. Genes inhabit a respectable scientific theory. Memes however are hardly even a hypothesis, though they have infected the minds of certain reductionists.
12. Penfield 1975, pp. xiii, xix, 52, 57–9, 76, 55, 54, 77.
13. Sacks 1985, pp. xii, 94.
14. Quoted in Hale 2002, p. 233, from Damasio 2000, pp. 108f.
15. Isted 1979, p. 5.
16. Terry Scott in Edelman & Greenwood 1992, p. 76.
17. Jay 1979, p. 126.
18. Hale 2002, p. 237.
19. Ib., p. 251; Damasio 2000, pp. 127, 242f.
20. Isted, p. 21.
21. Kapur 1977, p. 73. *Cf.* Damasio 2000, pp. 108f.
22. Kapur 1977, pp. 76f.
23. *Cf.* Douglas Ritchie's remarks about thinking, versus thinking in words, quoted in Hale, pp. 237f.
24. There are a variety of terms in use among brain specialists. To avoid confusion, declarative memory will here be termed 'explicit memory'; nondeclarative, implicit or procedural memory will here be termed 'tacit memory.'
25. As one speaks of the 'laying down' of crops for the following year.
26. Penfield 1975, p. 21.
27. Cytowic 2002, pp. 127–132.
28. Luria's S has been identified as D.C. Shereskevskii, Squire & Kandel p. 141. See Luria 1975, *passim.*
29. Standing 1973. Also clearly described in Rose 1993, pp. 116f.
30. Rose 1993, p. 117.
31. Squire & Kandel 2000, pp. 176–8.
32. Cytowic writes that memory 'depends on structural changes in synaptic connexions believed to take place outside the medial temporal lobe.' That is its location may be very widely spread, and certainly no specific location has been found for it. 'One often hears,' he writes, 'that memory

resides in the hippocampus. It does not. The hippocampus is essential for forming memories and providing salience so that events will be remembered, but memories are sown throughout the cortex.' Cytowic 1996, pp. 321, 323, 317, 319. Logically, however, if (as Bergson suggested) memory is merely communicated through the brain and is not within it, then naturally surgical removal of tissue does not affect it. Furthermore, perfectly reasonable physical explanations could be given: the stimulus may arouse memories which are, as it were, 'stored' far off in the brain.

33. Rose 1993, pp. 119f, 128, 320. Rose 1999, pp. 61–5.
34. Squire & Kandel 2000, pp. 176–8. They also say that 'although the amygdala is essential for the development of memories based on fear and other emotions, it is not known whether the memories themselves are actually stored there.' Ib., p. 170.
35. Squire & Kandel 2000, pp. 173, 176.
36. Squire *et al.,* 1991, p. 296.
37. Ib., pp. 407f.
38. For confirmation that pure consciousness 'really exists,' see Chapter 12.
39. Smythies 1993, p. 211.
40. Blackmore 1999, pp. 223f.
41. The quotation is from the Cambridge philosopher C.D. Broad writing in support of Bergson.
42. Huxley 1954, pp. 16f.
43. Ornstein 1975, pp. 19–22.
44. Blake 1958, p. 96.
45. Bergson 1988, p. 38. Quoted in Robbins 2000, pp. 28f.
46. Robbins 2000, p. 29.
47. I simplify here for the sake of clarity. Bergson insists on a clear distinction between memory and perception — the latter is bound to the present, that is to the plane of action which moves forward through time. Our brain is a mechanism which concerns itself with actions and reactions at that present point. Perception is therefore particularly vivid, but to operate properly it has to draw upon the plane of memory, where, Bergson writes, 'our mind retains in all its details the picture of our past life.' (Bergson 1988, p. 241.) At this moment the relevant memories are called into consciousness.
48. Robbins 2000, pp. 42f.

Chapter 5

1. Berger 1966, pp. 164f. Berger takes a Sartrean view of free will.
2. Sartre 1949, pp. 564f.
3. Bergson 1965, *passim.*
4. Blakemore 1988 pp. 253, 269, 255–267.
5. Libet in Libet *et al.,* 1999, pp. 48f.
6. Blackmore 1999, pp. 239, 245f.
7. Blauvelt in Libet *et al.,* p. 270.
8. Cotterill 1998, p. 344.
9. Mackintosh-Smith 2001, p. 75.
10. For a brief but interesting account, see Magee 1997, pp. 62f.
11. Ib., pp. 68f.
12. *Cf.* the eighteenth century French philosopher Maine de Biran. Jeffrey M Schwartz, pp. 133f of Libet *et al.,* 1999. Huw Price's suggestion is similar — that our experience as *agents* is the origin of our view of causality, Price 1996, pp. 157–9. Searle sees this as proof of free will's reality and indeed of

causality, Searle 2004, pp. 203f. Moreover it seems that Thomas Reid said much the same in 1790.
13. Libet *et al.,* 1999.
14. Ib., p. 52.
15. Cotterill 1998, pp. 340–2 refers to experiments by Carpenter and associates which, according to him, disprove the veto. He must be mistaken about this however. The veto in these latter experiments was not the product of a free choice, and what was measured was simply the speed of reaction time to an external command. The issue is not the reaction time, which even in the case of an internal command, cannot be of infinitely compressible length. The issue is the decision of the unconscious to start reacting before the conscious mind does so.
16. Libet *et al.,* p. 54. *Cf.* the observations of Eastern meditation, Bricklin in Libet *et al.,* p. 79.
17. Goswami 1993, p. 194. Searle 2001, pp. 290f.
18. Penrose 1999, pp. 135–7.
19. Libet *et al.,* p. 56.
20. Schwartz in Libet *et al.,* p. 124, 128.
21. David L. Wilson in Libet *et al.,* p. 196.
22. Elitzur 1995, p. 356.
23. Schwartz in Libet *et al.,* p. 142.
24. The intimate connexion between free will and consciousness is recognized in ancient Indian philosophy — but also in the theory of Sartre.
25. That is partially camouflaged or obscured.
26. Goswami 1993, pp. 109–111, 164–6.
27. Smythies 1994: pp. 179f. *Cf.* Lanier in Libet *et al.,* p. 264.
28. Laszlo 1993, pp. 98f. This second of Hall's experiments can be found in *Proceedings of the National Academy of the Sciences*, USA, Vol 88 (4), July 1991, pp. 5882–86. He refers, among other things, to J. Cairns *et al.,* writing in *Nature*, no 335, 1988, pp. 142–5. Hall's own previous research is in *Genetics* 126, 1990, pp. 5–16.
29. Firsoff 1967 pp. 9, 47f.

Chapter 6

1. *Gospel of Thomas*, §29.
2. As Magee points out to Ryle, Magee 1986, pp. 128–145.
3. The Buddha preached a doctrine of *anatta,* literally 'absence of the soul.' But the concepts of soul versus body, a spiritual versus a worldly existence, etc., are fundamental to his thinking.
4. Goswami 1993, p. 151.
5. Romanes 1895, p. 50.
6. Firsoff 1967, p. 55. His example, from which he concludes: 'The nervous system and the brain operate at a subatomic level.'
7. Griffin 1997, pp. 107f.
8. Wilber 1984, p. 19.
9. Wilber 1997, p. 85.
10. Schopenhauer 1970, p. 117.
11. Velmans 2000, p. 226.
12. Written in the 1930s. Teilhard was a Jesuit priest and palaeontologist, had a deep knowledge of science, sought to reconcile evolution with theology, and was forbidden by the Catholic Church to publish any of his philosophical works in his own lifetime.
13. Barrow & Tipler 1986, p. 197.
14. See Chapter 9, pp. 161f.
15. Barrow & Tipler 1986, pp. 197f.

16. Firsoff 1977, p. 126.
17. Firsoff 1967, pp. 103f, 57, 106.
18. Chalmers 1997, p. 28. Lockwood 1989, pp. 157–60, Maxwell 1978, *cf.* Russell 1927, p. 386.
19. Quoted in Wilber 1984, p. 142.
20. Griffin 1998, *passim.*

Chapter 7

1. Ramachandran & Blakeslee 1998, pp. 85, 106–9, 105.
2. Cytowic 1996, p. 222; Cytowic 2002, p. 111.
3. Ganzfeld research is performed *via* sensory deprivation. The subject wears translucent goggles, earphones which produce a white noise, and his/her body is cushioned so as to reduce tactile sensations. Thus the subject's vision, hearing and feeling are reduced to a uniform field which provides no *events* to which his / her attention can be drawn.
4. North 1997, pp. 67f.
5. Cytowic 2002, p. 114; Heron 1957.
6. Cotterill 1998, pp. 303–311. Dennett refuses to believe in 'filling in' because he thinks it might commit him to a belief in qualia.
7. Cotterill 1998, pp. 315, 311f, 315.
8. Mavromatis 1987, p. 225. See Oswald 1962.
9. The term 'eidetic' is a most fortunate invention, since it combines within it the ancient Greek for 'seeing' and for 'knowing.'
10. Cytowic 2002, pp. 106f. Originally Stromeyer & Psotka.
11. Mavromatis 1987, p. 241.
12. Schatzman 1980, pp. 18f, 29f, 175, 282, 278f.
13. Ian Wilson 1982, p. 220. Wilson is one of the most cautious yet fair-minded of writers on such topics.
14. See Green 1968, *passim.*
15. Mavromatis pp. 71–4. This is mental imagery which precedes dreaming, and is experienced while falling asleep.
16. Tyrrell 1953, pp. 89f.
17. Gregory 1971 p. 128.
18. Green & McCreery 1975, pp. 151f, 212. These authors call this a 'metachoric experience.'
19. Tyrrell 1953, pp. 11, 60–2, 91, 99.
20. Braude 1986, p. 173.
21. Tyrrell 1953, p. 23. A similar figure is quoted by MacKenzie 1987, p. 265. Hart *et al.,* 1956.
22. Braude 1991, p. 187.
23. Green & McCreery 1975, p. 80f.
24. Herbert 1985, p. 194.
25. Sartre 1949, p. 27.
26. Wallace 2000, p. 63.
27. Sartre 1949, p. 18.
28. Quoted and discussed in Vesey 1964, pp. 266–283. Russell 1921, pp. 10, 23.
29. Tallis 1999, pp. 246–9.
30. Bohm 1980, p. 209.
31. Quoted in Capra 1983, p. 155.
32. Toshiko Isuzu, 'Matter & Consciousness in Oriental Philosophies,' in Cazenave 1984 pp. 293–303.
33. Goswami 1993, p. 188.
34. Wallace 2000, p. 110.
35. Sharf 2000. Sharf not only denies the privacy of experience but also its very reality — while claiming that he does not do so!
36. Wallace 2000, pp. 73–6. Or consult some basic texts drawn from ancient masters in Bucknell & Kang.
37. Wallace 2000, pp. 115–119.
38. Sartre 1949, p. 22. My translation.
39. Ib., p. 22 footnote.

Chapter 8

1. Mermin 1990, pp. 110f.
2. Martin 1990, pp. 73–129.
3. Pagels 1984, p. 133.
4. Gamow & Stannard 1999, p. 115.
5. Quoted from Martin 1990, p. 77. For this famous experiment, and for the conclusions drawn, the reader may consult any popular account of quantum physics.
6. Or, to be more precise, any such measurement would be necessarily false.
7. Gribbin 1999, p. 29.
8. A good instance is Newton 2000, p. 177f, a point which he argues in detail, ib., pp. 86–105.
9. Bohm 1980, pp. 191f.
10. Gribbin 1999, pp. 83f, 511f, under the heading 'Vacuum polarization.' Davies & Gribbin 1992, pp. 136–142.
11. Davies 1988, p. 87.
12. Laszlo 1993, p. 147. Both David Bohm and Laszlo refer to the Quantum Vacuum as the ψ-field.
13. Laszlo 1993, pp. 88f.
14. quon = a quantum entity or event. The term is due to Nick Herbert 1985, p. 64.
15. Herbert 1985, pp. 24, 193–95, 25, 193.
16. John Wheeler and Bryce DeWitt are also involved in the popularization of this idea.
17. For instance Deutsch 1998, p. 51.
18. See for instance Gribbin 1999, pp. 271f. A particularly clear and thought-provoking account is Nadeau & Kafatos 56–59. But the possible references are endless!
19. Hodgson 1991, p. 339.
20. For instance Storrs McCall's *Model of the Universe*, Clarendon Press, Oxford 1994, reviewed in Clarke 1995B.
21. Despite much discussion, it is of course still unknown whether the Universe is infinite.
22. Goswami 1993, p. 76.
23. As we shall see below, the increase in universes on each occasion might well be infinite.
24. Namely in my novel *Time-Slip*, 1986.
25. Clarke 1995b, pp. 57f.
26. Penrose 2004, pp. 1031f, concludes that almost all interpretations of Quantum Physics depend upon some notion of conscious observer.
27. We do not need, for the purposes of the argument here, to explain these. Interested persons may consult, for instance, Gribbin 1999, p. 103, pp. 500–5, 532–4, or Huw Price, pp. 225–8.
28. Gribbin 1999, p. 505.
29. Stapp in Libet *et al.,* 1999, pp. 143–64: p. 158. See further Stapp 1993.
30. Stapp in Libet *et al.,* 1999, p. 152.
31. *Cf. ib.,* p. 163, where Stapp writes, 'our experiences are elements of the causal structure that do necessary things that nothing else in the theory can do.'
32. Ib., pp. 157, 159. See Chiu, C.B., Sudarshan, E. and Misra, B, 1977 'Time Evolution of Unstable Quantum States and a Resolution of Zeno's Paradox,' *Phys, Rev,* D 16, p. 520; Itano, W, Heinzen, D., *et al.,* 1990; 'Quantum Zeno Effect,' *Phys. Rev.* 41A, pp. 2295–300.
33. *Scientific American*, 'Frozen Light,' July 2001; *New Scientist*, 22 May 2004, pp. 32–5.

34. Nadeau & Kafatos 2001, p. 59. Also Newton 2000, p. 166.
35. Nadeau & Kafatos 2001, p. 58f.
36. *New Scientist* 9 March 2002, p. 28.
37. Stapp, in Libet *et al.,* 1999, p. 163, p. 161.
38. Some of these interpretations are as follows: 1) Reality belongs not to the quantum itself, but to the whole measurement situation.
    2) The World is created out of the act of observation — and at a nonlocal distance.
    3) The World is an undivided wholeness.
    4) The Many-Worlds Interpretation — the Everett multiverse — which violates the contrafactual definiteness assumption in Bell's theorem, because it has lots of contrafactuality and practically no definiteness.
    7) Consciousness creates reality — and it does so nonlocally.
    8) Duplex Universe. That is the superposition of half-realized tendencies, à la Heisenberg. See Herbert 1985, pp. 240–5.
39. Herbert 1985, pp. 249, 227.
40. That is the fact that nonlocal (faster-than-light) events occur.
41. Herbert 1985 pp. 230, 214.
42. Pagels 1985, p. 197.
43. Eddington pp. 28, 98.
44. Hodgson 1991, pp. 447, 371.
45. *Cf.* Herbert 1986, p. 44.
46. Hodgson 1991, pp. 383–5.
47. Newton 2000, p. 164.
48. This argument certainly does not put out of court certain kinds of anomalous situations, such as a smaller universe (Universe S) embedded or nested in a larger one (Universe L) — in the former of which the time-flow is in reverse (or at right-angles) to that in the larger one. For in neither universe would the time-flow be in two directions. Such a situation is theoretically possible. It would enable a developed creation to emerge at the end of a process (from the point of view of Universe S) but at the beginning of a process (from the point of view of Universe L). Provided separation between the Universes were adequately 'constructed,' no paradoxes would prevent such a situation.
49. The argument seems good. Nonetheless, we must not prejudge anything, and one could well wonder if the mind does not indeed 'signal into the past' in the context of free will. This is one possibility suggested by Libet's experiments, discussed in Chapter 5.
50. Chalmers 1996 p. 345.
51. Penrose 1995, particularly pp. 369–71, 409f.
52. Zohar 1990, p. 63–65.
53. Chalmers 1996, p. 119.
54. Chalmers 1995, footnote p. 208.
55. But perhaps he is merely suggesting that microtubules provide a physical prerequisite for consciousness, not that they are the whole answer.

Chapter 9

1. Green 1976, p. 1.
2. Charon 1983a, pp. 21f. These two theories are both accepted by physicists, despite the fact that they are mutually inconsistent. Despite many attempts to unite them, no generally accepted harmonization is yet available.

3. Barrow & Tipler agree that 'radial energy' is a properly scientific hypothesis, being verifiable or falsifiable, pp. 197–9.
4. Charon 1983a, p. 86. In all references to this book, the translations are mine.
5. Charon 1983c, p. 49. (Translation slightly altered.)
6. This locking-off is not total, according to Stephen Hawking's calculations.
7. Charon 1983a, pp. 83f, in which he refers to Wheeler *et al.,* 1973.
8. Charon 1983a, pp. 23, 88.
9. Charon 1983c, p. 67. Translation slightly altered to make it more idiomatic.
10. The leptons are the six elementary particles which are not quarks, that is the electron, muon, tau particle and their associated neutrinos. They are all point-like.
11. Charon 1983a, pp. 119, 234; 1983b, p. 74.
12. Charon's mathematical explanations can be found in *Théorie de la relativité complexe* and in *L'Esprit et la relativité complexe*.
13. Charon 1983a, p. 200.
14. Charon 1983c, pp. 76, 98f, 100.
15. This was of course many decades before virtual reality machines were thought of.
16. This window provides such fascinating experiences that he is tempted to spend the rest of his life watching at it. This is all the more convincing because the 'fascinating experiences' in question are to the person whose mind he is looking through of the utmost banality.
17. Schopenhauer 1970, pp. 68–70.
18. Meister Eckhart (1260–1327), quoted in Forman 1999, p. 148.
19. J. B. Phillips' translation of *I Corinthians 13*, quoted in Happold 1970, p. 194.
20. Capra 1983, p. 188.
21. Lucas 1973, p. 251.
22. Gribbin 1999, p. 24.
23. Smythies 1994, p. 184.
24. Smythies 1994, pp. 9ff.
25. Smythies 1993, p. 206; 1994, p. 12. Blackness is of course a positive colour. It is not an absence of experience, *cf.* Smythies 1956, p. 50.
26. Smythies 1967, p. 7.
27. See Honderich 1988. Smythies 1994, p. 96.
28. Smythies 1994, p. 149. *Cf.* Deutsch 1998, pp. 120f.
29. Smythies 1993, pp207f. See Harrison 1985.
30. Smythies 1993, p. 209, quoting Kenny 1970.
31. McGinn 1995, p. 229.
32. *Cf.* also Cazenave 1984, p. 365. Here, Willis H. Harman argues that mind must be spatially and temporally extended. For clairvoyance and telepathy indicate this. He adds: 'Mind exists in co-extensive unity with the world it observes.'
33. See Broad 1923, H.H. Price 1953, Smythies 1994, pp. 145–8.
34. Jackson 1977, p. 103. Quoted by Smythies 1993, p. 225. Jackson (p. 78) seems to think that sensations 'are located in parts of the body.' This is a fundamental error. They are located in the body image.
35. See Chapter 6, p. 88.
36. Actually it is certainly familiar but is still merely a supposition!
37. Smythies 1993, p. 225. 'Cryptic' is an unfortunate choice of terms; it simply means 'hidden.'
38. Ib., p. 226.

39. 'The resistance to taking mental events as spatial ... tempts us ... to associate them with what they are of, or what they represent, and hence to be lost for a location to which to assign them.' Honderich 1988, p. 88.
40. Smythies 1993, pp. 220, 225.
41. Smythies 1956, pp. 56f.
42. Smythies 1994, p. 163, where he mentions reincarnation as a possibility.
43. Lewin 2001, p. 151.
44. Smythies 1994, pp. 193–7.
45. Laszlo 1999, pp. 184, 186, 188f, 191–3.
46. Quoted in Eliade 1977, p. 595.
47. Olivelle 1998, p. 268.
48. I gather from Marcer himself that my description of his views in 1996 is correct. His thinking is at present centred on Creation, and its derivation from the QV. Interested readers should consult http://www.bcs.org.uk/cybergroup.htm.
49. Marcer 1992, p. 22.
50. Marcer 1995, pp. 4–12, 3. See the Berry or geometric phase, Anandan 1992.
51. According to Swami Vivekananda.
52. Marcer 1995, p. 3. Laszlo 1999, pp. 172–5.

Chapter 10

1. Nasr 1981, pp. 235f.
2. W. Paley, pp. 1–5.
3. Dembski 2000, pp. 257f, 262, 270.
4. This is normal for contemporary estimates of the universe's age.
5. Dembski 1998, p. 209. Quantum computation does not increase these chances, for quantum superpositions are *indeterminate* states (which eventually transform into determinate ones) Ib., p. 210 note 16.
6. Dembski 1998, p. 210.
7. Leslie 1989 p. 7.
8. An aeon is a billion years. With a touch of regret, I use billion in the American sense, that is = a thousand million, rather than in the old British sense = a million million. For the American usage has become almost universal.
9. Leslie 1989, p. 204, p. 3.
10. Laszlo 1993, p. 86.
11. For a fuller account of points 1–9, see Leslie 1989, pp. 3–6.
12. Laszlo 1993, p. 86.
13. Penrose 1989, pp. 342–4.
14. Barrow & Tipler 1986, p. 18.
15. Linde 1990, p. 177.
16. Barrow & Tipler 1986, pp. 524–541.
17. Stewart & Cohen 1997, p. 106.
18. *Cf.* Donald 1991, p. 164.
19. Quoted by Barrow & Tipler 1986, p. 123.
20. Stewart & Cohen 1997, pp. 160f, 112.
21. Dembski 1998, p. 60.
22. Behe 1996, pp. 196, 252.
23. Stewart & Cohen 1997, p. 63.
24. Barrow & Tipler 1986, pp. 562–4, 565f, 133.
25. Not that we have been looking for very long. Moreover, if we were to find such life, this would merely add force to the conclusions of the present chapter.
26. Behe 1996, p. 39. My italics.
27. Dawkins 1991, pp. 96f.
28. Quoted in Behe 1996, p. 39.
29. Behe 1996, pp. 79–85, 113f.
30. *Cf.* Barry G. Hall, 'How is an advantageous phenotype selected when it requires multiple mutations, none of which are

advantageous until all are present (that is only the last mutation to occur is actually selected)?' *Proceedings of the National Academy of the Sciences*, USA, Vol 88 (4), July 1991, p. 5882.
31. Behe 1996, pp. 72, 68, 114f, 185.
32. There are about 100,000 in complex creatures like ourselves. Hoyle 1996, p. 156.
33. Hoyle 1996, p. 133f. See also Hoyle & Wickramasinghe 1981.
34. Shapiro 1986, p. 128.
35. Dawkins 1991, pp. 54f, 57–60.
36. Of course, if each time one of the necessary answers were found, this gave the animal an adaptive advantage, then we might assent to Dawkins's idea. But it suffices to look at the complexity of the system to see that this is not *and cannot be* the case.
37. Dawkins 1991, pp. 59f.
38. Shapiro 1986, pp. 178–80.
39. Behe 1996, p. 221.
40. Laszlo 1993 p 126, quoting from Hoyle 1983.
41. Hodgson 1991, pp. 335–42. *Cf.* Dembski 1998, pp. 215f.
42. For instance Hoyle & Wickramasinghe 1988, pp. 138f.
43. *Philosophy Now,* 34, 2001/2, p. 42.
44. Quoted in Behe 1996, p. 222. *Cf.* Behe's own discussion of this issue, pp. 223–31.
45. That is the fundamental principle of evolution, that passing on the genes to the next generation is the prime necessity, quite overriding the survival of the individual.
46. Lanier in Libet *et al.,* 1999, p. 265.
47. This amazing creature fires a boiling hot solution at its enemies. See the interesting discussion in Behe 1996, pp. 31–6.

Chapter 11

1. See for instance Peterson 1996, pp. 145–227 for a clear and accessible introduction to these arguments.
2. See Craig 1979, Craig & Smith 1993, and (for a particularly clear and concise account) J.P. Moreland, in pp. 176–189 of Peterson *et al.,* 1996.
3. Craig & Smith 1993, pp. 4, 21f, 12–16.
4. Rudy Rucker is a descendant of the philosopher Hegel.
5. J.P. Moreland's account of Craig's argument, Peterson 1996, p. 179.
6. Le Poidevin 2003, p. 57.
7. Quoted in Moore 1990, p. 135.
8. Aristotle's word for the infinite (το απειρον) may be translated literally as 'the boundless,' since the Greek word περας signifies 'boundary, limit.' This seems admirably clear, as does the phrase for 'untraversable' (το ἀδυνατον διελθειν). In Physics III.6.207a Aristotle remarks (thinking evidently of the Eleatic philosophers): 'The fact is that the unlimited is really the exact opposite of its usual description; for it is not "that beyond which there is nothing," but "that which is always beyond."'
9. *Cf.* Craig & Smith 1993, pp. 24-26. See Moore 1990, p. 35.
10. Craig & Smith 1993, p. 33. See also p. 101.
11. J G Whitrow in Fraser 1968, p. 566.
12. Moore 1990, p. 49.
13. Quoted from Craig, in Peterson *et al.,* 1996, p. 183.
14. Quoted in Craig & Smith 1993, p. 34.
15. Barrow & Tipler 1986, pp. 601–8. Davies 1983, p. 11. Both quoted in Craig & Smith pp. 106f.

16. Craig & Smith 1993, p. 30.
17. Ferguson 1995, pp. 96f, quoting Jastrow 1992, p. 107.
18. A singularity is a point at which the laws of the Universe break down, and we do not know what might replace them. Before the Big Bang, and in its very early stages, the laws of the Universe do indeed break down: we have a 'singularity.'
19. Craig & Smith 1993, pp. 125, 143, 144.
20. That is 'Out of nothing nothing can be made,'
21. Craig & Smith1993, p. 146.
22. *Chandogya Upanisad* 6.2.2, Olivelle 1998, p. 149, Eliade 1977, p. 114. The passage continues: 'On the contrary, my dear, in the beginning there was being alone, one only, without a second. It thought, 'May I be many, may I grow forth ...'
23. Barrow 2000, p. 298.
24. Hawking 1988, pp. 139–141.
25. Ward 1996a, p. 295.
26. Ward 1996b, p. 16.
27. Shankara: *Viveka-Chudamani*, quoted in Huxley 1985 p. 22.
28. Hawking 1988, pp. 138f.
29. Experience proves that children are much brighter than most people think.
30. Attar 1985, p. 132. There is much more to this image than I have suggested here.
31. Spencer Brown 1969, pp. 104–6, as in Martin 1990, pp. 101f.
32. Martin 2003, pp. 85f.

Chapter 12

1. Armand Robin, 'La tortue,' *Ma vie sans moi,* © Editions Gallimard, Paris, 1940. My translation.
2. Deikman 2000, p. 75.
3. *Cf.* Velmans 2000, p. 173, 176.
4. *Cf.* W Harman 1994.
5. *Cf.* Eddington 1928, p. 283, where he says that it is through combining the viewpoints of many consciousnesses that 'the external world of physics arises.'
6. Damasio 2000, p. 309.
7. Searle 1999 pp. 73–83.
8. Hauser 2001, pp. 261–314. Surely however it would be humane to give them the benefit of the doubt.
9. Parfit 1985, p. 232.
10. Deren 1953.
11. See p. 23 above on Ibn al-Arabi's remark, and *cf.* Forman 1999, p. 120.
12. Borges 1998, 'The Disc,' pp. 477–9.
13. *Cf.* Stace 1961, pp. 79, 110f, where he makes a distinction between extrovertive and introvertive mysticism.
14. Cited in Happold 1970, pp. 130, 133f.
15. Cohen & Phipps 1979, p. 168.
16. Crookall 1969, p. 21.
17. Allen, pp. 30–34, quoted in Happold, p. 133.
18. Wilber 1984, p. ix.
19. Happold 1970, pp. 54f.
20. Stace 1961, p. 14f.
21. Entheogen: literally, a substance which generates the God hidden within it.
22. Smith & Tart 1998, pp. 105, 97–107.
23. Forman 1990, p. 12.
24. Ib., p. 13.
25. Philip Almond quoted in Forman 1999, p. 31f.
26. Forman 1999, pp. 44, 51f, 95.
27. Deikman 2000, p. 77.
28. Forman 1990, p. 39.
29. Stace 1961, pp. 113f, 227.

30. Rumi 1995, pp. 138f.
31. Stace 1961, pp. 155f, 126.
32. Forman 1999, p. 110.
33. Happold 1970, p. 273.
34. Stace 1961, p. 224.
35. Forman 1999, pp. 137f, 11–30.
36. Happold 1970, p. 214.
37. Forman 1999, p. 142, pp. 134–6.
38. Blacker & Loewe 1975, pp. 33f.
39. Whiteman 1961, p. 3.
40. Ward 1987, p. 104.
41. Forman1990, p. 127. See also Daniel C. Matt, ib., p. 121.
42. *Kena Upanishad* , Mascaró 1965, p. 51.
43. Stace 1961, pp. 162f.
44. Whiteman 1967, pp. 292–307.
45. Fleming 1995, pp. 62f.
46. Underhill 1991, p. 88.
47. Happold 1970, pp. 216f.
48. See Whorf 1956.
49. Wilber 1984, pp. 104f.
50. According to Radhakrishnan 1940, p. 28, *ânanda* signifies *freedom,*
51. Stace 1961, p. 338.

Conclusion

1. Whether one says 'outside' or 'within' depends on the definition in context of 'Universe.'

Bibliography

JCS = *Journal of Consciousness Studies*

Aleksander, Igor (1999) 'A NeuroComputational View of Consciousness,' in Rose 1999, 180–99

— (2002) *How to Build a Mind*, Phoenix, London

Alexander, Samuel (1966) *Space, Time and Deity*, Gifford Lectures, Macmillan, London

Allen, Warner (1946) *The Timeless Moment*, Faber, London

Anandan, J. (1992) 'The Geometric Phase,' *Nature* 360, 26 Nov, 307–313

Attar, Farid ud-Din (1985) *The Conference of the Birds*, Routledge, London

Barrow, John D. (1990) *The World within the World*, OUP, Oxford

— (2000) *The Book of Nothing,* Cape, London

Barrow, John D. & Tipler, Frank J. (1986) *The Anthropic Cosmological Principle,*OUP, New York & Oxford

Behe, Michael (1996) *Darwin's Black Box,* Simon & Schuster, New York

Benor, Daniel J.(1992 & 4) *Healing Research* (2 Vols), Helix, Deddington & Munich

Berger, Peter L (1966) *Invitation to Sociology*, Penguin

Bergson, Henri (1965) *Essai sur les Données immédiates de la conscience*, P.U.F., Paris 1965

— (1988) *Matter and Memory,* Zone Books, New York & London

Bermúdez, José Luis (1998) *The Paradox of Self-Consciousness* , MIT, Cambridge Mass. & London

Blacker, Carmen & Michael Loewe (1975) *Ancient Cosmologies*, Allen & Unwin, London

Blackmore, Susan J. (1999) *The Meme Machine,* OUP, Oxford

Blake, William, ed. J. Bronowski (1958) *A Selection of Poems and Letters*, Penguin

Blakemore, Colin (1988) *The Mind Machine,* BBC Publications, London

Bohm, David (1980) *Wholeness and the Implicate Order*, Routledge, London

Borges, Jorge Luis (1998) *Collected Fictions*, Penguin

Braud, William & Rosemarie Anderson (1998) *Transpersonal Research Methods for the Social Sciences*, Sage, London & New Delhi

Braude, Stephen E. (1991) *The Limits of Influence: Psychokinesis and the Philosophy of Science*, Routledge, London & New York

Broad, C. D. (1923) *Scientific Thought,* Routledge, London

Brown, Jason W. (2000) *Mind and Nature,* Whurr, London & Philadelphia
Bucke, Richard M. (1948) *Cosmic Consciousness*, Dutton, New York (originally 1901)
Bucknell, Rod & Chris Kang (1997) *The Meditative Way*, Curzon, Richmond
Buddhaghosa (1976) *Visuddhimagga: The Path of Purification,* Shambhala, Berkeley

Capra, Fritjof (1983) *The Tao of Physics*, Flamingo, London (revised ed.)
Cazenave, Michel (1984) *Science and Consciousness*, Pergamon, Oxford & New York
Chalmers, David J.(1995) 'Facing Up to the Problem of Consciousness,' *JCS* 2 no 3, 200–219
— (1996) *The Conscious Mind: In Search of a Fundamental Theory,* OUP, Oxford
— (1997) 'Moving Forward on the Problem of Consciousness,' *JCS* 4 no 1, 3–46
Charman, Robert A. (1997) 'The Field Substance of Mind — A Hypothesis,' *Medical & Scientific Network* no 63, April, 11–13
Charon, Jean-Émile (1977) *La Relativité complexe*, Albin Michel, Paris.
— (1983a) *L'Esprit et la Relativité complexe*, Albin Michel, Paris
— (1983b) *J'ai vécu quinze milliards d'années*, Albin Michel, Paris
— (1983c) *The Unknown Spirit*, Coventure, London
Churchland, P.M. (1984) *Matter and Consciousness: A Contemporary Introduction ...*, MIT, Cambridge Mass.
Churchland, P.M. & P.S. (1998) *On the Contrary*, MIT, Cambridge Mass.
Clarke, Christopher J.S. (1995a) 'The Nonlocality of Mind,' *JCS* 2 no 3, 231–240
— (1995b) 'Review of Storrs McCall: *A Model of the Universe,' Medical & Scientific Network* no 58, August, 57–9
— (1996) *Reality through the Looking-Glass,* Floris, Edinburgh
Cohen, J.M. & J.F. Phipps (1979) *The Common Experience*, Rider, London
Cornwell, John, ed. (1998) *Consciousness and Human Identity*, OUP, Oxford & New York
Cotterill, Rodney (1998) *Enchanted Looms: Conscious Networks in Brains and Computers,* CUP, Cambridge & New York
Craig, William Lane (1979) *The Kalâm Cosmological Argument,* MacMillan, London
Craig, William Lane & Quentin Smith (1993) *Theism, Atheism and Big Bang Cosmology,* OUP, Oxford
Craig, William Lane & J.P. Moreland (2000) *Naturalism,* Routledge, London & New York
Crookall, Robert (1969) *The Interpretation of Cosmic and Mystical Experiences*, Clarke, Cambridge & London
Cytowic, Richard E. (1996) *The Neurological Side of Neuropsychology*, MIT, Cambridge Mass.
— (2002) *Synesthesia: A Union of the Senses*, 2nd ed., MIT, Boston, Mass

Damasio, Antonio (2000) *The Feeling of What Happens*, Heinemann, London

Davies, Paul (1983) *God and the New Physics*, Dent, London

— (1988) *Other Worlds*, Penguin

Davies, Paul & J.R. Brown (1986) *The Ghost in the Atom,* CUP, Cambridge

Davies, Paul & John Gribbin (1992) *The Matter Myth,* Penguin

Dawkins, Richard (1991) *The Blind Watchmaker*, Penguin

Deikman, Arthur J. (2000) 'A Functional Approach to Mysticism,' *JCS* Vol 7 nos 11/12, 75–91

Dembski, William A. (1998) *The Design Inference: Eliminating Chance through Small Probabilities*, CUP, Cambridge & New York

— (2000) 'Naturalism and Design,' pp. 253–279 of Craig & Moreland 2000

— (2002) *No Free Lunch*, Rowman, New York

Dennett, Daniel C. (1993) *Consciousness Explained*, Penguin

— (1994) 'Instead of Qualia,' in A. Revonsuo & M. Kampinnen eds: *Consciousness in Philosophy and Cognitive Neuroscience*, Erlbaum, Hillsdale, N.J.

— (2000) 'It's not a Bug, it's a Feature,' *JCS* Vol 7 no 4, 25–7

— (2003) *Freedom Evolves*, Allen Lane, London

de Quincey, Christian (1999) 'Past Matter, Present Mind,' *JCS* Vol 6, Jan, 91–106

— (2000a) 'Conceiving the Inconceivable? (Discussion of Nicholas Humphrey's Theory),' *JCS* Vol 7 no 4, 67–81

— (2000b) 'The Promise of Integralism,' *JCS* Vol 7 nos 11/12, 177–208

Deren, Maya (1953) *The Divine Horsemen,* Thames & Hudson, repub. as *The Voodoo Gods*, Paladin 1975

Dershowitz, Alan (1994) *The Abuse Excuse, and Other Cop-Outs, Sob-Stories and Evasions of Responsibility*, Little, Brown, New York

Deutsch, David (1998) *The Fabric of Reality*, Penguin

Donald, Merlin (1991) *Origins of the Modern Mind*, Harvard UP, Camb. Mass. & London

— (2001) *A Mind so Rare*, Norton, New York & London

Duncan, Ronald & Miranda Weston-Smith (1977) *The Encyclopædia of Ignorance*, Pergamon, Oxford & New York

Dyson, Freeman (1989) *Infinite in All Directions*, Penguin

Eddington, Sir Arthur (1928) *The Nature of the Physical World*, Cambridge University Press, London

Edelman, Gil & Robert Greenwood (1992) *Jumbly Words, and Rights where Wrongs should be*, Far Communications, Kibworth

Einstein, Albert & L. Infeld (1938) *The Evolution of Physics: From Early Concepts to Relativity and Quanta*, Simon & Schuster, New York

Eliade, Mircea, ed (1977) *From Primitives to Zen*, Collins, London

Elitzur, Avshalom C. (1995) 'Consciousness can no more be Ignored,' *JCS* 2 no 4, 353–8

Farah, M.J. (1990) *Visual Agnosia,* M.I.T., Camb. Mass.

Ferguson, Kitty (1992) *Stephen Hawking: Quest for a Theory of Everything*, Bantam, New York

— (1995) *The Fire in the Equations*, Bantam, Toronto & London1995

Firsoff, V. Axel (1967) *Life, Mind and Galaxies*, Oliver & Boyd, Edinburgh

— (1977) *At the Crossroads of Knowledge*, Ian Henry, London

Fleming, Ursula (1995) *Meister Eckhart, the Man from Whom God Hid Nothing*, Gracewing, Leominster

Fodor, Jerry A. (1992) 'The Big Idea,' *Times Literary Supplement* 3 July

— (1998) *In Critical Condition*, MIT, Cambridge Mass. & London

— (2000) *The Mind doesn't Work that Way*, MIT, Cambridge Mass. & London

— (2003) 'Why would Mother Nature Bother?,' pp. 17–18, *London Review of Books*, Vol 25 no 5, 6 March

Forman, Robert K C. ed (1990) *The Problem of Pure Consciousness*, OUP, Oxford & New York

— (1998) 'What Does Mysticism Have to Teach Us?' *JCS* 5 no 2, 185–201

— (1999) *Mysticism, Mind, Consciousness*, State University of New York, Albany

Fraser, J.T. (1968) *The Voices of Time,* Penguin

Gallagher, Shaun (2000) 'Review of José Luis Bermúdez's *The Paradox of Self-Consciousness* ', JCS Vol 7 no 7, 45–50

Gamow, George & Russell Stannard (1999) *The New World of Mr Tompkins*, CUP, Cambridge

Goswami, Amit (1993) *The Self-Aware Universe,* Simon & Schuster, London & New York

Green, Celia (1968) *Lucid Dreams*, Hamish Hamilton, London

— (1976) *The Decline and Fall of Science*, Hamish Hamilton, London

Green, Celia & Charles McCreery (1975) *Apparitions*, Hamish Hamilton, London

Gregory, Richard L. (1971) *The Intelligent Eye*, Weidenfeld, London

Gribbin, John (1999) *Q is for Quantum*, Phoenix, London

Griffin, David Ray (1997) *Parapsychology, Philosophy and Spirituality*, State University of New York, Albany

— (1998) *Unsnarling the World-Knot*, University of California, Berkeley

— (2001) *Reenchantment without the Supernatural*, Cornell, Ithaca & London

Grim, Patrick (1991) *The Incomplete Universe*, MIT, Cambridge, Mass.

Haggard, Patrick & Helen Johnson (2003) 'Experiences of Voluntary Action' *JCS* Vol 10 nos 9/10, 72–83

Hale, Sheila (2002) *The Man who Lost his Language*, Penguin, London & New York

Happold, F.C. (1970) *Mysticism: A Study and an Anthology*, Penguin

Harman, Willis (1994) 'The Scientific Exploration of Consciousness,' *JCS* 1 no 1, 140–8

Harrison, Jonathan (1985) *A Philosopher's Nightmare*, Nottingham University Press, Nottingham

Hart, H. *et al.* (1953–6) 'Six Theories about Apparitions,' *Proceedings of the Society for Psychical Research*, Vol 50, pp. 153–239

Hauser, Marc (2001) *Wild Minds: What Animals Really Think*, Penguin

Hawking, Stephen W. (1988) *A Brief History of Time,* Bantam, London & New York

Hebb, Donald O. (1952) 'The Role of Neurological Ideas in Psychology,' *Journal of Personality* 20, pp. 39–55

Herbert, Nick (1985) *Quantum Reality: Beyond the New Physics,* Rider, London & Melbourne1985

— (1986) 'How to be in Two Places at the Same Time,' *New Scientist* 21 Aug, 41–44

Heron, W (1957) 'The Pathology of Boredom,' *Scientific American* 196, 52–6

Hobson, J. Allan: (1999) *Consciousness*, Scientific American Library, New York

Hodgson, David (1991) *The Mind Matters,* Clarendon, Oxford

Honderich, T. (1988a) *A Theory of Determinism: The Mind, Neuroscience and Life Hopes*, OUP, Oxford

— (1988b) *Mind and Brain,* OUP, Oxford

Hoyle, Fred (1983) *The Intelligent Universe*, Michael Joseph, London

Hoyle, Fred & N.C. Wickramasinghe (1981) *Evolution from Space,* Granada, London

— (1988) *Cosmic Life-Force*, Dent, London

— (1996) *Our Place in the Cosmos*, Orion, London

Hoyle, Fred & G. Burbidge & J.V. Narlikar (2000) *A Different Approach to Cosmology*, CUP, Cambridge

Humphrey, Nicholas (1992) *A History of the Mind*, Chatto, London

— (1995) *Soul Searching: Human Nature and Supernatural Belief*, Chatto, London

— (2000) 'How to Solve the Mind-Body Problem,' *JCS* 7 no 4, , 5–20, 98–112

Hunter, J.F.M. (1956) 'The Concept "Mind,"' *Philosophy* 61, 439–451

Hutto, Daniel D. (1998) 'An Ideal Solution to the Problems of Consciousness,' *JCS* 5 no 3, 328–43

Huxley, Aldous (1985) *The Perennial Philosophy*, Grafton, London (originally Chatto 1946)

— (1954) *The Doors of Perception*, Chatto, London

Isted, Charles R. (1979) *Learning to Speak Again After a Stroke*, King Edward's Hospital, London

Jackson, Frank (1977) *Perception: A Representative Theory*, CUP, Cambridge
Jastrow, Robert (1992) *God and the Astronomers,* Norton, London
Jay, Peggy E. (1979) *Help Yourselves: A Handbook for Hemiplegics and their Families*, Ian Henry, Hornchurch
Johnson, Raynor C. (1971) *Watcher on the Hills*, Pilgrim Books, Norwich
Johnson-Laird, P.N. (1988) *The Computer and the Mind*, Fontana, London
Josephson, Brian D. & V.S. Ramachandran, eds (1980): *Consciousness and the Physical World,* Pergamon, Oxford & New York

Kapur, Narinder (1977) *Injured Brains of Medical Minds*, OUP, Oxford & New York
Kenny, Antony, ed. & trs. René Descartes (1970) *Philosophical Letters*, OUP, Oxford
Kripke, Saul A. (1980) *Naming and Necessity*, Harvard University, Cambridge, Mass

Lanier, Jaron (1995) 'You Can't Argue with a Zombie,' *JCS* 2 no 4, 333–347
— (1997) 'Death: The Skeleton Key of Consciousness Studies?,' *JCS* Vol 4 no 2, 181–5
Laszlo, Ervin: (1993) *The Creative Cosmos*, Floris, Edinburgh
— (1999) *The Whispering Pond*, Element, Boston, Mass. & Shaftesbury
Lem, Stanislaw (1983) *A Perfect Vacuum*, Harcourt, New York & London
LePoidevin, Robin (2003) *Travels in Four Dimensions*, OUP, Oxford
Leslie, John (1989) *Universes,* Routledge, London
Lewin, Roger (2001) *Complexity*, Phoenix, London
Lewis, David (1983 & 1986) *Philosophical Papers,* Vols 1 & 2, OUP, Oxford
— (1986) *On the Plurality of Worlds,* Blackwell, Oxford
Lewis, Harry A. (1998) 'Consciousness: Inexplicable — and Useless too?,' *JCS* Vol 5 no 1, 59–66:
Libet, Benjamin, Anthony Freeman, & Keith Sutherland (1999) *The Volitional Brain: Towards a Neuroscience of Free Will*, Imprint Academic, Thorverton (i.e. *JCS* Vol 6, nos 8–9)
Lighthill, Sir James (1972) *Artificial Intelligence: a General Survey,* Scientific Research Council Report, London
Linde, Andrei D. (1990) *Particle Physics and Inflationary Cosmology,* Academic Press, Boston, Mass
Lockwood, Michael (1989) *Mind, Brain and the Quantum*, Blackwell, Oxford
Lowe, E.J.: (1995) 'There are No Easy Problems of Consciousness,' *JCS* 2 no 3, 266–271

Lucas, J.R. (1973) *A Treatise on Time and Space*, Methuen, London
Luria, Aleksandr R. (1975) *The Mind of a Mnemonist*, Penguin

McGinn, Colin (1995) 'Consciousness and Space,' *JCS* 2 no 3, 220–30
— (1997) *The Character of Mind*, OUP, Oxford (New Edition)
MacKenzie, Andrew (1987) *The Seen and the Unseen*, Weidenfeld, London
Mackintosh-Smith, Tim (2001) *Travels with a Tangerine*, John Murray, London
Magee, Brian (1986) *Modern British Philosophy,* OUP, Oxford
— (1997) *The Philosophy of Schopenhauer*, revised edition, OUP, Oxford
— (1998) *Confessions of a Philosopher*, Orion, London
Marcer, Peter J.: (1992) 'The Physical Foundations of Computer Science: Challenging the Accepted Wisdom,' pp. 20–2, *Computer Bulletin*, Vol 4, Part 4, Sep/Oct
— (1995) 'The Need to Define Consciousness — A Quantum Mechanical Model,' pp. 3–15, *Consciousness: The Big Issue*, Symposium, ed A.M. Fedorec & P.J. Marcer, University of Greenwich
Martin, Graham Dunstan (1981) *The Architecture of Experience: A Discussion of the Role of Language and Literature in the Construction of the World*, Edinburgh University Press, Edinburgh
— (1990) *Shadows in the Cave: Mapping the Conscious Universe,* Penguin
— (2003) *An Inquiry into the Purposes of Speculative Fiction — Fantasy and Truth*, Edwin Mellen, Lewiston & Lampeter
Mascaró, Juan, trs. (1965) *The Upanishads*, Penguin
Mavromatis, Andreas (1987) *Hypnagogia*, Routledge, London
Maxwell, Grover: (1978) 'Rigid Designators and Mind-Brain Identity,' *Perception & Cognition*, ed. C.W. Savage, University of Minnesota, Minneapolis
Mermin, N. David (1990) *Boojums All the Way Through*, CUP, Cambridge & New York, 1990
Merrell, Floyd (1991) *Unthinking Thinking: J.G. Borges, Mathematics and the New Physics,* Purdue University Press, Lafayette, Indiana
Midgley, Mary (1995) 'Interview' with Anthony Freeman *re The Ethical Primate*, *JCS* 2 no 1, 67–75
— (1999) 'One World but a Big One,' in Rose 1999, 246–270
Moody, Todd C (1994) 'Conversations with Zombies,' *JCS* 1 no 2, 196–200
— (1995) 'Why Zombies won't stay Dead,' *JCS* 2 no 4, 365–372
Moore, A.W. (1990) *The Infinite*, Routledge, London & New York
Moravec, Hans (1988) *Mind Children: The Future of Robots and Human Intelligence,* Harvard University Press, Cambridge Mass.

Nadeau, Robert & Menas Kafatos (2001) *The Non-Local Universe*, OUP, Oxford
Nagel, Thomas (1979) *Mortal Questions,* CUP, Cambridge
Nasr, Seyyed Hossein (1981) *Knowledge and the Sacred*, Edinburgh University Press, Edinburgh
Newton, Roger G. (2000) *Thinking about Physics*, Princeton University Press, Princeton & Woodstock
North, Anthony (1997) *The Paranormal*, Blandford. London
Nozick, Robert (1981) *Philosophical Explanations,* OUP, Oxford

Olivelle, Patrick (1998) *Upanishads*, OUP, Oxford & New York
Olson, Eric T. (1998) 'There is No Problem of the Self' *JCS* 5, nos 5/6, 645–57
Ornstein, Robert E. (1975) *The Psychology of Consciousness*, Cape, London
Oswald, I. (1962) *Sleeping and Waking*, Elsevier, Amsterdam

Padmasambhava (1998) *Natural Liberation,* trs. B. Alan Wallace, Wisdom, Boston, Mass
Pagels, H.R. (1984) *The Cosmic Code: Quantum Physics as the Language of Nature,* Penguin
Paine, Thomas (1938) *The Age of Reason*, Watts, London
Paley, William (1809) *Natural Theology*, J. Faulder, London
Parfit, Derek (1985) *Reasons and Persons,* OUP, Oxford
Penfield, Wilder (1975) *The Mystery of the Mind,* Princeton University Press, Princeton
Penfield, Wilder & H. Jasper (1954) *Epilepsy and the Functional Anatomy of the Human Brain*, London
Penrose, Roger (1989) *The Emperor's New Mind,* OUP, Oxford & New York
— (1995) *Shadows of the Mind,* Vintage, London
— (1999)*The Large, the Small and the Human Mind,* CUP, Cambridge, pbk
— (2004) *The Road to Reality*, BCA (Cape), London
Peterson, Michael, *et al.* (1991) *Reason and Religious Belief*, OUP, Oxford & New York
— (1996) *Philosophy of Religion: Selected Readings*, OUP, Oxford & New York
Pinker, Steven (1998) *How the Mind Works,* Allen Lane, London
Polanyi, Michael (1967) *The Tacit Dimension*, Routledge, London
Polkinghorne, J.C. (2000) *Faith, Science and Understanding*, SPCK, London
Popper, Karl (1976) *Unended Quest: An Intellectual Autobiography*, Fontana, London
Price, Henry H. (1953) 'Survival and the Idea of Another World,' *Proceedings of the Society for Psychical Research*, Vol 50, 1–25. Also pp. 1–33 of Smythies 1965.
Price, Huw (1996) *Time's Arrow and Archimedes' Point*, OUP, Oxford & New York

Radhakrishnan, S. (1940) *Eastern Religions and Western Thought*, OUP, Oxford

Ramachandran, V.S. & Sandra Blakeslee (1998) *Phantoms in the Brain*, Fourth Estate, London

Ramachandran, V.S. & W. Hirstein (1997) 'Biological Functions of Consciousness and Qualia,' *JCS* 4, nos 5/6, 429–57

Regis, Ed (1992) *Great Mambo Chicken and the Human Condition*, Penguin

Ridley, Brian K. (2001) *On Science*, Routledge, London

Robbins, Stephen E. (2000) 'Bergson, Perception, and Gibson,' *JCS* Vol 7 no 5, 23–45

Roberts, Bernadette (1984) *The Experience of No Self*, Shambhala, Boston

Robin, Armand (1940) *Ma vie sans moi,* Editions Gallimard, Paris

Romanes, George John (1895) *Mind and Motion and Monism,* Longman's, London & New York

Rose, Hilary & Steven (2000) *Alas, Poor Darwin,* Cape, London

Rose, Steven (1991) 'What the Chick can Tell us ...' in Squire *et al.*1991, 392–412

— (1993) *The Making of Memory,* Bantam, Toronto & London

— (1999) ed. *From Brains to Consciousness?* Penguin

Rowe, William L. (1975) *The Cosmological Argument,* Princeton University Press, Princeton

Rucker, Rudy: (1980) *White Light*, Virgin, London

— (1982) *Infinity and the Mind: the Science and Philosophy of the Infinite*, Paladin, London

— (1986) *The Fourth Dimension and How to Get There*, Penguin

Rumi, Jalaluddin (1995) *The Essential Rumi*, trs. Coleman Barks, Penguin

Ruse, Michael (2002) 'Darwinism and Atheism,' W. Mark Richardson *et al.*, pp. 140–153, *Science and the Spiritual Quest*, Routledge, London

Russell, Bertrand (1921) *The Analysis of Mind*,

— (1927) *The Analysis of Matter*, Kegan Paul, London

Ryle, Gilbert (1963) *The Concept of Mind*, Penguin

Sacks, Oliver (1985) *Migraine*, Duckworth, London

Sartre, Jean-Paul (1949) *L'Etre et le Néant*, Gallimard, Paris

Schatzman, Morton (1980) *The Story of Ruth*, Duckworth, London

Schopenhauer, Arthur (1970) *Essays and Aphorisms*, Penguin

Schrödinger, Erwin (1992) *What is Life,* with *Mind And Matter & Autobiographical Sketches,* CUP, Cambridge

Schwartz, Jeffrey M: (1999) 'A Role for Volition and Attention in the Generation of New Brain Circuitry ...' *JCS* 6 (8–9), 115–42

Searle, John R. (1980) 'Minds, Brains and Programs,' *Behavioral and Brain Sciences* 3, 417–457
— (1984) *Minds, Brains and Science*, BBC, London
— (1992)*The Rediscovery of the Mind,* MIT, Camb. Mass. & London
— (1995) 'Consciousness, its Irreducibility,' in *Oxford Companion to Philosophy*, ed. T. Honderich, OUP, Oxford
— (1997)*The Mystery of Consciousness,* Granta, London
— (1999) *Mind, Language and Society,* Weidenfeld, London
— (2000) 'Consciousness, Free Action and the Brain,' *JCS* Vol 7 no 10, 3–22
— (2001) *Rationality in Action*, MIT, Camb. Mass.
— (2004) *Mind*, OUP, Oxford & New York
Searle, John R, & Walter Freeman (1998) 'Do We Understand Consciousness?'*JCS* Vol 5 nos 5/6, 718–33
Shannon, Claude & Warren Weaver (1949) *The Mathematical Theory of Communication*, University of Illinois Press, Urbana
Shapiro, Robert (1986) *Origins: A Skeptic's Guide to the Creation of Life on Earth,* Summit, New York
Sharf, Robert H. (2000) 'The Rhetoric of Experience and the Study of Religion,' *JCS* Vol 7, nos 11/12, 267–287
Shear, Jonathan & Ron Jevning (1999) 'Pure Consciousness,' *JCS* Vol 6 Feb / March, 189–209
Shear, Jonathan: ed. (1997) *Explaining Consciousness: The Hard Problem,* MIT, Cambridge Mass. & London
Sheets-Johnstone, Maxine (1998): 'Consciousness: A Natural History' *JCS* 5 no 3, 260–94
Sheikh, Anees *et al* (1996) 'The Somatic Consequences of Consciousness,' p. 140ff of Velmans 1996
Sherrington, Charles Scott (1906) *The Integrative Action of the Nervous System*, Constable, London
Smith, Allan L. and Charles T. Tart (1998) 'Cosmic Conscious Experience and Psychedelic Experiences: A First Person Comparison.' *JCS* Vol 5 no 1, 97–107.
Smythies, John R. (1956) *Analysis of Perception*, Routledge, London
— (1965) ed. *Brain and Mind*, Routledge, London
— (1967) ed. *Science and ESP*, Routledge, London
— (1993) 'The Impact of Contemporary Neuroscience and Introspection Psychology on the Philosophy of Perception,' pp. 205–231 of Edmond Wright ed. *New Representationalisms*, Ashgate Publishing, Avebury
— (1994) *The Walls of Plato's Cave*, Ashgate Publishing, Avebury
Spencer Brown, G. (1969) *Laws of Form*, Allen & Unwin, London

Squire, Larry R. (1987) *Memory and the Brain*, OUP, Oxford

Squire, Larry R. & Eric R. Kandel (2000) *Memory: From Mind to Molecules*, Scientific American Library, New York

Squire, Larry R. *et al.* (1991) *Memory: Organization and Locus of Change*, OUP, London & NY

Stace, Walter T. (1961) *Mysticism and Philosophy*, Macmillan, London

Standing, Lionel (1973) 'Remembering Ten Thousand Pictures,' *Quarterly Journal of Experimental Psychology* Vol 25, 207–22

Stapp, Henry P. (1993) *Mind, Matter and Quantum Mechanics*, Springer-Verlag, New York

— (1999) 'Attention, Intention, and Will in Quantum Physics,' *JCS* 6 (8–9), 143–164

Stewart, Ian & Jack Cohen (1997) *Figments of Reality*, Cambridge UP, Cambridge & New York

Stromeyer, C.F. & J. Psotka (1970) 'The Detailed Texture of Eidetic Images,' *Nature* 225, 346–349

Tallis, Raymond (1999) *The Explicit Animal: a Defence of Human Consciousness,* Macmillan, London (reprint)

Teilhard de Chardin, Pierre: (1955) *Le Phénomène humain*, Seuil, Paris

Thalberg, J. (1983) 'Immateriality,' *Mind* 92, 105–113

Tipler, Frank J.: (1995) *The Physics of Immortality: Modern Cosmology, God and the Resurrection of the Dead*, Macmillan, New York & Basingstoke

Turing, Alan (1950) 'Computing Machinery and Intelligence,' *Mind* 59, 433–60

Tyrrell, G.N.M. (1953) *Apparitions*, Duckworth, London, rev. ed.

Underhill, Evelyn (1991) *Practical Mysticism*, Eagle, Guildford

Velmans, Max (1996) *The Science of Consciousness*, Routledge, London & Philadelphia

— (2000) *Understanding Consciousness*, Routledge, London & Philadelphia

Vesey, G.N.A. (1964) ed. *Body and Mind*, Allen & Unwin, London

Voorhees, Burton (2000) 'Dennett and the Deep Blue Sea,' *JCS* Vol 7 no 3, 53–69

Waismann, Friedrich (1951) 'Verifiability,' pp. 117–144 of A.G.N. Flew, ed. *Logic and Language*, Vol I, Blackwell, Oxford

Wall, Patrick D. (1977) 'Why do we Not Understand Pain?,' in Duncan, Ronald & Miranda Weston-Smith, 1977, 361–8

Wallace, B. Alan (2000) *The Taboo of Subjectivity*, OUP, Oxford & New York

Ward, Keith (1996a) *Images of Eternity*, Darton, London 1987, republished as *Religion and Creation*, Clarendon, Oxford

— (1996b) *God, Chance and Necessity*, Oneworld, Oxford

Weed, Laura E. (2003) *The Structure of Thinking: A Process-Oriented Account of Mind*, Imprint Academic, Exeter

Wheeler, John A., C.W. Misner & K.S. Thorne (1973) *Gravitation*, Freeman, San Francisco

Whiteman, J.H.M. (1961) *The Mystical Life*, Faber, London

— (1967) (as Michael Whiteman) *The Philosophy of Space and Time and the Inner Constitution of Nature*, Routledge, London

Whorf, Benjamin Lee (1956) *Language, Thought and Reality*, MIT, Cambridge, Mass.

Wigner, Eugene P. (1967) *Symmetries and Reflections,* MIT, Cambridge Mass. & London

Wilber, Ken (1984) *A Sociable God*, Shambhala, Boulder & London

— (1984) *Quantum Questions*: *Mystical Writings of the World's Great Physicists*, Shambhala, Boulder & London

— (1997) 'An Integral Theory of Consciousness,' *JCS* 4 no 1, 71–92

Wilson, Ian (1982) *Reincarnation?* Penguin

Wolpert, Lewis (1993) *The Unnatural Nature of Science*, Faber, London

Zohar, Danah: (1990) *The Quantum Self*, Bloomsbury, London

Zukav, Gary (1980) *The Dancing Wu Li Masters*, Fontana, London

Index

Andrew Welburn

Rudolf Steiner's Philosophy

and the Crisis of Contemporary Thought

The Austrian-born philosopher Rudolf Steiner (1861–1925) created a vast legacy of practical work in Waldorf education, biodynamic agriculture, Camphill communities and many other artistic and scientific areas.

The foundation of all these approaches is a highly developed system of thought with which Steiner addressed philosophical issues. Many of these issues were also tackled by a number of contemporaries, notably the phenomenological school represented by Edmund Husserl and others.

Seeking to clarify his moral thinking, which he termed 'ethical individualism,' Steiner offered a challenging view of knowledge: not as an abstract and objectified reality, but as a form of relationship between the knower and the known. By this measure, all genuine knowledge is experiential and thus intimately involved with, and capable of changing, the world. Equally, there is no world 'out there,' since every individual is a participant in reality, and there are no morally neutral acts or thoughts.

Andrew Welburn presents a fascinating insight into the radical nature of Steiner's thinking. He examines Steiner's inheritance of ideas from Johann Wolfgang von Goethe, his attempt to break out of Cartesian dualism and Kantian idealism, and his challenge to the conventional framework of European philosophy.

www.florisbooks.co.uk

David Lorimer

Radical Prince

The Practical Vision of the Prince of Wales

This is the first book to provide an explanatory overview of the Prince of Wales' philosophy, revealing the coherence of his ideas on ecology, organic agriculture, holistic health, religion, architecture and education.

David Lorimer outlines the radical thinking that underpins the Prince's vision and the ways in which he has translated this into practical projects with The Prince's Trust, The Prince's Foundation, The Duchy of Cornwall, the Prince's Foundation for Integrated Health and the Prince of Wales' International Business Leaders Forum.

www.florisbooks.co.uk